DATE DUE

| | | | |
|---|---|---|---|
| | | | |
| | | | |
| | | | |
| | | | |
| | | | |
| | | | |
| | | | |
| | | | |
| | | | |
| | | | |
| | | | |
| | | | |

# FINNISH IMMIGRANTS IN AMERICA 1880–1920

A. WILLIAM HOGLUND

AYER COMPANY, PUBLISHERS, INC.
SALEM, NEW HAMPSHIRE 03079

Reprints Editions, 1992
Ayer Company, Publishers, Inc.
Salem, New Hampshire 03079

Editorial Supervision: Steven Bedney

---



SCANDINAVIANS IN AMERICA

See last pages of this volume for titles.

Manufactured in the United States of America

---

**Library of Congress Cataloging in Publication Data**

Hoglund, Arthur William, 1926-
Finnish immigrants in America, 1880-1920.

(Scandinavians in America)
Issued in 1957 in microfilm form as the author's thesis, University of Wisconsin, under title: Paradise rebuilt.
Reprint of the ed. published by University of Wisconsin Press, Madison.
Bibliography: p.
Includes index.
1. Finnish Americans--History. I. Title. II. Series.
[E184.F5H58 1979] 973'.04'94541 78-15182
ISBN 0-405-11639-X

# FINNISH IMMIGRANTS IN AMERICA 1880–1920

A. WILLIAM HOGLUND

# FINNISH IMMIGRANTS IN AMERICA 1880–1920

THE UNIVERSITY OF WISCONSIN PRESS

MADISON–1960

Published by
*The University of Wisconsin Press*
430 Sterling Court
Madison 6, Wisconsin



Printed in the United States of America by
the Vail-Ballou Press, Inc., Binghamton, New York

# PREFACE

In this study I deal with the Finnish immigrants in those areas of thought and action which were most important in the lives of any immigrant group. I emphasize especially their many organizations which pursued different ideals and aspirations for a better and happier life. At the same time I try to show how their heritage from Finland was reshaped in America. Lastly, I look at the immigrants' reassessment of their organizational endeavors after a generation of effort. Although my study thus emphasizes one nationality group, I hope that the pitfalls of fileopietism have been avoided.

The preparation of this study has indebted me to many persons and institutions and I can only start to single out those who have been helpful and generous.

This study was begun at the suggestion of my major professor, Dr. Merle Curti, who felt that I should employ my familiarity with the Finnish language to open up aspects of immigrant life closed to those not so endowed. Otherwise, I might have kept the door closed even to myself in learning about an immigrant group's past. I am also grateful for his critical examination of my chapters during the preparation of the study in its original thesis form at the University of Wisconsin.

My parents tolerated and supported me generously as a graduate student in efforts which often seemed to bring me no closer to a completed study.

I also want to indicate some of my other debts. There are the ten fellow graduate students who sweated to help sort out needed newspaper volumes from over 4,500 volumes which were stacked in the basement of the State Historical Society of Wisconsin. My requests for information and materials were serviced by librarians at about a dozen institutions located from Massachusetts to Minnesota. Newspaper publishers in Duluth, Superior, Ironwood, Hancock, Ashtabula, and Brooklyn made available files and photographs. In Hancock Dr. Armas Holmio made special arrangements to keep open the Finnish American Historical Library. Members of the Finnish Historical Society of Hiawatha Land in Crystal Falls opened their archives for my use. Dr. Rafael Engelberg, former director of the Suomi Seura in Helsinki, sent me photographs and original "America letters."

Especially deserving of my appreciation are the scores of individuals who gave or lent source materials of all kinds and provided transportation, lodging, and other assistance.

My latest debts are to the American Philosophical Society in Philadelphia for a grant which enabled me to travel for further research and locating illustrations and to Mr. Randall Sale, cartographer at the University of Wisconsin, for the maps.

I must also acknowledge with appreciation the permission granted to quote from the following copyrighted material.

E. P. Dutton & Co., Inc., New York: *Kalevala: The Land of the Heroes,* trans. by W. F. Kirby, Everyman's Library, 2 vols. (New York, 1951).

Routledge & Kegan Paul Ltd., London: Aino Tuomiokoski, "Finnish [Proverbs]," *Racial Proverbs: A Selection of the World's Proverbs Arranged Linguistically,* comp. by Selwyn Gurney Champion (New York, 1938), pp. 134–40.

Mr. Lewis Beeson, Michigan Historical Commission, Lansing: Aili Kolehmainen Johnson, "Finnish Labor Songs from Northern Michigan," *Michigan History* XXXI (September, 1947), 331–43.

National Bureau of Economic Research, New York: *International Migrations,* I: *Statistics,* ed. Walter F. Willcox (New York, 1929).

If I have failed to mention any specific indebtedness, I hope that this book is proof that I have not regarded lightly any of the courtesies extended to me.

A. W. H.

*October, 1959*

# CONTENTS

# ILLUSTRATIONS

# FINNISH IMMIGRANTS IN AMERICA 1880–1920

*Elysium is sought and all associations*
*have their own roads to find the way there.*

New Yorkin Uutiset, July 24, 1912

CHAPTER I

# RURAL EXODUS

*In modern days the flow of population takes two directions. It is away from rural areas, partly to overseas countries in the form of emigration, and partly to towns and industrial centres within the same country.*

O. K. KILPI[1]

By 1900 Finland's people were changing the mode of rural life celebrated in their epic *Kalevala.* Their mythical Sampo, magic mill of abundance, now was being rebuilt with the help of modern industry. Thousands of Finns left the countryside for the rising industrial and commercial centers, while many more stayed to reorganize farm life. Still others left the farms, and even the cities, of Finland to seek their fortunes in America, where most of them would become industrial workers. It was clear, as the nineteenth century ended, that Finnish life was undergoing a major change.

Before 1900 arrived, Finns had experienced a kind of awakening. In all areas of activity they found new purposes and vistas. As one English traveler wrote, art, literature, industry, commerce, and politics were revived. She said that after the "repose of centuries" the nation was roused to self-consciousness.[2]

During the awakening, political life, especially, was invigorated. Starting in 1863 after fifty-odd years of inactivity, the four-estate Diet henceforth was the center of politics. In it the nationalist elements fought for recognition of the Finnish language by official institutions, like courts and schools, which had until then used almost exclusively the Swedish spoken by about one-tenth of the population. Of like concern to the Diet were economic issues which reflected the class interests of political groups from the Right to the Left. The Diet also was the focus of movements to extend the suffrage. Partly intensified in the struggle with Tsarist Russia, all this growing political awareness led to independence and civil war by the time of World War I.

The stirring of intellectual and cultural life was shown clearly by the spreading literary activity with its new ideas and aims. Heralding new themes from the time of its formation in 1831, the Literary Society collected Finnish folklore and poetry and published the epic, *Kalevala.* Its work stimulated the creation of a Finnish literature. Alexis Kivi's *Seven Brothers,* a literary milestone in 1870, gave overtones of social realism to the literature of the ensuing decades. Finnish newspaper publishers made prose a literary form increasingly common.

Religious life was altered, and in its role of chief educator the Church gave way to new educational agencies. From about 1825 the Lutheran State Church, which enrolled over ninety percent of the people, was swept by a series of evangelical and pietistic revivals. In education and social welfare the State Church lost dominance, and in 1906 it lost political representation as one of the four estates in the Diet. It had been largely instrumental in maintaining literacy through its confirmation classes and reading examinations. Now, however, said Johan Snellman, father of Finnish nationalism, a developing society needed "other teaching than the ordinary religious instruction given by the church. . . ."[3] So in the 1860's the beginning was made for a national system of grammar schools separated from the Church.

Adults found educational opportunities in the new libraries, lyceums, and folk schools which were partly inspired by the People's Enlightenment Society formed in 1874. Other opportunities for mental endeavor and expression were found in reform activities, temperance societies, trade unions, and coöperatives. No longer did newspapers have reason to complain as they had in 1850 that there was no "associative life" such as temperance and women's societies might provide.[4]

New ways and ideas were hastened by industrial developments, which from about 1870 became noticeably important. Several decades earlier, of course, Finns had started to pave the way for such enterprises by amassing capital, building canals, and erecting factories and sawmills. Around 1860 the forest industries received impetus from the discovery of processes to convert wood pulp. The Finnish government helped new industry by chartering companies, organizing banks, issuing currency, and undertaking railroad construction in 1858. It also espoused economic liberalism by permitting workers to move about freely and by ending the guild system and the restrictions on the number and type of factory mills and workshops. In such ways, then, the economy became industrialized.

Most people, however, did not enter the new industries, but remained in agriculture, which also underwent accelerated changes. They farmed less than 10 percent of the country's surface, their fields lying among tree-covered mountains, rocky hills, and lakes, as well as in the more open terrain of the coastal and valley regions of southwestern Finland. During the century after about 1750 the state took measures to combine scattered landholdings into individual farm units. With the development of foreign shipping, urban markets, and the wood industries, farmers relied more than they had on cash incomes earned by selling dairy and forest products, and even by working for lumber companies during the wintertime. As a consequence, farm households became attached to the money economy, and rural bank deposits appeared. Farmers spent money for agricultural machinery and other products of the factories.[5] By 1865 there were 612 country stores and by 1900 they numbered 4,391.[6] During the 1890's and later a novelist complained that his countrymen had become spendthrifts. In earlier times, he said, people lived frugally and only occasionally bought city goods, but now they found it impossible to live so simply, and stores had appeared like mushrooms. Now they cast away wooden utensils for ware of tin, and even silver and porcelain. They also discarded homespun folk costumes, as cheap and shoddy, for those made from factory-spun fabrics.[7] Without any question, city ways were undoing country ways.

Besides the new patterns of rural living, changes in the rural class structure developed. In 1815 the landowners constituted over one-half the total number of rural household heads, but in 1901 they represented less than one-fourth. During the nineteenth century the landless rural classes had increased in number faster than the landowners until growing concern was felt over the presence of the landless. Between 1815 and 1875, for example, one group of tenant householders increased almost twice as much as did the landowners, while the landless workers increased over five times. By 1901 the landless who tilled no land on their own account represented forty-three percent of all household heads and the tenants who rented land represented thirty-four percent. The growth in the number of the landless, however, was not uniform. It was greatest near the growing southern cities. In the provinces of Häme and Uudenmaa the landowners actually decreased in number. Although virgin land was settled, particularly in Oulu, the new farm owners did not reverse the decreasing proportion of landowners. Everywhere, by the end of the nineteenth century, the landless had few opportunities except to become laborers, either on farms or in cities.[8]

When urban industry developed, the cities attracted landless workers from the countryside. Government statisticians compiled data showing how internal migration increased urban population at the expense of the rural areas. Such data revealed that in 1910 almost eighty-one percent of the rural residents lived in their parish of birth, but that only about forty-two percent of the urban dwellers lived in their parish of birth.[9] Those who had left their birthplace were most numerous in the cities of southern Finland. In the province of Uudenmaa the capital city, Helsinki, showed most growth by attracting landless workers from nearby communes and provinces. It attracted rural youth, for instance, through its expanding markets. Young men working as drivers of farm produce wagons learned about city life on their market visits. Finally they moved to the city and took jobs which paid more cash than they had earned on the farms.[10] Others escaped to the city from famine, unemployment, or family difficulties in rural areas. Chiefly the landless and unmarried moved cityward, because they were least encumbered with property and family responsibilities.

Although most of the population was still rural in 1900, urban growth in population was more noticeable than rural during the past century. Between 1800 and 1850 the urban population represented five or six percent of the total population; by 1900 it was over twelve percent. At the same time, the total population continued to grow, numbering 832,659 in 1800, 1,636,915 in 1850, and 2,655,900 in 1900. During the years from 1800 to 1850 the urban and rural populations doubled, and each increased at about the same rate. But in the next half century the urban population rose more than 200 percent, from 105,496 to 331,200; the rural population increased over 60 percent, from 1,531,419 to 2,324,700.[11] Just as the rural population decreased in relative importance, agricultural occupations also became less important in comparison with urban occupations. The new urban centers of employment, however, did not absorb all rural migrants, because thousands of them left Finland for the cities of America.

While nearby rural migrants found work in the southern cities, rural migrants from the more distant northwest found work in far greater numbers, not in Finnish cities, but in American industrial centers. Between 1893 and 1920 the provinces of Vaasa and Oulu provided over sixty percent of all emigrants who left the country.[12] During the years between 1882 and 1902, over 103,000 left the two provinces for America and around 2,000 went south to Helsinki.[13] But whether or not the migrants left Finland, they came from the same rural classes and regions, and they left the countryside for similar reasons. In this period of migration industrial growth was not absorbing all comers fast enough, especially during the famine years and the periods when even Helsinki had unemployment. Then, too, those living closest to the southern cities had the best opportunities to enter new jobs as they appeared. So the more distant rural areas sent their migrants overseas.[14]

After about 1860 the vanguard of thousands of Finnish immigrants started to arrive in the United States. In earlier decades mainly a few seamen had found their way to the New World. Much earlier in the seventeenth century Finns had helped to found New Sweden at the mouth of the Delaware River, but they did not pave the way for any sustained immigration from Finland. Hence, the immigrant arrivals of the 1860's really opened the way for the main period of Finnish immigration, which reached its peak at the opening of the twentieth century.

Before the 1880's few statistics were kept on the number of persons leaving Finland for America. One Finnish economist estimated that from 1865 through 1882 12,000 emigrants left the country.[15] From July, 1871, through June, 1883, American officials recorded 1,942 Finnish arrivals. Between July, 1883, and June, 1920, they recorded 257,382 arrivals.[16] During the years from 1883 through 1920 Finnish officials issued 310,136 passports to emigrants destined, with few exceptions, for North America.[17] In part, the discrepancies between the figures are accounted for by the fact that all passport applicants did not leave Finland, nor did they all land in the United States. Then, too, in the early years American officials probably did not list all Finnish arrivals, but instead included them with the Russians. On the other hand, there were unrecorded emigrants who left without passports. Officials in both countries, however, agreed that Finns reached America in their greatest numbers during the late 1890's and the following decade.

But not all Finns remained in the United States. In the years from 1893 through 1920 the Finnish government reported that 273,735 passports were issued and that between 1894 and 1920 incomplete tabulations showed 35,698 Finns had returned from abroad. During the period between 1894 and 1914 it reported that data from steamship companies showed the departure of 244,584 emigrants and the return of 100,897, who represented about forty-one percent of those departing. To be sure, some of the returnees again entered the United States. Official American data supported the Finnish statistics. Between July, 1910, and June, 1920, officials reported 61,347 arrivals at American ports. In the same period they recorded the departure of 20,545 Finns, who represented over one-third of the new arrivals.[18] Hence, roughly between thirty and forty percent of the immigrants did not find permanent homes in the United States.

The Finns traveled back and forth between Finland and America via England. Occasionally they went via Germany. As the Finland Steamship Company, founded in 1883, had a virtual monopoly on shipping between England and Finland and had the sole right to sell tickets of the transatlantic lines, Finnish travelers naturally went through England.[19] They usually left from the port of Hanko, near Helsinki, probably on the *Urania, Arcturus,* or *Titania.* Landing at Hull, they took the train to Liverpool or Southampton where they boarded ships of lines like the Allan, Cunard, American, and White Star for New York, Boston, or Quebec. Watching emigrants leave Hanko, an English traveler said that he was more pleased looking at the barrels of butter readied for shipment at the wharves than at the emigrants, "collected like sheep," whose "passports, tickets and goods were examined as though they belonged to beasts." [20] Describing the ship which took him from Hanko to England, an immigrant pictured it as a pigsty. Conditions were little different on the steamer which he boarded in England for New York. Passengers, he said, were roughly grasped by their necks, "as though they were prisoners," and they had to offer bribes to get service.[21] Emigrants, in general, traveled third class without the comforts and services of the first and second class passengers.

Few Finns—perhaps numbering only in the hundreds—were ever solicited directly in Finland by American agents. In 1891 the American vice-consul reported that steamship companies and labor contractors did not solicit emigrants in Finland.[22] In 1904 another consul said that steamship companies did not urge emigration, but canvassed only among emigrants who were already leaving the country. He stated, moreover, that no "foreign agitation or other artificial methods of raising the number of emigrants" had been noticed in Finland.[23] Undoubtedly in part because of the official American ban against the importation of contract labor, the solicitation of Finnish emigrants seldom occurred.

During the American Civil War the solicitation of Finnish miners in Norway inaugurated the mainstream of immigration from Finland to the United States. In 1864 the Quincy Mining Company, located in the Copper Country of northern Michigan, sent two agents to solicit miners from Norway. Consequently, in the two ensuing decades perhaps between 700 and 1,000 Finns came via Norway to the United States.[24] Although few in number, these arrivals made Michigan better known to their homeland, and the state became the first major center for the much greater numbers of emigrants leaving unsolicited from Finland.

On a few other occasions, agents also solicited for laborers and settlers. In 1873 the English-operated Allan Line, which transported emigrants from Finland to England before Finns set up their own line, hired an agent who contracted to secure men for a Swedish employment agency in Duluth, Minnesota. The agent secured a few hundred Finns and Swedes, who, however, refused to accept employment through the Duluth agency because they feared working on railroads in Indian territory and recognized no obligation since they had paid their own fares. During the early 1870's, the Allan Line helped European agents of the Northern Pacific Railroad to attract a number of Finns. In 1907 farm officials sent an agent to scour northern Europe for settlers who would take up abandoned farms in New York State, but Finnish officials barred his solicitations.[25] In addition, there were other instances when proposals were made to import men from Finland, but nothing was done to implement such plans.

As direct solicitation was rare, friends and relatives already in America assumed added importance in directing the arrival of immigrants from Finland. The first letters to them from the Old Country very likely asked for tickets and information about America. Immigrants often granted such requests, but at the same time the cautious ones absolved themselves of responsibility for anyone's leaving Finland. From Minnesota an uncle wrote his nephew, who had requested a ticket, not to blame his benefactor if things did not turn out well in the new country since the uncle would not "guarantee that it would always be good over here." He emphasized, moreover, that newcomers faced language difficulties, hard work, and the dangers of intemperance in America.[26] Between July, 1907, and June, 1920, American immigration officials reported that 55,366 of the 95,516 Finnish arrivals intended to join relatives and 31,898 planned to meet friends. In the same period 63,046 paid their own passage and 29,052 traveled on tickets bought by their relatives.[27] Agents encouraged such purchases of tickets by relatives already in America: in December, 1909, one agent in Negaunee, Michigan, advertised his services and listed the names of over seventy persons who had bought tickets through him for friends and relatives in Finland.[28] The Finland Steamship Company reported that in the five-year period between 1905 and 1909 it had sold 55,002 tickets for travelers westward bound from Finland and that two-fifths of the tickets had been bought in America.[29] Besides selling tickets in New York, agencies like the Nielsen and Lundbeck firm and the Finland Steamship Company Agency forwarded funds from America to Finland. No doubt such funds helped their recipients find a way to America.

Departing emigrants received little sympathy in Finland. Churchmen, writers, and public officials were generally critical and hostile. The critics had little understanding of the emigrants, who came primarily from the lowest ranks of society. Emigration occurred, so to speak, outside the sphere of the educated and ruling classes, who failed to appreciate why the emigrants departed. As long as they failed to understand that it was the desire for better working opportunities which impelled departure, critics were apt to regard emigrants as unthinking adventurers, and even as traitors and moral laggards.[30]

In opposing emigration, critics maintained that it created various dangers. They did not develop the point made by a journalist who visited America in the 1890's, that Finland gained by losing the morally bankrupt, but instead they emphasized the moral dangers, as well as the economic and national perils, attributed to emigration.[31] Members of the Diet were told that emigration represented an economic loss which outmatched the cash remittances sent from America. Addressing his estate in 1891, a bishop declared that emigration drained needed labor from agricultural areas. He said that no one had to leave Finland to find land; besides, departure violated the Biblical injunction to remain and work in one's native country. Three years later a member of the peasant estate deplored the draft-age emigrants who forsook their parents and fatherland while patriotic men fulfilled their military obligations. Upon his return from America, Akseli Järnefelt, a journalist, declared that patriotism and emigration did not belong together. During the national crisis in 1899, Juhani Aho wrote a story about the sons who, on proposing to leave Finland, were told by their outraged father that only effeminate weaklings left the young and old in the hands of the foe; needless to say, the sons remained at home. Although churchmen believed that emigration weakened love of country, they stressed even more the point that it weakened moral bonds. At their meetings and in the Diet they were unwilling to recognize marriages contracted by Finns in America. They expressed fears that Finnish men committed bigamy in America and forgot their "American widows" and children, who became public charges in Finland. Besides stressing the broken family ties, churchmen and others maintained that the "American widows" succumbed to merrymaking and sin, sons became undisciplined, and daughters were ruined in the absence of paternal guidance. If Finland suffered in such ways, critics saw complete ruin for those who stayed in America.[32]

According to the critics of emigration, their countrymen found perils in America, and they suggested that correct information about American conditions might deter further departures. As a result of their stay in America during the 1890's, Akseli Järnefelt and Matti Tarkkinen wrote pamphlets describing the supposed plight of Finns in the United States. To them America represented a virtual graveyard; departure from one's fatherland was self-destruction and Finnish nationality found its burial ground in

America where immigrants lost their best heritage. This was true, according to the pamphleteers, because immigrants misunderstood American freedom as license and abused it by irresponsibly rejecting their religious ties and marital obligations. They even forsook Finnish honesty and filled the prisons. Drunkenness, said the two writers, was the worst result of the misunderstood freedom. American economic conditions, maintained the two journalists, were disappointing; for the few successes that Finland heard about there were thousands of failures in America. In their view miners and other workers suffered from hard work, low pay, shameful diseases, and many accidents. An eight-hour day in America tired a worker more than a fourteen-hour day in Finland. In fact, said one of the writers, a twelve-hour day was a positive good in Finland for it taught a man to work during working hours and to rest when his work was done. Because of their nationalist bias, the pamphleteers concluded by suggesting that prospective emigrants would be better off remaining in their own country.[33]

Officials tried to discourage emigration as early as 1873, when the Senate urged pastors to issue warnings against emigrating. But in 1898 a Senate committee declared that emigration could not be prohibited.[34] Consequently, officials tried to discourage emigrants in other ways or to counteract the effects of emigration. Finnish marriages in America and dependents left behind in Finland by emigrants mainly concerned the clerical estate. Other emigrant matters of official concern were inheritances, financial transfers, shipping conditions, and military conscription. Emigration was also associated with land tenure, and the view was expressed that securing land for the landless would reduce departures. Various land reforms were started, but the major reform did not come until 1918, after the peak period of emigration. In the 1880's officials began to compile data on emigration, and in the next two decades they increased the range of their statistical work. Legislators endorsed studies on the causes and effects of emigration, but they did not succeed in sponsoring a study until after World War I. In so doing, they marked the change in attitude toward the emigrants.

Gradually, critics became less condemnatory of the emigrants. Under his Swedish family name of Järnefelt, Akseli Rauanheimo in 1899 wrote his pamphlet criticizing the emigrants, but by 1904 he had changed his views and observed that warmer feelings existed between Finns on both sides of the Atlantic. In 1908 he wrote that in earlier years critics had denounced emigrants as thoughtless traitors, without first considering the reasons which impelled their departure. Another writer noted in 1926 that there was more friendliness toward American Finns and America than there had been two decades earlier, when America was commonly pictured as a land where people drank, lived dissolutely, rejected God, and acted like wild beasts. As views changed, writers, clergymen, and officials sought friendlier relations with the American Finns. In 1912 and after the war, groups in Finland encouraged immigrants from America to visit the Old Country. Finnish musicians, clergymen, and journalists crossed the ocean to cultivate the Finns in America.[35] In part, their friendliness had developed from gratitude for immigrant relief sent to Finland during difficult years and, in part, from sympathetic concern for immigrant organizations. Whatever their reasons for seeking immigrant friendship, however, the former critics could no longer condemn those who left Finland as traitors, moral degenerates, and irresponsible adventurers without endangering their contacts in America.

With the changed attitudes toward the Finns in America came increased emphasis on the economic reasons for emigration. To be sure, already during the 1890's critics had connected emigration more or less incidentally with famine, low wages, and unequal land distribution, but they had stressed mainly moral and patriotic considerations. In contrast to such critics, in 1914 the national legislature approved its labor committee's categorical repudiation of the earlier criticism which blamed emigration upon adventurousness, moral irresponsibility, and weakened patriotism. Instead, drawing upon data assembled in the preceding two decades, it declared that economic conditions accounted for emigration. Its report regarded emigration as the natural outgrowth of a half century of change in Finnish agriculture.[36]

Noting the agricultural changes, officials and other observers became less fearful of migratory landless workers. They increasingly accepted as inevitable the presence of workers without land. Willingly or not, they recognized them in 1906 by admitting the propertyless to the suffrage. Three or so decades earlier prohibitions were removed on the free movement without bond of landless workers. In 1899 Yrjö Koskinen rejected the idea of providing land to all the landless.[37] Under the circumstances, this meant that the landless workers were free to travel wherever they could find employment.

Those concerned with the landless saw that persons without land had to find work even if it meant leaving Finland. As a labor paper observed in 1903, emigration would continue as long as wages, hours, and working conditions were less attractive in Finland than in America. In 1888 a baroness said that the solution of "the problem of the landless people" was basic to understanding reasons for emigration. Speaking in 1910, a member of the national legislature declared that emigrants and urban workers came from the same landless element. Economists concluded that emigration resulted from the failure of a fairly rigid agricultural system to provide land or otherwise to sustain a rapidly growing population.[38] In other words, neither rural nor urban employers hired all the landless moving about.

Without question, emigration was essentially the departure of the landless from rural areas. To be sure, people increasingly emigrated from urban areas, but they did not outnumber the rural emigrants; then too, many of the urban emigrants had originated in rural areas. Between 1893 and 1920, passports were issued to 273,366 emigrants of whom 236,507 left rural communes.[39] In the seven years before 1900 the urban emigrants were over 7 percent of the total, and their percentage doubled during the decade of World War I. During the years 1893–1920 about 60 percent of all emigrants at one time followed agricultural pursuits, or had parents who were employed in agriculture. They included 14,774 landowners, 66,593 landowners' children, 7,112 tenants, 25,710 tenants' children, 72,271 cottagers and landless farm workers, and 609 others in agricultural employment. The remaining emigrants included 2,422 merchants and clerks, 4,613 seamen, 13,614 handicraftsmen, 4,022 factory workers, 16,962 domestic servants, 32,878 without fixed occupations, 2,717 public officials and employees, and 9,438 in miscellaneous or unreported occupations.[40] Most emigrants were not only landless, but also lacking in industrial experience. They had only their labor to sell.

To find a livelihood was imperative, although it meant emigrating and drawing censure from one's native country. Immigrant writers challenged their critics in Finland who said that emigration was prompted by unpatriotic, immoral, and godless motives. One pastor even found Biblical sanction for emigration.[41] If they gave their reasons for leaving Finland, most immigrants gave economic ones. As most of them arrived with less than fifty dollars, they came anxious to earn money and expecting to return speedily to Finland with a fortune. In 1890 an immigrant told American consular officials that he had no friend but "de dollar" in the United States. Later another immigrant recalled his reason for coming in terms of an old saying which stated that one could "cut gold with a wooden knife" in America. Others expressed themselves somewhat differently and said that they came to seek "something better."[42]

Behind these dreams of riches was the feeling that it was hard to make a living in Finland. In the 1880's the American consul in Helsinki emphasized famine and the lack of work as motives for emigration. Immigrant writers declared that the lower classes came to America because they found it easier to earn their bread and not because they were depraved. Debating the causes of emigration, an immigrant temperance society resolved in 1907 that the reasons were "fundamentally economic" and it deplored the condition of the working classes who worked long and hard for low wages in Finland.[43] Certainly, many came to America with high expectations of making their livelihood more easily than in the Old Country.

At the same time, however, Finns found other immediate reasons for leaving. Looking for change and adventure, many young people sought escape from rural seclusion and parental domination. One critic complained that children threatened to go to America whenever their parents disciplined them.[44] Between the years 1899 and 1905 Finns also found reason to flee the restraints imposed by the Russian government; hundreds sought to escape military conscription or political persecution by emigrating. Others left because of restrictions placed upon their associative and publishing activities. Many, no doubt, were attracted to America by the presence of friends and relatives.[45]

In a sense, the Finnish awakening was the underlying reason for emigration. Since it led to the breakdown of the isolated, self-contained rural household, the awakening led people to reject the old farm order and its outlook. It raised the possibility of earning money in industry for a livelihood which offered more than did subsistence agriculture. It reduced not only the economic, but also the social, functions of the rural household. People often thus formed some organization to take over social leadership from the household. The awakening also brought forth intellectual currents which went beyond rural folklore and wisdom. In other words, Finns awoke and discovered a chance to leave the farm and to pursue ideas and ways which were hitherto unknown.

Entering industrial life in America, Finnish immigrants broke with their country ways. If they were little touched by the awakening in Finland, the act of departure surely roused them. Physical survival, if nothing else, made them seek mastery of a way of life which was more urban in America than in Finland where agriculture retreated more slowly. When the new life was mastered, the immigrants finally found their America.

CHAPTER II

# NEW FOLKWAYS

*Forge our happiness*
*With the same enthusiasm;*
*Work in common effort*
*With iron will!*

EMIL ELO [1]

In general, Finnish immigrants had little experience with the precise, literate, and organized minds of the modern world. Their wisdom was embodied in folk traditions which were being displaced in the awakening. Usually formalized as verse, proverb, song, and hymn, the folklore represented intimate face-to-face trading of minds. Of course, the many found the literary world through the Bible, Catechism, and perhaps the almanac; the few also found it occasionally through other books. When writers preserved the oral folklore, they recorded the wisdom of the many, the untutored, and the lowly of the countryside. But they did not endorse a mere return to the old. Instead they championed the awakening and its literary values and retreat from a self-contained rural society. Everyone did not accept the awakening in the same degree, and many did not come to a full realization of it until after they had crossed the Atlantic. The folk traditions, especially verse and song, nonetheless helped immigrants master their problems in a society in which rural folkways no longer sufficed.

During the nineteenth century folk traditions were disappearing in Finland. Foreign visitors to the country reported that in the new business age picturesque folk costumes were cast away; even traditional head dress gave way to the printed kerchiefs sold by traveling peddlers.[2] Early in the century Elias Lönnröt and others started to transcribe the oral literature before it should be lost. When he began his collection of the *Kalevala* runes, he found that the bards who had preserved them for generations were passing away. He had to improvise when runes could not be discovered to provide the gaps in the narrative. In 1868 one reviewer of the first American edition of the *Kalevala* said that the minstrels were fast disappearing because "the prosaic spirit of commerce, with the distracting influences of a busy civilization would soon make the people forget their songs." [3] Examining Finnish poetry in the 1890's, one scholar noted that its sources were "gradually drying up." This situation resulted, he said, from the "new times, contact with other peoples, and external influences [which tend] to depreciate the spontaneous work of minds that are leaving or have already left their primitive conditions." [4] Before the folklore was entirely lost, however, Finns assembled one of the largest collections of riddles, charms, songs, ballads, proverbs, and incantations.

In the folklore collections the proverbs disclosed the character of the passing rural society which revolved around the family household. As critiques or guides for social control proverbs emphasized discipline, marriage, and child rearing: "Love is a flower which turns into fruit at marriage"; "A man has plenty of time to choose a wife"; "From sleep to sleep the child; from work to work the bride"; "The rod does not break bones"; "The frost brings the pig home."

Restraint in speaking was valued where primary relationships dominated and people lived intimately: "Much talking in the world; little knowledge"; "His tongue is not burnt with porridge who quarrels with old women"; "The sword destroys a man, the tongue a thousand."

Industriousness and frugality were valued where the soil yielded grudgingly: "He who holds all holidays suffers all hungers"; "One does not get rich gaining but saving"; "When can the lazy work? In the autumn there is much mud, in the spring much water, in the winter biting cold, in the summer burning heat."

In the hard struggle for survival, however, Finns found consolation and exhortation: "There is good where we are not"; "One cannot jump higher than one's head"; "Even the sun does not shine long from one side"; "Even a crust is bread"; "Some have luck, most have summer, all have God."

There was distrust of society beyond the family. The state was little known except as personified by the sheriff, the soldier, or the tax collector: "The law is as it is read," that is, "it is read in nine ways and always right"; "Let the king be heard but not seen." Class antagonisms between gentry and peasant and between rich and poor found expression: "It will not do to go berrying with the gentry; they take both berries and basket"; "The illness of the rich is known to all, but not even the death of the poor"; "Even the masters have their master—God."

But this proverb-ridden life changed in Finland. Family life was partly replaced by associative life. Plowing a furrow began to give way to turning a lathe. State power lost some of its remoteness through universal suffrage. So it was appropriate to observe: "There is nothing as it was [in olden days] except sleep and hunger."[5]

In preserving the proverbial image of a bygone life, romantic nationalists found strength for the future. Having the romantic "appreciation of ancient rusticity," they saw "a golden age of novel customs" in the *Kalevala.* Under the inspiration of their folklore studies, they helped formulate Finnish nationalism as a new "purposeful doctrine," for folklore seemed to embody "those national differences and characteristics upon whose cultivation Finland's future would depend."[6]

If the romantic writers gloried in the past, the writers of realism and naturalism celebrated the immediate workaday world. In 1870 Alexis Kivi offered a realistic motif in his celebrated novel, *Seven Brothers.* He suggested that the peasant could not escape from the world of reality into some unreal world of adventure, but must return to realize his desires by work and struggle. The brothers could not escape the compulsion of learning the A B C Book. They returned from their forest retreat to begin family life and undertake improved farming. By learning to read they satisfied the Church. The youngest brother marked his return to society by helping start one of the first public grammar schools, and he also learned to pen weekly correspondence for the local newspaper. In showing at the close of his story the brothers' increased interest in mental growth, Alexis Kivi keynoted the intellectual ideals of the awakening. Those ideals included high regard for the grammar schools which were actually being inaugurated during the decade in which he wrote his novel.[7]

When the first immigrants left Finland, formal schooling had already begun to supplant their folk training. From the 1860's the four- and six-year grammar schools grew in numbers, and attendance increased. Henceforth the home and church became less important as centers for training in elementary reading. Officials issued data showing increased literacy, but they did not indicate what proportion of the population had had formal public schooling. In 1880, out of each 1,000 persons who were fifteen years and older, 15 were educated beyond grammar schools, 85 could read and write, 670 could read, and 230 could neither read nor write. Thirty years later out of each 1,000 persons in the same age group, 37 were educated beyond grammar schools, 419 could read and write, 346 could read, and 198 could neither read nor write.[8] During the three decades the proportion of those able both to read and write had increased almost five times. No doubt this change was due mainly to the increased attendance at the new public schools. As emigrants came mainly from youthful ranks, it was probable that they had had greater opportunities for education in Finland than the adult population in general.

When immigrants arrived from Finland, American officials reported that most of the newcomers could read and write. Between July, 1899, and June, 1910, under 2 percent of the new arrivals fourteen years old and older could neither read nor write. During the same period over 26 percent of all immigrant nationalities in the same age group were illiterate.[9] But there are no statistics on immigrant school attendance.

Only part of the immigrants, however, had had some schooling. In 1908 an immigrant striker told Minnesota's governor that he had attended school only three days, but had learned to read through self-study. He insisted, moreover, that he went "to school all the time in the poor man's fight for life." [10] In May, 1913, the immigrant-operated Work People's College, located near Duluth, reported that over one-third of its 136 students had never been to school. Of those who had attended grammar school over one-third had not graduated. Since almost three-fourths of the student body were in their twenties, they came from the adult group most likely to have attended school during childhood. Although only about two-thirds had previous school experience, all of them undoubtedly were at least able to read.[11] It should be noted, however, that an even smaller proportion of all immigrants who came to the United States had attended school.

Since most emigrants left northern rural areas which were

slowest to develop schools, many of them never had the educational opportunities of the towns and cities or of the urban and rural communes in southern Finland. Visiting a northwestern area of emigration, one journalist pointed out that the schools there were less numerous than in the south.[12] In the academic year 1871–72, out of every 100 rural school-age children only 3 were in school while 15 out of every 100 urban school-age children were enrolled in school; during the year 1901–2, in the same groups 37 rural and 78 urban children attended school.[13] So the chances were that less than 50 percent of the emigrants before 1900 had schooling, but the percentage increased among those emigrating after the start of the new century. The percentages undoubtedly increased when new schools were organized where none had existed before.

Likewise other aspects of the awakening appeared most slowly in northern rural areas and in greatest strength in southern urban Finland. However, the towns and coastal areas of northern Finland also embraced the awakening faster than their rural hinterlands. For various reasons southern Finland took the lead in the awakening. There, first, new industry appeared, railroads spanned distances, and industrial cities sprouted. There farmers first modified land uses and acquired new machinery. There the capital city of Helsinki became the country's political, educational, and cultural center. For instance, it was the chief center for publishing newspapers and periodicals. When the library movement developed, the southern provinces had the greatest number of books and libraries per capita. Fewer than 10 percent of the members of the leading temperance organization came from the northern provinces of Oulu and Vaasa. The two provinces also gave the lowest percentages of votes to the socialists. But they were not entirely isolated from the general ferment. After 1900 their dairy farmers supported coöperatives. Earlier in the century rural areas in Vaasa, Oulu, and elsewhere were swept by religious revivals like the Laestadian and pietistic movements. In contrast, southern Finland favored more evangelical movements and was stirred by the religious problems of urban living. Then, too, city churches faced more competition than rural churches from secular associations. In short, the more remote rural areas lagged in accepting different aspects of the awakening. Indeed, their isolation was not entirely broken until the twentieth century.[14]

Understandably, then, rural life was colored by provincialism. In older times physical isolation had accentuated differences in dress, speech, and behavior. Such isolation meant that certain traits like pugnacity, stubbornness, and taciturnity became associated with those living in particular regions. Frugality, for example, was associated with the people in the parish of Laihia: it was said that twenty-five years after lads caught fish in a brook, women drew water from the brook for fish stew.[15] The people of Northland (Pohjanmaa), which included most of Oulu and Vaasa, were regarded as especially provincial. According to one immigrant, at the end of the nineteenth century the Northlanders "were still leading lonely and isolated lives" and "not much interested in or aware of anything that took place outside their own province." [16] Hence, the champions of the awakening early frowned upon provincial Northland for its tardiness in developing with the rest of modern Finland.

Those early champions of Finnish nationalism, Yrjö Koskinen, Zacharias Topelius, and Johan Snellman, stressed the cultural and economic isolation of their native Northland. In 1869 Snellman wrote about the strong sense of independence and industriousness which made the Northlanders unwilling to learn by associating with other people. He said that the people of no other area did so little reading, except for religious and devotional literature; moreover, that, although the area had about one-third of all Finns, newspaper publishers and book sellers had little contact with them. In 1856 Yrjö Koskinen, later senator, declared that the northern culture did not progress equally with the rest of Finland. The Northland needed new farming methods, improved transportation, and more "cultural enlightenment." In 1843 Zacharias Topelius said that the Northlanders were very proud, independent, and prone to passionate action. He felt that conquest of a barren land instilled such traits.[17] To these three men provincialism thus meant isolated, self-sufficient, rural living. In their view, to awaken was to depart from the old provincial farm life.

When they left the Northland, emigrants drew attention to those provincial traits which supposedly impelled their departure. In 1891 the Diet gave a common explanation that emigration arose partly from the Northlander's inherited love of adventure. Although political and economic grievances led to emigration from

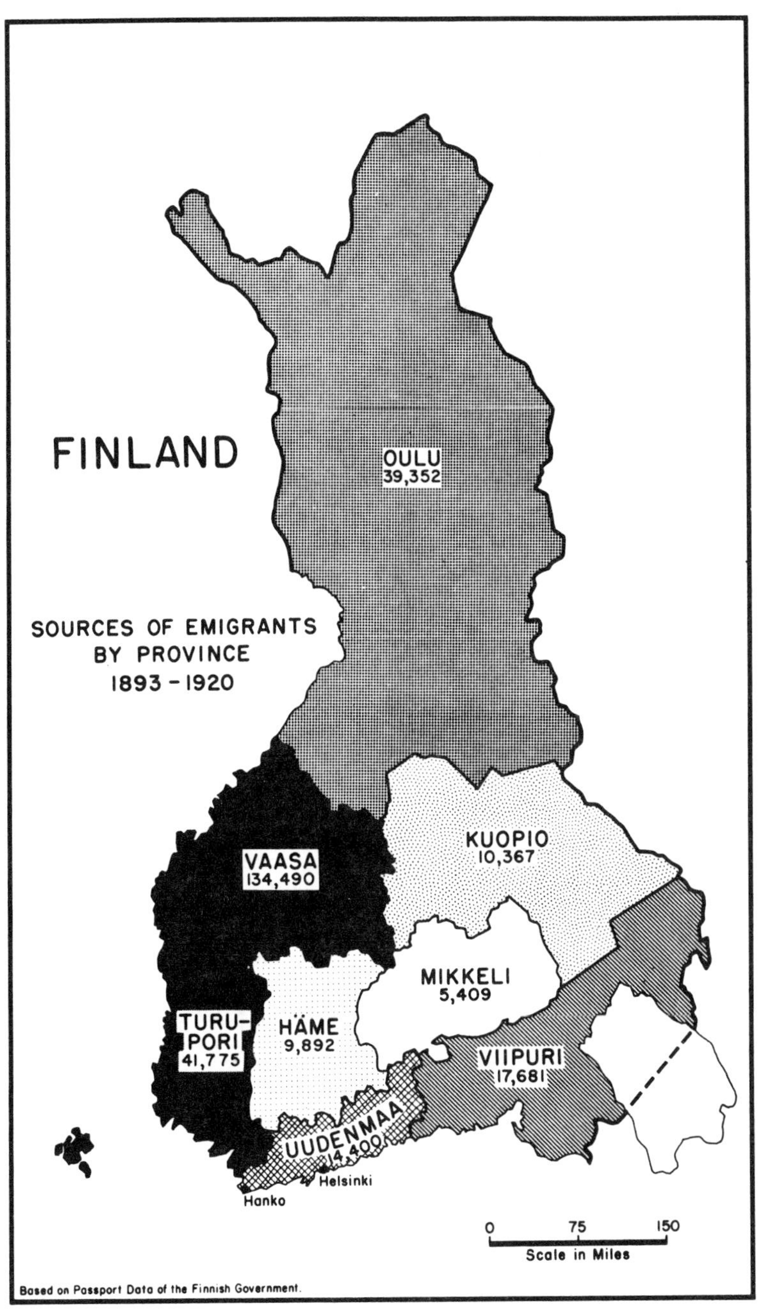


*Map of Finland showing origin of emigrants by province*

*Hotel in Hanko, Finland, that housed emigrants awaiting ship departure*

*Steamship* Urania *taking 509 emigrants from Hanko to England in 1893*

all over Finland, an immigrant pastor claimed, the fact that the largest number of immigrants came from Vaasa and Oulu was due to the character of the Northlanders. That character, he wrote, revealed strong adventurousness and boldness and a strong love of freedom as proved by their desire to own land.[18] Since Northlanders began to settle in America before socialism appeared in Finland, immigrant socialists later attributed the hostility or indifference of the firstcomers to their rural background. According to the socialists, these firstcomers had thus created a "Gibraltar of conservatism" in the Cape Cod area of Massachusetts. In Ashtabula, Ohio, one correspondent attributed the existence of over twenty different organizations to the rural origins of the immigrants. He explained that, since so few immigrants came from cities, where they might have learned the value of labor unity, they separated into divergent groups in America.[19] Immigrants, however, did break away from their rural backgrounds.

After reaching America, the immigrants discarded or modified their folk traditions. It goes without saying that they found new ways in America and barriers to organizing a New Finland. Even if they took up farm life immediately upon their arrival in America, they found that American farming differed from Finnish. Most newcomers to America found little need to use arts suitable for self-sufficient rural households. Entering the mine and mill, men found few occasions to show their skills in horseshoeing, butchering, and wood carving. Entering domestic employment, women found little occasion to show their skills in weaving, buttermaking, and milking. The new arrivals needed more often to learn and use new skills, even if only how to push an ore car or to open a tin can. When they moved to farms, immigrants without money for all the desired goods and services often resorted temporarily to their old skills as jacks of all trades.

Farmers in the cutover lands of the Great Lakes region, for example, drew in the beginning on their experiences in the Northland, but their old ways were eventually replaced or modified by new ones. They cut logs and built hay barns in the fashion of their native Northland. Such barns could be built with little cash outlay for labor and materials. But when the immigrant farmers and their children prospered, they ceased copying the old ways, increased their farm operations, and built modern barns like American farmers who produced for a cash market.[20] With cash, they did not have to rely on their own resources for sustenance. And so they, too, retreated from the old ways of farm life as the miners, the mill operators, and the domestic servants had done.

In other ways the immigrants also retreated from rural customs. Newly arrived women who came with homemade folk costumes, soon dressed in factory-made dresses, or for economy's sake they might wear homemade dresses of factory prints. If immigrants used foods found in Finnish menus, like breads, fish, coffee, and dairy products, they used what was common and relatively inexpensive in America, and they probably used more wheat than rye bread and more real coffee than substitutes. Probably the use of the *sauna,* or steam bath, was their most common and distinctive transfer of folkways from Finland. Not every family, however, acquired a *sauna;* finances were limited, houses were too close to permit construction, and renters did not wish to build on someone else's land. In towns and cities they used mainly the commercial steam baths operated by their fellow countrymen. Immigrants who turned to farming after an industrial apprenticeship often built private bath houses on their land.

Among other customs immigrants modified were their holiday habits. Like native-born Americans, they celebrated Easter, Christmas, and Fourth of July. They also observed Saint John's Day, which originally had honored sun gods in pagan Finland, but now marked the return of summer in June. The celebration of such festive occasions no longer depended on finishing farm tasks, but on whether or not one's shift in the mine or shop conflicted. As one writer said, it was hard to celebrate Christmas accompanied by factory sounds.[21] Since the immigrants were scattered in many communities, summer holidays like Saint John's Day and Fourth of July became reunions which were sponsored by some organization. Festive occasions were often used by societies to promote causes associated with the awakening. At festivals and other entertainments the societies provided music for folk dances, like the polkas and schottisches, in the hope of raising money and attracting youthful new members. So the moments of recreation also helped change their customs.

In their organized retreat from rural ways immigrants continued to draw on the rural symbolism of farm life and its folklore.

References to pigs, cows, knives, and birch ladles, for example, appeared in their imagery. Because its possession was important in Finland, the cow came to represent anything highly regarded. Said one immigrant woman, it was like getting a cow when she received a love letter. Beyond using rural similes, immigrants applied rural symbolism in a naturalistic examination of human life and society, which they compared to the physical world with its cycles of birth, growth, and decay. Foremost they drew on that age-old simile comparing daylight and darkness with knowledge and ignorance. Knowledge was like the light which came from the rising sun of the east. In turn, it released energies to fight sin and evil arising in the new industrial order. Sin and evil cast autumn-like clouds over human life, which bloomed like a spring flower and then faded in the fall. Spring liberated nature from the chains of cold winter; man also needed springtime to free himself from economic oppression, King Alcohol, and moral sin. To find liberation men and women therefore called for organized struggle to meet the problems of living in an industrial society. Their images of rural commonplaces had grown smaller and more remote from rural actuality.[22]

In trying to master their problems immigrants found instruction and entertainment in the symbol of the untutored countryman. When immigrants started organizing and publishing, they used the symbol to promote their new purposes. The untutored countryman thus provided periodical titles like the *Rascal, Rogue, Shoepack,* and *American Matthew*. In verse, song, and story entertainment and instruction came from the untutored hero who matched wits with his supposed social betters and with persons showing pretension, arrogance, and conceit. Sometimes the hero was represented as in his native Finland; at other times he was an immigrant.

Many a story was told about John or Matt who outwitted the gentry in Finland. John, for example, was sent to fish for a master who ordinarily did the fishing himself. John secured a big catch of fish whose heads and tails he took to the master while he hid the bodies. Outraged, the master asked for the rest. Pretending ignorance, John said that he had assumed the rest was useless and inedible, because he had had nothing to eat but heads and tails in the master's household.[23]

In America the immigrant Matt or John also showed wit. He

outwitted the pesky lice or the arrogant boss in the lumbercamp. Once John was characterized as "Sven Duva, the Younger," a veteran of World War I. (Like the hero of Johan Runeberg's patriotic verses, Sven Duva learned soldiering by always doing the wrong thing, but at the crucial moment the country bumpkin did not fail like those who had supposedly learned soldiering in the right way.) [24] The newly arrived immigrant who had not yet learned American ways also drew pointed comments from more experienced and sophisticated persons whose foolish and "high toned" pretensions, in turn, created mirth. A newcomer was dismissed as a greenhorn by a poet for asking what was the source of power for streetcars.[25] The urbane also repeated dialect stories to suggest the newcomer's provincial origins. But even if Finns poked fun at the untutored hero, in reality at themselves, they were looking further and deeper.

To master new situations the immigrants drew on their folklore. From their abundant oral traditions of song, verse, and proverb, they drew intellectual fodder. From the *Kalevala* legends they took the name Sampo, the magic mill of abundance, and bestowed it with high hopes as the name of coöperative, temperance, business, and other enterprises. They also found additional reassuring titles in the *Kalevala*. Bent upon organizing to meet common problems, the newcomers in America found that proverbs continued to be useful as critiques for social behavior. With little family life or none at all, immigrants discovered that organized life outside the home had become urgent. Since proverbs had taught discipline in rural Finland, the immigrants used them again for social control.

As the parent had once taught his child through proverbs, the organization now taught its member through proverbs. Although organized activity was relatively new among them, the immigrants learned to participate and help each other through common endeavor. Hard-working organizers of associations were advised by a writer that "Industriousness conquers hard luck." A correspondent endorsed the new coöperative store in Weirton, West Virginia, and agreed with the saying, "God helps those who help themselves." From Maine another reporter applied the saying, "A new broom always sweeps cleaner," to the energetic new preacher who organized a church sewing club to secure finances. When a socialist local failed to receive outside speakers or actors for a celebration, they relied on their own resources, for surely "A cat finds its claws on the tree." When many a hall was dedicated to temperance or socialism, the members observed, "One's own home; one's own master." Using such halls for lectures, sponsors reminded patrons, "Learning does not push one into a rut and knowledge does not thrust one from the road." Proverbs thus exhorted the immigrants to new efforts.

The organizations felt that not all immigrants were disciplined and that many needed fatherly admonition. On one occasion bachelors who protested criticism of their drinking and inadequate support of a socialist local, were told by their lady critic, "The dog who is hit with the hoe yelps." In Newport, New Hampshire, the agitation committee disciplined socialist members because "He who saves the whip, hates his child; but he who chastens his wife, loves her." From quarters hostile to socialism but sympathetic to other causes, one newspaper warned of the dangers of spreading socialism and complained, "The plague still catches." Since organizers of rival associations assumed the worst about each other, they traded reprimands publicly and exploited any hint of misbehavior, for surely "There is no smoke, if there is no flame." When immigrants began to marry and raise families, their organizations hoped to keep the children from straying away by arranging classes because "The oldster is master of what is learned in youth." [26] No matter where they turned, immigrants had appropriate proverbs bidding them accept the organized discipline so new to them.

To promote organized discipline immigrants also drew on the art of speaking. They were not satisfied merely to converse intimately with friends and kin, but, unlike the pastors, few were experienced in speaking before public groups. So when congregations and societies were organized, immigrants found reason to practice their speaking talents. Each association had organizers who learned to speak publicly and arouse attention and who went on "missions of conquest" to enlist their fellow immigrants. As one churchman said, America was the land for home mission work because the immigrants were not attached to regular church life as they had been in Finland. This situation caused pastors and laymen to tour as far west as the Pacific Coast in the hope of forming new congregations. One such missionary reported that during three months in 1890 he traveled 6,800 miles to visit twenty-three communities.

Temperance workers also made similar tours. In 1901 Kalle Ojajärvi described himself as an unschooled speaker who addressed about 4,000 listeners on his tour covering almost 6,000 miles. On the socialist circuit the most famous "agitator" probably was Martin Hendrickson, who had first promoted temperance during the 1890's before turning to socialism in Massachusetts. On his nine-month tour in 1907 he reported covering 13,000 miles and reaching an audience of about 45,000 in 122 immigrant centers.[27] Indeed the lecture tour gave opportunities for those wanting to speak.

Speakers proved attractive, certainly in part, because of their colorful language and behavior. Kalle Ojajärvi hoped that he had not said "crazy things" when obliged to use "forthright language." Martin Hendrickson defended his use of "raw language" as necessary to attract attention and was criticized by a correspondent for evidently believing in the proverb, "The words of the poor are not believed except when they swear." Another speaker gained attention among critics who alleged that he thumped his fists on the coffin during a funeral oration. Upon reaching the pulpit, Pastor Arthur Heideman once took off his shoes and socks and proceeded to trim his toenails while he discoursed to his congregation.[28] Without any doubt, such speakers, pastors, and preachers satisfied their audiences, because people flocked to hear addresses lasting two hours or longer.

When they started organizing, Finns found many occasions which required speakers. They needed chairmen capable of conducting meetings. Two national temperance organizations, for example, strove to develop chairmen by providing manuals which contained the rules and even complete speeches for use on appropriate occasions.[29] Organizations also encouraged their members to develop such varied oral talents as recitation, declamation, singing, and dramatic speech. They sponsored debating societies and discussion groups; a few had the *juttutupa,* or "chatter room." Through such subsidiary clubs the parent groups hoped to train members as speakers.

In Erie, Pennsylvania, a temperance society discussed why all its members did not participate in meetings and entertainments. It concluded that their inexperience was the reason and decided that henceforth each discussion session would have practice speeches by members. Then the group as a whole would try to develop mental agility by examining such topics as what were the merits of temperance and social reform, which sex had more pity towards the other, and whether wealth, love, or beauty was most important for marriage. If everyone practiced debating, speakers surely would be developed.[30]

To develop both oral and literary expression, immigrant societies used the *nyrkkilehti,* which means literally "fist paper." The paper consisted of original and borrowed poems, stories, essays, and anecdotes. Its editors made one handwritten copy, which was then presented orally at some evening entertainment. Numerous religious, temperance, socialist, and other organizations issued the *nyrkkilehti,* but probably the temperance and socialist groups prepared it most commonly. Each tried to entertain and instruct according to its particular aims. Calling itself the "Blockhead," one socialist fist paper urged workers to seek knowledge, contribute writings to future issues, and buy the latest socialist literature. Editors of a temperance fist paper welcomed contributions mainly from all the "water boys" in order to show the value of combatting intemperance and to satisfy "laughing nerves"; they accepted contributions about broken homes, sordid drunkards, and unsullied, innocent youth. After presenting the sober messages, editors of the different fist papers enlivened their pages with anecdotes stressing courtship and marital matters. At first, under enthusiastic sponsorship, most fist papers appeared regularly. As time passed, editors began to complain of editorial burdens and the lack of contributions. Issues appeared less regularly until finally their preparation was permanently suspended.[31]

During the prime of the fist papers, their sponsors encouraged the arts of declamation and writing and also urged regular literary publishing. Immigrant writers observed that such papers served as bridges to newspaper publishing because they stimulated writing and aroused interest in newspapers.[32] Societies increasingly depended upon newspapers which published reports about local events written by correspondents who were usually designated by the organizations. Meanwhile the full-time newspaper editors and writers provided the varied literature which local talent and limited leisure could not sustain on a regular basis in the fist papers. When immigrants found occasion to write, they usually found acceptance in some newspaper. Perhaps inevitably, the fist papers gave way to the newspapers.

In the transition to a more literary culture, immigrants used poetry which originally had not been written down. Instead it was transmitted orally from bard to bard and from generation to generation. Like the *Kalevala* runes, the oral verses achieved literary form only after collectors transcribed them. This poetry was found among the unschooled. In the *Kalevala* Väinämöinen says,

*That I sang so much in childhood,*
*And when small, I sang so badly.*
*I received no store of learning,*
*Never travelled to the learned.*
*Foreign words were never taught me,*
*Neither songs from distant countries.*[33]

With literary training poets developed their art more and more as a means of written expression. But poetry was still created by all immigrant ranks, including those who came to America with little schooling.

On countless occasions immigrants revealed their untutored poetic tradition in its new literary forms. Various publications contained thousands of verses written by their readers. Still others wrote verses for almost any occasion—from birthdays to funerals and from divine invocation to strike advocacy. In a list of original books by immigrants the works of poetry numbered over one-half of the prose titles.[34] Editors and pastors, however, wrote most of these books. Their greater literary experience gave them tools, and their positions gave them the time, to write poems longer than one or two pages.

Both poets and editors realized that poetry was a medium of expression for the unschooled. In 1902, aroused by Russian actions in Finland, Matti Johansson, who was a temperance advocate, issued a booklet of verse in which he apologized for his lack of schooling. His verses, he said, were those of a simple "common man" whose words were

*Born in the heart,*
*Untouched by schooling,*
*Unguided by learned precepts.*

Editors stated that they welcomed the work of such men even though the form did not meet the "standards of the learned." One editor said he was publishing a poem which he could not understand, hoping that its publication would encourage better work from the contributor.[35] Still another editor accepted a poem from a poet who explained that since his lack of education made him unable to punctuate verses he had added various marks of punctuation at the bottom of his sheet. The editor said that just enough of them had been sent.[36] But another poet, Eelu Kiwiranta, was not encouraged by the editors.

As one of the unschooled poets, Eelu Kiwiranta assured the publication of his verses by printing them on his own hand press. According to his autobiographic verses, he came from unhappy, poverty-stricken circumstances in northern Finland where he had no chance to attend school. After serving in the army, he worked in a mill where the girls scorned his occasional advances, for

*Coming as a rustic*
*In the mill girls' minds*
*He was completely mad.*

Then he came to the "land of gold," but finding little wealth in the mines of Michigan, he moved to a farm. In his leisure he wrote verses which disclosed his lively interests, especially in matters of the heart although he was a married man of fifty. Most of all, he expressed his love for freedom from the burdens of hard toil, low pay, and hypocrisy.

The poet Eelu Kiwiranta said that he started farming to escape "mine slavery." Men shoveled ore into cars which they pushed to the shaft. "Hurry up!" rang constantly in their ears. Not even at night did he feel free, because the whistle never failed to call him back to work in early morning. Then he bought a farm in the cutover lands near Nisula, Michigan. On the farm he found no bosses, little income, and no unemployment and there

*No worldly tumults reached his ears;*
*He enjoyed quiet and peace.*

Yet he was not entirely isolated, because he often left the farm in the hands of his wife while he toured the countryside and sold his verses.

In his verses Kiwiranta matched wits in the manner of the countryman John or Matt. He examined everything which he felt represented sham, pretension, and hypocrisy among his fellow immigrants. He derided the "high toned" wives of the mine drillers for setting themselves apart from the women whose husbands had less desirable, lower-paying jobs in the mines. With his poems of love, he said, he drew the applause of youth but the fury of the clergymen, to whom

> *. . . came no memory of their past youth*
> *Instead they saw only an adulterous scene.*

He intimated that Laestadians took the name of the Lord in vain by jumping and yelling in their services. Weak-minded persons drew his censure for enriching the pockets of numerous agents and promoters. Though he shared dreams of economic betterment with the lowly, he stated that the socialist leaders were disqualified from representing workers, because they started disorders and acted like bloodhounds. The poet claimed that he was neither socialist nor capitalist, but only a worker seeking a better life. In other verses he urged workers to awaken and unite in comradely endeavor to secure their just share from the capitalists. But socialists, churchmen, and others criticized him in effect for failing to spell out the program of action whereby immigrants might gain a better life. He distrusted modern routine and organization and, unlike other poets, was not willing to accept, champion, and follow decisions of an organized group. For a time he joined the Laestadians and even sold subscriptions for two newspapers, but later ended his connections with them all. Yet he recognized the contemporary challenges, and in his own way he helped make the transition from an oral to a literary culture.[37]

In their organizing endeavors immigrants associated their poetic traditions with vocal and instrumental music. They found this possible because much verse, such as the *Kalevala,* was chanted to the accompaniment of a stringed instrument, the *kantele.* The couplets of the untutored poets were often sung. It was commonplace to provide poetry and music at any group affair for home, church, hall, or outdoors. Concerts were also arranged. Music societies even performed for listeners other than immigrants: in 1903 a glee club from Calumet, Michigan, sang before a Chicago audience of 6,000 at a benefit performance for the famine-stricken of Finland.[38] All told, Finns had hundreds of choral groups.

To add to their own original verses and songs, immigrants imported suitable books from Finland or reprinted selections from them. Such borrowings included the folk songs and the patriotic songs of the awakening: songs in praise of rustling pines, glistening lakes, sun-lit nights, and shrewd carefree wits. Immigrants also used the folk tunes from Finland for their original verses. Pastors and organists came to promote church music and former army musicians came to help organize bands, either as independent groups or as subsidiaries of fraternal, temperance, or socialist clubs.[39] Most important, perhaps, immigrants adopted the annual festival of the People's Enlightenment Society begun during the 1880's in Finland. The festival organized thousands, both as performers and listeners, in praise of song and verse.

From the 1890's immigrants increasingly sponsored festivals in connection with their summer holidays and annual organizational meetings. In 1897, for example, the Finnish National Temperance Brotherhood started the first of its annual festivals, which drew upwards of ten thousand persons at a time.[40] Such organizations made certain that the festivals would occur annually and would attract brass bands and choral groups. They also stimulated rivalry among poets for the honor of having their verses recited on such occasions. Through poetry everyone was urged to support the purposes of the festival sponsors who helped immigrants cope with their problems. In this way poetry gave direction to Finns during their stay in America.

With verse and song immigrants reminded each other of their departure from the Old Country and their entrance into a strange new land. They pictured themselves as wanderers, seekers, and even tramps who were separated from their homes and who drifted in search of new ones. One of them wondered whether the wandering immigrant would ever find a new home again. This sense of homelessness was based on reality since most immigrants were unmarried youths who had left their homes in Finland. The emphasis on home and childhood also reflected the general concern with the lessening importance of family life. Strange new circumstances in America, moreover, contributed to the feeling of isolation and rejection. Understandably, many a poet felt that America was a strange country with dark roads for the orphan who might find consolation in memories of his Northland. Editors of a song book for immigrants included the lines,

*An immigrant did I become*
*Homeless now I wander;*
*Like an orphan I roam*
*Ever remembering my birth land.*

Homeless and unschooled, one young Finn came to America in his twenties and sang his ballads in carefree fashion. As he sang his song of the wanderer, he spoke of moving like a bird and hopping trains from state to state in the West. The town of Bessemer, Michigan, he decided, was best of all places in the Midwest and the Pacific Coast.[41] Like birds, also, most other immigrants moved about in search of jobs.

According to the poets and songsters, the wandering immigrant came easily to grief and lost himself in the strange new land. Rejected, penniless, and unable to speak English, he met many pitfalls. One churchman confessed:

*I roamed about lost for many years*
*and sank deeper into a sinful wilderness.*

Peace on earth was not promised to the immigrant by the devotional song which described man as a visitor out of place in the wrong world. On Sunday morning, said a poet, men found their way to church but by evening lost their way and entered saloons. One poet told how an immigrant lad had left his happy home to seek gold in America, but, alas, he found whiskey, which killed him, and news of his death killed his mother in Finland. Other poets found the wandering immigrant falling victim to economic injustice. Although there were homes and food aplenty, a poet declared that justice denied them to the forsaken wanderer. Another described how the wanderers were enslaved to work day and night while others reaped the fruits of their toil.[42] Life, however, was not all so dark.

Verse and song sought to renew hope in the minds and hearts of the immigrants. Poets assured church members that their earthly trials were only temporary. A religious song told them that they were on earth only as visiting strangers whose real homes were on distant shores in heaven. A hymn assured the oppressed who found no peace on earth that in heaven there was no want of food and clothing. Though homeless and forsaken, a poet confided, some day the poor would master their plight and find springtime with homes and freedom on earth. Another dreamed:

*Although as hoboes on a boxcar roof*
*We sing our many songs,*
*One day in a Pullman we shall ride,*
*Drawing great puffs of smoke.*

In the spirit of those experimenting with a utopian community, the leader sang beckoning immigrants from the outside world of misery and hate:

*No one yearns for the world*
*When he makes his home with you.*

By fighting intemperance, one songster believed, the traveler in life would protect both home and family. A poet agreed and hopefully saw the return of happiness to the home when liberation came from the chains of drink. Indeed, the home had become the symbol of the paradise looming behind dark clouds.[43]

Hoping to find paradise, immigrant organizations gave their clarion calls in verse and song. In different ways they expected to find happiness somewhere and sometime for mankind, and their particular organizational aims were identified with the individual immigrant's search for a better life. Everyone, they declared, must awaken and make a real effort to achieve enlightened happiness. Through song books major organizations proclaimed, "Awaken, unite, and struggle!" Each promised final entrance to paradise. "To struggle!" called the poet to his people of the *Kalevala,* and he urged them to raise the "flag of knowledge" with

*A new Sampo, a new spirit*
*Which would bring victory yet.*

As in the Old Country, they must raise "Finnish spirits" anew for greater achievement. They must rise from the darkness of drunken stupor, work-ridden minds, and sinful souls. They must find light through united effort to the shores of eternity, to freedom from intemperance, and to the new economic order. As the organizations said again and again:

*Unite, strengthen!*
*This alone assures victory.*

Then no more would the immigrant find himself alone, hopelessly enchained and wandering in darkness.[44]

When he shared the organization's search for paradise, the immigrant certainly had removed himself from his old rural ways and ideas. The organization increasingly was accepted by him as his foster parent. As the teacher taught by linking the familiar with the unfamiliar, so now the new parent by drawing on rural traditions charted the way in a nation retreating from the farm faster than the Old Country. Through associative activity in America the Finnish immigrant found a new home, a paradise built with his Old Country heritage in his New World environment.

CHAPTER III

# ASSOCIATIVE SPIRIT

*We see groups of people as though nervous, roving in support of diverse endeavors. It [the immigrant people] seeks spiritual satisfaction in several different churches and sects which support the same faith. It reveals national and political aims in all sorts of leagues and in joining the ranks of political parties and it seeks economic security in diverse secret societies and common enterprises.*

HEIKKI ANIAS [1]

As soon as they came to America, Finnish immigrants sought each other's companionship. In their trials they found solace through informal contacts among themselves. Next they developed their companionship into formal organizations. As they organized to meet common problems in their new circumstances, the Finns sought fulfillment of varied aspirations in numerous associations ranging from small independent clubs to nationwide leagues. Then with messianic fervor they endorsed mental improvement and proclaimed that organized minds were power. By seeking mastery of their own minds through the organizations, the immigrants finally found their America and intellectual independence from Finland.

Ordinarily immigrants did not join organizations other than those of their own making. Of course, in newly developing industrial areas there were few associations for anyone to join; and if any such groups existed, language barriers and unfamiliarity kept out the immigrants. But in some areas, particularly in western mining regions, employers helped immigrant religious and temperance organizations by giving them funds, land, and the use of buildings. For instance, in Soudan, Minnesota, one iron mining company gave land to the Finnish temperance society, and in Michigan's Copper Country the Calumet and Hecla Company gave land and funds to newly organized churches, including the Finnish. Such assistance, however, was far outmatched by the contributions made by the Finns when they really became interested in organizing.

When they began to organize, the immigrants awoke in the associative spirit suggestive of the awakening in Finland. Some renewed the associative interests which they had acquired in Finland and others actually developed such interests for the first time in their lives only after leaving the Old Country. But they all usually affirmed the belief that knowledge is power. Everywhere, wrote an immigrant, there was talk about the era of enlightenment and reason. To liberate themselves from the oppressive darkness of ignorance Finns found hope in mental discipline. In this spirit a temperance writer declared that mental exercise led to happiness. Until the mind had found the way to happiness, it was discontented. History showed, he added, that the way was found by forming ideals and by humanistic endeavors. Intensive thought, according to the Unitarians, brought liberation from authoritarian religions. One socialist paper proclaimed that the thinking slave had found the road to freedom, and a socialist poet promised that one day man would know everything and thus master nature. Dedicating a school, a Lutheran pastor urged the spread of enlightenment in a religious spirit. Echoing the clergyman's sentiments, a poet later declared that knowledge which was gained at the school brought light and assurance in daily struggles. Besides, knowledge must be used, said the school's director, because the desire for knowledge was God-given.[2] Knowledge surely, then, represented power to the immigrants.

To promote knowledge immigrants published and read newspapers which offered all sorts of new ideas as well as old ones. The editors of the first newspapers, printed by private entrepreneurs for business purposes, tried to solicit the largest possible clientele by often opening their columns to writers who appealed to readers of many different opinions. It was not uncommon for editors to espouse religious and other doctrines which they later in part or entirely exchanged for new ones. Newspaper writers thus moved closer to temperance, social reform, and even socialism. In the early 1900's private publishers in Michigan and Massachusetts tolerated, at least temporarily, editors who discovered merit in liberal religion and socialism. Finding more than one intellectual home as an editor, lecturer, and pastor, Johan Lähde worked at various times for religious, temperance, and socialist papers.[3] Another newspaper worker, John Harpet, who came to America in 1886 as a nine-year-old lad, served on various newspapers which espoused religion, liberalism, socialism, conservatism, and Finnish nationalism.[4] When newspapers printed reports and stories about how some John or Matt had found religion, temperance, or socialism, they were not merely promoting causes, but reflecting the real experiments of immigrants in discovering new intellectual vistas.

Besides reading newspapers, churchmen, socialists, and temperance advocates stimulated themselves intellectually by starting libraries, often nothing more than a corner in a home or a hall, which they stocked with books on health, astrology, physics, biology, economics, language, sex, sociology, and history, as well as fiction, old and new. In addition to the libraries, they sponsored hundreds of lectures. With truth, a satirist pictured the agitator who was dissatisfied with having spoken on no more than fifteen subjects in his evening's address on capitalism, materialism, theosophy, confirmation, baptism, free love, distribution of wealth, and new social communities.[5] To test their knowledge of such subjects rivals debated on the same platform. Many a listener left reassured of the power of both the spoken and printed word.

In addition, a few speakers and writers sought to explore what might be termed "pure mind." To attain mental power, one promoter offered a correspondence course in hypnotism through which anyone could master the human mind and overcome illness, intemperance, and class oppression. Seeking "eternal truths," a theosophist offered a pamphlet which charted planetary influences governing human behavior and fortunes. From the ranks of the utopian socialists Matti Kurikka gave advice on mental powers. Rejected by the Finnish Socialist Federation, he ended his career as an editor dreaming of new panaceas for the woes of mankind. He advocated the theosophical quest for truth in the mysterious past unsullied by contemporary strife. His paper advertised that since it did not represent any party or sect but ordinary reason and love of truth, socialists, suffragettes, theosophists, and temperance advocates alike could accept its columns.[6] Most Finns who praised reason, however, preferred to struggle in behalf of their convictions through organizations.

Intense, indeed, were the debates over various ideas and causes. Sensing the intellectual intensity, in 1903 a correspondent observed that a war of words was sure to ensue whenever two or three Finns met.[7] Editors, in particular, traded verbal blows and were ready to think the worst of each other. According to one of them, his fellow journalists were the worst scoundrels that could be found among the immigrants.[8] Tempers flared especially when ideas that were supposed to be sacred and time-tested were challenged.

Obviously, the religious ideas of the immigrants represented something of the old that was challenged. Yet in America religious activity took on new forms: old church ties were renewed or new religious choices were made. Since no State Church existed, immigrants were free to consider whether or not they wanted to re-establish church connections. Consequently, they debated the merits of synodical and episcopal church organization and the desirability of maintaining friendly ties with the State Church of Finland. Critical editors denounced the State Church, its clergy, and tithes, expressing fears that clerical arrogance and authoritarianism might be transferred to America. Defenders of the State Church said that only those trained in the traditions of the old church were qualified to direct the building of religious organizations in America. They warned that unschooled laymen and even drunkards had entered immigrant pulpits in the absence of state control. They worried also when immigrants formed competing Lutheran groups, left the Lutheran fold for Unitarianism, Congregationalism, and Methodism, did not join churches, or sought the pamphlets of the agnostic Robert Ingersoll. So vigorous were the religious debates that courts occasionally had to settle disputes on jurisdiction over church properties.[9]

Since the religious disputes involved not only matters of church organization and theology but also of morality, people found doors opening to other areas of thought when they looked at the social behavior of immigrants. Disturbed by saloon life, they examined the problem of intemperance, which they attributed to the absence of economic well-being or of respect for the Divine. Then their concern over intemperance led to the search for remedies. Consequently, temperance and social reform entered their horizons and eventually socialism drew their attention. As they found new ideas, they had more causes over which to debate, and finally they had reasons to form organizations other than congregations.

In organizing into like-minded groups, most persons sought the power which they felt came from the possession of knowledge. Finnish Americans certainly realized that their life was one of organization. To be heard effectively, said an immigrant pastor, the individual, especially in America, had to join numerous societies. Another commentator observed that his era belonged to the societies and associations. In America, he felt, the spirit of association was noticeably strong since practically everyone belonged to some organization. Finnish organizations sprouted like mushrooms for, as one woman said, associative activities became second nature to her compatriots. Still others observed that in keeping with the spirit of the times, they were busily organizing to pursue enlightenment.[10]

Although the associative spirit had spread increasingly in Finland, it had not by 1900 acquired wide currency in many rural parishes. Since immigrants came mainly from such areas, their organizational energy in America impressed observers. Already in the 1890's an observer noted that the immigrants talked incessantly about their common endeavors. Before they numbered more than a few score in a community, he added, they were sure to organize more than one society.[11]

Indeed, the Finns formed thousands of such organizations as congregations, temperance societies, benefit associations, choral groups, socialist locals, library clubs, coöperative enterprises, and a host of others. Nor were they satisfied with one of a kind in a community: factions withdrew and formed rival associations. While their independent local groups usually had limited purposes and functions, their national federations had more comprehensive ones. Consequently, the national organizations eventually dominated Finnish-American institutional life.

Immigrants first organized along religious lines. The first completely Finnish congregation was probably formed in the early 1870's by Minnesota Laestadians who had started to hold meetings in the previous decade. In 1867 Laestadians also had joined other Finnish, Swedish, and Norwegian Lutherans in forming a congregation with a Norwegian pastor in Hancock, Michigan. These

Lutherans were disciples of Lars Laestadius, who had conducted revivals in Lapland until his death in 1861. Typically the group had lay preachers, rejected elaborate church rituals, and preferred hymn singing, Biblical reading, and oral confession of sins at services. Quarrels ensued, and in 1871 the Laestadians withdrew from the Hancock church to form a new congregation in nearby Calumet under Salomon Korteniemi, a lay preacher. In 1879 they legalized their church as the Apostolic Lutheran, a name adopted by other Laestadian congregations. During the next two decades, Johan Takkinen, layman, and Arthur Heideman, seminarian, extended the influence of the Calumet congregation to other Laestadians. But not until 1908 did some of the Apostolic Lutheran congregations start holding common meetings. In this way independent congregations developed new sects or factions because of differences on theology and disagreement of personalities. The Apostolic Lutherans established themselves especially in the rural areas of Michigan and Minnesota.

Although the Laestadians withdrew, the Lutheran church of Hancock was still supported by adherents of the State Church of Finland. When the Finns increased in number, they gained control of the church by purchasing the shares of the Swedes and Norwegians. As a result, they formed the first Finnish Evangelical Lutheran congregation in America. In 1876 they received their first pastor from Finland. After seven years in America, Alfred Backman returned to Finland and was replaced by Juho Nikander, who arrived in 1885 and served until his death in 1919. Largely under the leadership of Nikander, the Finnish Evangelical Lutheran Synod was formed in 1890. The Synod Lutherans showed strength in Michigan, Minnesota, Oregon, Ohio, and Pennsylvania.

Not all Lutherans, however, were willing to join the Synod, which felt close to the State Church of Finland. In 1890 dissidents withdrew from the Synod congregation in Calumet and formed a new one to which they invited as pastor William Eloheimo, who had helped organize the Synod. Later he left this congregation for Ironwood, Michigan, where he formed a new church organization. Eventually his group joined with a church body from Ohio and other independent Lutheran congregations to form the Finnish National Evangelical Lutheran Church in opposition to supporters of the State Church of Finland. Uniting in 1898, the National

Lutherans drew support from communities in such states as Michigan, Minnesota, Ohio, and Wyoming.

Other critics of the State Church also organized independent congregations, but they remained outside the Lutheran fold. Mainly in Ohio and Massachusetts, Finnish Congregational churches appeared associated with their American counterparts. In Minnesota appeared Unitarian groups under the leadership of Risto Lappala, who had found the faith in Boston. Scattered groups of Methodists and Baptists were organized, partly by those who had found the new faiths in Finland. Such independent groups, however, were a handful compared to the three main bodies of Lutherans.[12]

Between 1890 and 1910 Finns were most active in forming new congregations. By 1900 they probably had 100 or more congregations. In the next decade they formed at least 143 new ones, of which about 60 joined the Synod. According to federal church censuses, in 1906 the three Lutheran groups had 239 congregations with 31,188 members, and ten years later they had 245 congregations with 33,478 members. In 1906 the Synod Lutherans had 105 churches with 12,907 members, the National Lutherans had 66 churches with 10,111 members, and the Apostolic Lutherans had 68 churches with 8,170. During the following decade both the National and Apostolic Lutherans lost members. Using figures which were larger in 1911 than those of the federal census in 1916, one pastor issued data which indicated that about one-sixth of all immigrant churchmen were outside the three major Lutheran groups. Although the various figures did not distinguish between the foreign-born and native-born members, it was estimated that two out of every three immigrants, and maybe more, remained outside the churches.[13]

After forming their first congregations, Finns organized their first temperance societies. Sometimes the temperance societies worked closely with congregations in maintaining common buildings. Around the early 1880's Finns had joined Swedish and Norwegian temperance societies in Michigan, Ohio, and elsewhere. After 1884 they set up their own societies, the first one in Ashtabula, Ohio.[14] With their next society in 1885 at Hancock they started the first of several societies which united as the Finnish National Temperance Brotherhood in 1888. During the following year dissenters from the Brotherhood united under the name of the Friends of Temperance. In 1896 and 1902 two other leagues were started in states east and west of Michigan. Rivalries developed in the 1890's, a decade in which more new societies were organized than in any other. When the Brotherhood banned dancing and certain other activities, discontented members formed rival societies. By 1900 there were 150 societies with 6,550 members, and in 1908 there were 200 societies with 11,200 members.[15] About half the members belonged to the Brotherhood, which had its main strength in Michigan. The remaining half belonged to the three other leagues or were independent. Although the temperance forces grew after the 1890's, they started to lose strength when socialist locals emerged after 1900.[16]

From the 1890's Finns formed workingmen's societies, which were later replaced by socialist clubs. Just as temperance and church groups had coöperated, now temperance societies worked occasionally with the new labor organizations. When about 1905 some temperance societies became socialist, often bitter fights ensued over hall ownership from the members opposing the transformation of such societies. Among the first workingmen's clubs was the Imatra Society of Brooklyn, New York, formed in 1890 as a mutual benefit association for workingmen. It maintained a hall and supported social, educational, and other causes. By 1903 the Imatra Society headed a league of about thirty local associations, mainly in eastern states. At Fitchburg, Massachusetts, in 1894 immigrants also had formed an independent mutual aid society, Saima, which later became socialist. In Rockport, Massachusetts, in 1899 Finns organized their first, though short-lived, socialist club in America. After the turn of the century, other socialist clubs appeared as organizers made converts and socialists arrived from Finland. Except for the parent local in Brooklyn, most of the Imatra associations became socialist, as did Michigan members of a short-lived labor league that had been formed in 1903. By 1906 there were over 50 socialist clubs, with about 2,000 members, which formed the Finnish Socialist Federation. In 1913 the Federation had 260 socialist locals with a paid membership of 12,651. In April, 1914, it reported nearly 15,500 members, but within a few months it lost perhaps over 3,000 members to the ranks of industrial unionism, which drew support especially in Minnesota and states farther west. By 1915 the membership was below 10,000.[17] Although its membership rose again, the Federation in 1920 once more lost members in the schism over the issue of communism. The Federation drew some of its strongest support in Massachusetts, New York, and Michigan.[18]

In addition to maintaining the major religious, temperance, and labor organizations, immigrants promoted many other associations. Besides supporting subsidiary groups of the major organizations in music, dramatics, and athletics, they also established independent societies in such activities. They developed various coöperatives, youth clubs, insurance companies, and benefit societies. From the 1880's nationalistic-minded persons, especially, sponsored benefit societies and fraternal orders. In 1882, for example, San Francisco Finns formed a benefit society to aid sick members and to provide funeral escorts for the deceased because unlike other nationalities, its representative recalled, Finns had been noticeable for their lack of festive funeral escorts.[19] To enhance their reputations immigrant nationalists formed in 1898 a secret benefit society, the Knights of Kaleva, and organized the Ladies of Kaleva in 1904. During World War I the two groups reported about 100 locals, and in 1911 they had an estimated membership ranging between three and four thousand.[20] Membership in such groups was usually combined with membership in the major organizations.

Although indebted to their Old Country, Finnish immigrants developed independence in organizing their associative life. As individuals, they came with varied experiences and aspirations which helped guide their entry into organized activities. But like other immigrants, Finns modified their ideas of organizations brought from Finland to fit their new circumstances and changed needs.[21] It was not surprising, then, that they showed increasing self-reliance in developing their activities. Besides importing literature from Finland, they set up their own publishing houses. In addition to attracting pastors, editors, and other organization specialists, they went about training their own. Consequently, largely untrained and inexperienced laymen found important roles in the various organizations. From their response to new experiences in America really came the sense of independence.

Finding literary nourishment in their native country, immigrant associations imported books and newspapers from Finland. All immigrant publishing houses sold such literature. Editors copied from imported Finnish newspapers and journals; publishing houses reprinted editions which had originally appeared in Finland. In such fashion, for example, readers obtained works of Jack London and Arthur Conan Doyle. Various societies imported songbooks which they copied. For its classes in 1910 the Finnish National Temperance Brotherhood recommended twenty-eight titles, of which over half came from Finland.[22] Recalling their first years in America, one socialist wrote that New York socialists watched events in Finland so closely that they had regarded as their virtual mouthpiece a newspaper which was published in Helsinki.[23] Yet the socialists, like other immigrants, turned their attention more and more to their own publishing efforts in America.

Distance, if nothing else, forced immigrants to develop newspapers that could serve them more effectively than those imported from Finland. Becoming avid newspaper readers in America, immigrants could not depend upon the haphazard delivery of old imported papers. Newspaper reading was a new experience for most immigrants from the countrysides of Europe.[24] In 1899 a journalist declared that there was more newspaper reading among Finns in America than in Finland.[25] Satirically a correspondent noted that, since newspaper reading had increased so much in America, it was no longer possible for one to convey his thoughts even to his neighbors except through newspaper columns.[26] To satisfy the need for reading material, private publishers began to issue scores of weeklies in the two decades after 1876. But their papers did not last more than a few years except for a few like the *Uusi Kotimaa* ("New Homeland") and *Siirtolainen* ("Immigrant"). The history of most publications, said one journal, was a "Nice name, short life, and early death."[27] This situation changed, however, when organizations began to issue their own newspapers.

Although private publishers continued to promote papers like the *Pohjan Tähti* ("North Star"), *New Yorkin Uutiset* ("New York News"), *Amerikan Sanomat* ("American Tidings"), and *Päivälehti* ("Daily Journal"), after about 1900 organizations were not satisfied with such publications and instead issued their own organs. The private papers which survived did so partly by permitting their columns to be used by competing organizations. Such a policy, however, did not entirely satisfy the organization-minded, who felt that a newspaper should serve the interests of only one group; moreover, said one churchman, only papers clinging to firmly established principles could survive.[28] Private publishers found it harder to continue and a publisher declared in 1910 that he had closed his publishing house because financing was difficult to obtain unless one were connected with some party cause.[29] Synod Lutherans depended on their *Amerikan Suometar* ("American Finn"), National Lutherans published the *Auttaja* ("Helper"), and socialists owned the *Työmies* ("Workingman") and *Raivaaja* ("Pioneer"). Various associations also had monthly and quarterly publications besides newspapers. But whether or not immigrants read organizational newspapers and journals, they all shared in developing literary independence from Finland.

Newspapers trained writers in terms of life in America. As the press provided an outlet for the articulate, hundreds became correspondents who reported community events and the affairs of local organizations. In a satirical vein, one writer complained that editors needed an eight-day week to read the countless local letters reporting newborn babies, dead horses, and lost pigs. These letters came in such increasing numbers to one newspaper that the editors had to reduce the space devoted to general news and events in Finland. When they learned English, editors and writers often drew copy from American newspapers and press services. In 1916 an editor stated that ten years before, his paper had taken its copy mainly from sources published in Finland, but now it was different, he said, because the staff was better able to interpret events in America. Editors were caricatured as men who carried shears ready to clip articles for translation and who upon entering the house of a host would immediately set to clipping an article by Theodore Roosevelt.[30] By such clipping, indeed, editors broadened the sources of ideas for their readers.

Besides newspapers, private Finnish publishers like August Edwards of Ashtabula, Ohio, printed short, paper-bound reprints and translations of stories and verses which came from sources in Finland or America. They also offered dictionaries and grammars to help people master the English language. In addition to issuing similar works on language, the organizations published yearbooks and journals with original writings, society reports, and didactic messages. Such volumes were often like almanacs. They appeared for anniversary celebrations and other festive occasions and for holidays like Christmas, Easter, May Day, and Saint John's

Day. Through these varied publications the immigrants increased their awareness of immediate concerns.

Disappointed by these publications, several writers called for a creative literature produced by Finnish Americans. They had in mind original novels and short stories. As one editor said in 1908, until then immigrant publishers had produced few original works besides small booklets, dictionaries, poetry collections, and annual calendars.[31] To encourage more original writing literary societies were organized. But even without such societies, which proved to be short-lived, creative literature became more abundant. From about 1890 immigrants had issued original verses, essays, tales, and short stories. In the first years of the new century they even published original novels. But critics were not satisfied: for instance, in 1912 one critic described the first novels as "weedy."[32] During the decade of World War I and the 1920's Finns, drawing mainly on immigrant themes, produced most of the original work—novels, memoirs, and histories—which served as the capstone to an independent literature.[33]

In addition to the intellectual nourishment offered by literature from Finland, the immigrants themselves were important as carriers of ideas to guide organizations. They could not easily forget their intellectual experiences in Finland. Language barriers, moreover, forced them to attempt their intellectual rehabilitation first in terms of experiences gained in Finland. The few learned men—clergymen, speakers, and editors—were essential to the new immigrant organizations and enjoyed a status which they probably had not had in Finland. The immigrants found, however, that learned men came in too few numbers. Therefore, they felt forced to train organization men from their own relatively untutored and inexperienced ranks. In doing so, they found the basis for a new intellectual leadership.

Starting in the 1870's, various pastors and lay preachers arrived to give religious leadership. They came partly in response to immigrant invitations. From Finland the Apostolic Lutherans secured as pastor Arthur Heideman, who was seminary trained, and lay preachers like Salomon Korteniemi and Johan Takkinen. Alfred Backman was the first seminary-trained pastor who came to America and he was replaced by another trained clergyman, Juho Nikander; both worked for the Synod Lutherans. During the years between 1876 and 1921 about eighty pastors came from the State Church of Finland. Fifty-five of them served an average of only seven years in America.[34] In 1902 the National Lutherans called two pastors from Finland and two more in 1917. From Finland also came missionaries to work mainly among seamen in New York and San Francisco and occasionally in immigrant communities. Although few in number, the seamen missionaries represented the only sustained effort by agencies in Finland to send clergymen to America.

Clergymen, however, were not the only ones who arrived to help develop institutions. Helping immigrants organize were various writers, speakers, and university students. In 1876 Adolf Muikku, a university student, started the first Finnish-language newspaper in America. Later other students joined the staffs of leading immigrant newspapers. Aiding temperance organizations were Karl Tolonen, a pastor who arrived with experience gained as the head of a temperance society in Finland during the 1880's, and Juho Jasberg and Isaac Sillberg, both formerly active in temperance work in Finland. After about 1900 the immigrant arrivals included socialists like Matti Kurikka, Frans Syrjälä, Wilho Boman, and Antero Tanner, who recalled in 1904 that until then most of the socialist leaders had already been active in Finland. Organizations were also aided by such arrivals as singers, bandsmen, gymnasts, and actors. They also received visiting church dignitaries, musicians, and speakers. During 1908, in response to its third request, the Finnish National Temperance Brotherhood received a speaker from Finland.[35] But in the main, organization specialists came voluntarily as immigrants rather than as agents sent at the request of organizations in America or Finland.

Even though hundreds of persons with organizational experience arrived, immigrants were disappointed that more did not come and that some of the arrivals did not stay long. When the political atmosphere became freer in Finland, various editors and speakers returned home. Among them were Eero Erkko, a nationalist editor, and Taavi Tainio, a socialist writer; both of them entered the newly reorganized legislature in Finland. So many pastors returned to Finland, said the directors of the Lutheran Synod, that their seminary had to train new ones from immigrant ranks. Unable to make definite promises about salaries, National

Lutheran spokesmen in 1908 sought without success for pastors from Finland. For a year lack of a director postponed the start of temperance training classes for speakers and teachers. Since immigrant ranks included few who had received more than an elementary education, a temperance speaker explained, it was hard to find a proper director. Socialists with similar problems reported that they lacked agitators and that experienced speakers and editors returned to Finland. When coöperatives appeared, their leaders complained about the scarcity of trained and experienced store managers.[36] Not only on the top levels, but also on the lower levels, immigrants reported their lack of trained organization personnel.

Local societies emphasized their lack of trained personnel by encouraging members to become speakers, writers, actors, and singers, for they needed persons able to entertain, teach, and conduct meetings. As laymen commonly had not conducted religious affairs in Finland, congregations lacked not only pastors, but also experienced laymen. In Finland, for example, the clergy cared for the religious training of children while in America laymen largely conducted Sunday schools. The need for such laymen was emphasized in 1903 by the annual meeting of the National Lutherans. In 1895 one writer warned that without trained clergy local groups would lose enthusiasm for joining congregations, and he advised encouraging lay preachers. Temperance and socialist societies also encouraged their membership to practice speaking, singing, and acting. As such arts were essential to their common enterprises, one promoter urged Finns to practice them at an affair sponsored by New York temperance advocates.[37] Not only did the smallest of local societies stress the need for oral skills, but they also solicited members able to do secretarial work, write reports, and keep financial accounts. Bookkeeping and arithmetic hence became important subjects for training classes held by various organizations. To overcome their lack of trained personnel local societies encouraged and even financed attendance at such classes by their members.

From the 1890's, immigrants set up schools to train personnel for their organizations. In Hancock, Michigan, in 1896 Synod Lutherans opened a school and later started the seminary branch, which ordained its first clergymen in 1906. The school included a general academic department for young students and adults. During its first fifteen years it had over five hundred students.[38]

Like the Synod Lutherans, the National Lutherans in 1903 opened their own school, called the Folk School, in Minneapolis and later moved it to Smithville near Duluth. As they kept control only of the seminary branch, anyone could buy stock in the school. Consequently, disputes arose over courses and teachers. Failing to secure full control in 1906, the National Lutherans did not have another seminary until World War I. They had lost control to the socialist-minded stockowners, who in 1907 changed the school into the Work People's College. Under its new administration the school offered courses ranging from socialist doctrine to bookkeeping and attracted nearly seven hundred students by 1914, when the industrial unionists secured full control.[39] The school also developed correspondence courses, as did private schools operated by entrepreneurs. In the meantime additional immigrants were reached by other educational ventures.

Besides the schools, organizations created varied educational aids. In addition to their newspapers, they provided handbooks on the conduct of meetings, and their local societies maintained libraries with books for self-study and discussion clubs for practice in public speaking. On the national and regional levels, organizations sponsored scores of training courses and institutes. In 1900 Lutherans of Calumet, Michigan, arranged lectures on varied subjects. During the winter of 1904 the Finnish National Temperance Brotherhood offered its first lecture courses to train personnel. At its annual meetings the Brotherhood also held lecture sessions for students of public speaking. In an effort to develop potential organizers, an early socialist lecturer addressed about five hundred persons in one series of talks repeated in ten or more communities.[40] After World War I midwest coöperatives maintained summer courses to train their personnel. As such courses and institutes lasted only a week or two, they reached many people whom time, family duties, employment, and limited finances precluded from full-time attendance at the schools.

In part, the schools and training sessions must receive the credit for developing new organizational personnel. Although they mainly trained immigrant adults, by World War I they had also trained adults who were born in America or who had arrived as immigrant children to be reared in the United States. Outmatching the number of pastors who came from Finland, were about a hundred men, both native and foreign-born, ordained by the immigrants between 1900 and 1920. Some of those ordained had studied at Finnish or Swedish schools in America. Others had attended schools which were not maintained by immigrants: among these was Wilhelm Leeman, who arrived in 1900 at the age of eighteen years. He worked for four years in a quarry before starting studies at the Boston Evangelical Institute and becoming a Congregational minister in 1907. During the years between 1906 and 1920 the Lutheran Synod ordained about forty men who had attended its seminary, and in 1924 its president declared that ten of its then fifty-five pastors had been trained in Finland while most of the rest had studied at the seminary. By 1925 an educational director in another field, coöperative businesses, asserted that three-fourths of the managers were trained in the summer courses operated by the Central Co-operative Exchange in Superior, Wisconsin. Since its first course held in 1919 over 70 percent of the forty-three students had entered coöperative service.[41] But in general, immigrant training did not lend itself readily to such statistical presentation, for most training was piecemeal and unmarked by the awarding of degrees or certificates. Instead, it was measured by the increasing participation of the relatively untutored immigrants in organized activity.

Religious activities first offered opportunities to the untrained and inexperienced immigrants. To maintain congregations in America laymen learned to become trustees of church properties, Sunday school teachers, and participants in various church meetings. Laymen also filled pulpits. Revivals in Finland, of course, had produced lay preachers who held meetings, but they stayed within the State Church, at least formally. On coming to America, the Laestadians organized independent congregations with respected lay preachers like Johan Mursu who, five years after becoming a Laestadian at the age of twenty-eight, in 1880 arrived without schooling in Minnesota. During the debates of the 1890's, Synod Lutheran pastors cited examples of little-trained men organizing congregations. Recalling those debates, one writer said that practically anyone could become a pastor and many wanted to do so. Another writer gave the example of the Finnish tailor, gifted with speaking abilities, who, after two weeks of study, was ordained by a Norwegian Conference in Minneapolis before he entered the pulpit in Calumet.[42] Pointing out such pastors was meant partly as criticism of the National Lutherans, who said that they accepted clergymen with little or no seminary training. Besides religious work, laymen also found opportunities in other fields.

Like the churches, temperance and socialist societies attracted many who were untutored and inexperienced. Publishing its handbook in 1906, the Finnish National Temperance Brotherhood declared that because many Finns had become acquainted with organized group activities only after arriving in America, it felt obliged to instruct them on the conduct of meetings. Studying the Brotherhood in 1911, one writer concluded that many of its leaders had acquired their knowledge through self-study: one such leader was Juho Jasberg whose self-improvement had begun in Finland. Among socialists, also, there were similar individuals. On its staff in 1909 and 1910, one socialist paper reported, there were no editors with formal training. Among the socialist converts was a man who came to the United States in 1903 at the age of eighteen years. Having attended only confirmation classes in Finland, he found work as a laborer. About 1905 he began to write articles and poetry for the socialist press and joined socialist organizations in 1906. Upon the formation of a socialist club in Bogota, New Jersey, the local correspondent reported that only six of the twenty-one new members had had previous membership in the Socialist Party.[43] When inexperienced persons entered organizational activities in such ways, they represented the advance of the spirit of awakening.

Released from inactivity and drawn into organizational activity, immigrants developed vigorously their sense of self-direction and independence. Their activity in the view of one author was almost unbelievable, for immigrants with little previous experience in Finland, he continued, were much livelier than they had been in the Old Country in forming all sorts of organizations. Suddenly in America, as a pastor also observed, immigrants learned to pursue vigorously different ideas leading in all directions. It was as though they had cast off the restraints of wardship and awakened to new aspirations. Another observer agreed that in America immigrants had often learned for the first time to take part in associations enthusiastically because they had had few such opportunities in Finland.[44] Upon awakening, immigrants found the sense of independence which guided their organized efforts, for imbued with the desire to act immediately, they could hardly depend upon direction from Finland.

When religious endeavors roused them, Finns found that they had to work under new conditions in America. As there was no State Church, they discovered the need for new methods. Individuals were free to organize congregations with or without affection for their old church in Finland. Nor, said one pastor, could they rely for religious direction on Finland, where clergymen knew little about America. No one could compel support of churches in America. There were no state-enforced tithes or religious tests for incorporating as church bodies. Instead, each congregation had full authority to run its own affairs. Since religious support was on a voluntary basis, church groups found new ways of organizing and raising money. Pastors, particularly, realized that their salaries depended on voluntary contributions from congregations and felt that the American system was degrading, in contrast to the system in Finland. Congregations hence had to select trustees who administered finances and properties. They arranged varied money-raising functions like evening entertainments, sewing clubs, and bake sales. As preaching did not suffice to attract members, said one pastor, they arranged different activities like choirs, discussion circles, and Sunday schools. Working among seamen in New York, one missionary was reprimanded by his superiors in Finland for introducing too many activities of an earthly nature. Besides such varied activities, churches found special reason to support church newspapers, for as one pastor observed, immigrants were scattered and often could be reached best through a press which served as a pulpit. Comparing immigrant churches with religious organizations in Finland, an observer in the Old Country noted that immigrants were avid newspaper readers and, hence, their churches had the strange role of publishing newspapers to spread the evangelical message.[45] As newspapers in this manner reinforced the various church activities, laymen became even more active participants in the conduct of religious matters in America.

In terms of religious doctrines the immigrants also found new directions or emphases. Although the Apostolic Lutherans split into factions in America just as in Finland, they did not always parallel the views of the sects in the Old Country. When they published in 1880 what was perhaps the first Finnish book issued

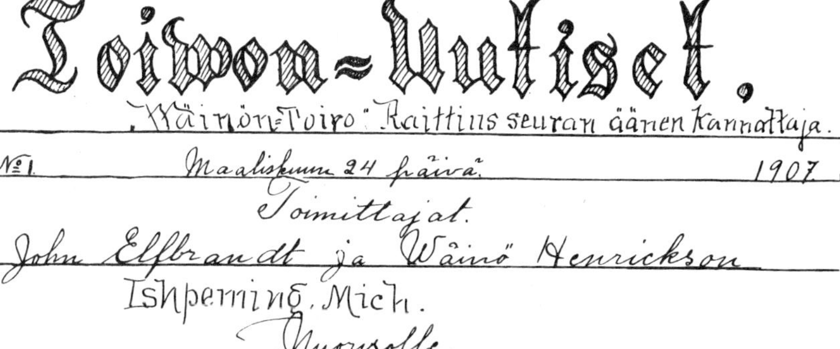

# Toiwon-Uutiset.

„Wäinön Toivo" Raittius seuran äänen kannattaja.

№ 1. Maaliskuun 24 päivä 1907.

Toimittajat.

John Elfbrandt ja Wäinö Henrickson

Ishpeming, Mich.

## Nuorisolle.

Tämä aika sun vaatii kasvattamaan
jaloksi, suureksi tahtosi, tuntos.
Tämä aika sun vaatii uhraamaan
isänmaallesi intosi, kuntos.

Waan vieläkö raukka viipyä voit
ilon aljojen kurjien luona?
Sä henkesi hehkunko sammua soit,
kun halpa se oisi vaan kuona.

Nyt juuri kun tarmoa tarvittais,
sinä etsitkö huumetta hurjaa
Nyt kun kahleita katkoa sais,
sinä suositko orjuutta kurjaa?

Sinä maljasi juotko, kun kansamme jo
väkijuomien orjana huokaa?

**Nyrkkilehti (*"fist paper"*) *issued by a temperance organization in Ishpeming, Michigan***

AMERIKAN

# Suomalainen Lehti.

A. JOHN MUIKKU

All Kinds of Job Printing

Suomesta.

*An early issue of the first Finnish-language newspaper published in the United States*

# TYÖMIES

AMERIKAN SUOMALAISEN TYÖVÄESTÖN ÄÄNENKANNATTAJA

TIISTAINA HUHTIKUUN 22 P. — APRIL 22 1913

Volume X. — Kymmenes vuosikerta

Varapresidentti selittää taasen sosialismia

Kaivosmiesten lakko Saksassa

11,000 jo lakossa

California ei aio perääntyä

Denverissä, Colo.

Belgian hallitus on alkanut pahoin horjua

# RAIVAAJA

Raivaajalla on enemmän tilaajia kuin toisilla Idän valtioiden suomalaisilla sanomalehdillä yhteensä

Raivaaja has a larger circulation than all the Finnish Newspapers of the Eastern States combined

Lauantaina, Toukok. 3 p. — Saturday, May 3

The only Finnish Daily in the East.

No. 102, 1913 — Yhdeksäs vuosik. Vol. IX

TYÖNANTAJAT PAKOTETAAN NEUVOTTELUIHIN

Panaman kanavaa valmistellaan yhä suuremmalla voimalla

KUMOUKSELLISET SURMANNEET 148 IHMISTÄ

Californian senaatti hyväksynyt japanilaisvastaisen lain

LASITYÖLÄISET VOITTANEET LAKKONSA

Toollisuus-valtioissa kuolee enimmän pieniä lapsia

MAANANASTAJAT MYRKYTTÄNEET INDIAANEJA

# TOVERI

Lännen suomalaisen työväestön äänenkannattaja.

ORGAN OF THE FINNISH WORKERS IN THE WESTERN STATES. THE ONLY FINNISH DAILY IN THE WEST.

LAUANTAINA 3 P. TOUKOK.— SATURDAY 3 MAY 1913

1913 — KUUDES VUOSIK.

Yleisiä uutisia

100,000 laista matkalla

itävalta-

Suuri kaivosmiesten lakko

Törkeää sananvapauden sortamista

Taas suuri työtaistelu alkanut

# TYÖKANSA

The only Finnish newspaper in Canada. Published every week-day. Advantageous paper for advertisers.

Balkanin liittolaiset

Satamatyöläisten lakko

Aito virallista menettelyä

# PELTO ja KOTI

FARM — HOME

May — Hancock, Mich. — Toukok.

# Toveritar

# SAKENIA

# VÄKÄ-LEUKA

Elokuun 1 p. — August 1 — 1912

Puhevapaus Amerikoissa.

*Bannerheads show the varied publications issued by socialist organizations before World War I*

*Men going to work in the steel mills of Monessen, Pennsylvania*

*The lumber camps of Rock, Michigan, attracted Finns*

in America, the author liberalized an important tenet of the Laestadian interpretation of the Ten Commandments. His change drew criticism in Finland though one critic conceded that in "free America" such a modification was feasible. After leaving the Lutheran Synod in the early 1890's, Pastor William Eloheimo wrote a Bible-like book revealing the Universal Kingdom through the prophet William. Even though his leadership was accepted in forming churches hostile to the Synod, his book was not accepted by many fellow immigrants. Generally, however, immigrants modified their religious orientation mainly by emphasizing the social gospel. Impelled by varying degrees of evangelicalism, they were concerned with saving people from social evil. Accordingly, Synod Lutherans were close to the Finnish National Temperance Brotherhood in taking action to remedy, or in merely calling attention to, a social problem. Except for temperance work, most churchmen were content to warn people away from social evil through newspapers and sermons. Unlike church publications in Finland, immigrant religious publications printed general news in addition to church matters. Since newspapers had become as essential as food, one writer declared that only a church paper provided the real truth about happenings in a moral light.[46] Examining events even led a few churchmen to advocate reform by means of some variety of socialism, but most did not go beyond the progressivism of Theodore Roosevelt. Such attempts to interpret life in America, nevertheless, drew the church-minded immigrants further away from the Finland which they had known.

Like churchmen, temperance advocates found new directions. As language barriers kept them outside many leisure-time activities, they found special opportunities to mingle socially in their own temperance halls. In Finland temperance work was directed towards political action; in America time had to elapse before immigrants were eligible to vote for prohibition. Unlike temperance societies in Finland, immigrant associations in America were often closely allied with church groups. Immigrant temperance workers recalled that in Finland pastors were not known for their active leadership in the crusade against liquor. It was different in America where, for example, in Conneaut, Ohio, one pastor noted that the members of the congregation and of the temperance society were virtually the same and that they used a common building. Partly to escape this church connection and the ban against dancing, societies were formed outside the Finnish National Temperance Brotherhood. The rivalries among such groups, according to one writer, distinguished temperance work in America. After his five-year stay in America another writer concluded that during the 1890's temperance work was livelier among immigrants than it was in Finland. Sharing this view was the temperance historian who recalled his visit to America. He said that in 1895 the immigrant membership in temperance societies totalled three thousand, or almost one-third of the membership in Finland, although all immigrants did not total one-tenth of the Old Country's population. He noticed that the meetings of the immigrant associations, unlike the societies in Finland, used passwords and more rituals. Immigrant societies also offered insurance services which were lacking in Finland.[47] Like the church groups, temperance groups had developed more varied methods than their counterparts in Finland.

Like the temperance societies, the socialist associations altered their activity in America. The name of the Finnish Socialist Federation was based on that of the American Socialist Party, while its counterpart in Finland was the Social Democratic Party. The first society of immigrant socialists, however, reportedly used the Social Democratic label before it was adopted in Finland. Like the temperance advocates, immigrant socialists found that immediate political action was less feasible than carrying on educational and social programs. Developing a practical program, therefore, they helped establish coöperatives. Before coming to America, few immigrants had had direct experience with coöperatives, which emerged in Finland mainly after 1899 with the aid of government funds and with university-trained leadership rather than with socialist. Consequently, an immigrant socialist newspaper felt that coöperatives in Finland were not generally oriented towards workers.[48] To avoid such a situation in America, socialists gave most impetus to forming coöperatives among Finnish Americans. And as a result their non-political program was strengthened.

Like the temperance advocates, immigrant socialists appeared very active to observers in Finland. In 1910 socialist sources in Finland declared that immigrant socialists were more passionate in their debates than Finnish socialists. According to one report, it was as if a disease afflicted the immigrants, because everyone wanted to speak. Another report said that Finland had less intense debates because America offered more "vigorous circumstances." Those circumstances produced endless resolutions, elections, and referenda. After his visit to America one writer declared that he found no returning immigrants who were satisfied with socialist activity in Finland, because they regarded the Old Country socialists as too slow and reformist. This view resulted, he believed, from the fact that immigrants were schooled in class conflict with Morgan and Rockefeller.[49] If Finland prepared the immigrants for socialism, America ripened them.

Immigrant socialists probably developed their liveliness mainly because of concern with industrial unionism, which broke their ranks in 1914. At this time no bitter rift existed between skilled and unskilled workers in Finland undoubtedly because, compared to America, Finnish industry had not created large unorganized forces of unskilled workers. Then, too, in America antiparliamentary views were largely associated with disillusionment over craft unionism. On the other hand, in Finland such sentiments rose from disillusionment with the failure of the leading party, represented by the Social Democrats, to secure acceptance of its program in Parliament. Studying American labor conditions through English-language sources, Kaapro Murros received credit for introducing immigrant readers to the newly organized Industrial Workers of the World. In 1907 Leo Laukki arrived as an émigré and former leader of general strikes in Finland to become the leading champion of industrial unionism, which drew support largely from Finns of the Midwest and Northwest. Eastern socialists generally opposed the inroads of industrial unionism because, according to one socialist editor, they had stronger backgrounds in socialism, labor unionism, and urban life. On the contrary, he said, western Finns came largely from rural areas where socialist and labor activity was little known. Another writer declared that, before coming to America, eastern Finns were already more familiar with craft unionism and thus more readily accepted it as craft industries were strongest in eastern states. Lacking such experiences, other immigrants entered the lower-paying, unorganized mass industries in the West and, hence, became more inclined towards industrial unionism.[50] So bitter was the debate between the easterners and westerners that they parted company in 1914. No wonder, then, that industrial unionism set immigrant socialists apart from their counterparts in the Old Country.

Although developing independence in such various ways, the association-minded immigrants could not escape their backgrounds in Finland. Yet they felt unable to rely upon Finland for intellectual sustenance and instead tried to create their own literature and to devise new methods of organizing. Above all, they developed new, self-reliant leaders from their own untutored and inexperienced ranks, for the urgency of their concerns required immediate action. Whether they sought bread, made love, or entered politics, Finnish immigrants expected fulfillment of their hopes through organized self-effort.

CHAPTER IV

# BREAD

*Newly arrived Finns and Scandinavians rarely have any money other than that required by the United States laws. Sometimes they bring $50 or $100, but they come here to work, and it is only after they have become familiar with things here and have put by some money that they finally settle down to stay.*

U.S. INDUSTRIAL COMMISSION REPORT [1]

Finnish immigrants were not exceptions among the Europeans who came to seek their fortunes in America. Whether or not the quest for money was their immediate reason for leaving Finland, they found that in America survival depended on finding a job. Few, if any, were wealthy enough for a life of idle pleasure in America. In their struggle for bread, moreover, both men and women found that riches did not come for the asking. They moved about in search of jobs; they organized for economic betterment. If they did not give up during their first five years in America, it was probable that most of them would never quit the country, for it was a lifetime job to master their economic problems and opportunities.

Although seldom solicited by employers, the Finns found jobs in America. Employers who did solicit sought out Finnish workers already in America more often than they encouraged them to leave Finland. But in contrast to real estate agents, employers seldom placed advertisements in Finnish-American publications. Without question, the most important solicitations occurred when employers offered jobs at newly opened places of work. In the 1860's the recruiting of Finnish miners from Norway to work in the copper mines of Michigan paved the way for many more immigrants who came without any further solicitation by employers. During the 1880's, when iron mines were opened in Michigan and Wisconsin, mining companies made efforts to attract Finns who were already in America. By 1911 Finns were almost one-fourth of the workers on the Gogebic Iron Range and most of them had arrived without any effort on the part of employers who had induced the first group of Finnish arrivals.[2] Once immigrants found such job openings, they spread the word among themselves. The firstcomers reported working conditions to friends and relatives in Finland. Then they introduced the newcomers from Finland at the employment offices. As Finns generally did not stay long in their first jobs, they looked for new positions. Finding work in new places, they served as scouts for those left behind. In the immigrant press local correspondents also reported employment conditions. Through their own channels of information, hence, immigrants mainly learned about employment opportunities.

To find jobs in certain fields, however, immigrants used employment agencies. In Duluth and elsewhere such agencies helped men find seasonal work in harvesting and lumbering. In the cities, especially New York, they aided women to secure domestic employment. Women operated six of the nine Finnish employment agencies advertising in 1914 in New York. Before leaving Finland, women could also read the advertisement of the agent who offered them his assistance at Ellis Island to find temporary housing and domestic work.[3] In the main, however, immigrants found work on their own initiative in the expanding industrial areas.

Upon arrival in New York, the immigrants usually headed for communities dominated by some major industry which needed unskilled laborers. They started out as low-paid laborers and then looked around for other opportunities. Mining was their first major occupational field: copper in Michigan; iron in Minnesota, Michigan, and Wisconsin; lead, gold, silver, and coal in the mountain states; and coal also in Pennsylvania. At the Lake Erie ports of Ohio men unloaded boats with their cargoes of ore from the north. The ore was then shipped to the steel mills of Ohio and Pennsylvania, where men also found employment. They found other jobs in the textile mills, furniture plants, and marble quarries of Massachusetts, the lumber camps from Maine to Washington, and the salmon fisheries of Oregon. In New York, Chicago, and other cities men entered trades such as carpentry, and women found work as domestic servants. On rare occasions both men and women entered business and professional fields. Upon ending their industrial careers, thousands became farmers.

Among the newly developed industrial areas Finns first sought Michigan and Minnesota. Because the state of Michigan had attracted them first during the 1860's when copper mines were opened, the West was best known to latecomers from Finland. After the Civil War, industrialists started new mines and lumber camps in the West for which they needed laborers. During the 1880's and 1890's they started extensive mining operations in Minnesota. After the new century opened, they continued expansion of their labor forces and so Finns still arrived westward bound. During the fiscal years between 1901 and 1920, 40 percent of the arrivals from Finland gave their destination as Michigan and Minnesota, and 31 percent indicated Massachusetts and New York.[4] By this time enough immigrants had stopped along the way leading westward to make eastern communities better known. So employment conditions led Finns to settle in a northern tier of states from the Atlantic to the Pacific, with the focus in the Great Lakes region.

Since Finns were only a fraction of the total American labor force that came from Europe, they rarely appeared in occupational figures issued by official agencies. According to the United States Immigration Commission, they were the most numerous foreign-born group among the workers in certain mining districts of Michigan and Minnesota.[5] In 1920 federal census enumerators made an exception and reported almost 15,000 immigrant farm operators of Finnish nativity. Everywhere, however, the Finns were too few in number to warrant tabulation by occupation in the published federal censuses.

In their own tabulations the immigrants revealed that they were chiefly attracted to basic industries. When, during the year 1898, editors undertook the compilation of occupational and other data on immigrant communities, their correspondent in Red Lodge, Montana, for instance, revealed that coal mining was the chief means of support for 263 men, 124 women, and 114 youths under eighteen years of age and that only 7 persons were in business. From Worcester, Massachusetts, in 1903 another census taker reported the presence of 1,306 Finns who drew their livelihood mainly from wire mills and foundries; a few worked in building construction, and 13 operated grocery stores and shops. According to a survey made in 1907, there were 2,958 Finns in the iron city of Ishpeming, Michigan. Those who were employed included 908 miners, 62 mechanics, 45 business proprietors and clerks, 49 odd-job workers, 18 saloon keepers and waiters, 6 professionals, and 30 farmers.[6] Such tabulations showed pointedly that in particular communities immigrants worked mainly as wage earners in some major industry.

At the same time, moreover, industrial employers dominated other aspects of immigrant life, more commonly in isolated mining, lumber, and mill centers than elsewhere. Companies maintained housing, stores, and other services for workers: by 1900, for example, Michigan mining companies were reported as having bought "substantial amounts of residential acreage around their properties" for housing purposes.[7] Although the availability of such services might influence their search for work, workers were first concerned with wages and conditions of employment.

Within each industry workers entered a hierarchy of jobs. They found that jobs were scaled according to wages and skills and also in terms of the physical exertion and discomfort involved. At the top of the hierarchy were the positions held by the superintendents, foremen, and machine operators. On the bottom were the numerous unskilled laborers. In the copper mines the most numerous were the underground workers like the trammers who filled and pushed the ore cars to the mine shafts. On the ore docks the most numerous were the laborers who used shovels to help empty ore boats. Other industries, likewise, hired most workers for jobs requiring sheer physical power and paying least money.

As most immigrants were rural laborers, Finns entered the hierarchy mainly as unskilled laborers. They had little else beyond their capacity to do physical labor for bargaining with employers. During the fiscal years from 1899 to 1910 American officials classed over 60 percent of the Finnish men as general laborers, one of the highest percentages among all immigrant groups. In 1911 the United States Immigration Commission reported that, on reaching America, Finns of the Minnesota iron ranges had had the highest percentage of general laborers in comparison with other immigrant groups. It said that they generally were among the bottom ranks, especially in the underground mines, while relatively more of them were moving up in the open pit mines. In the copper mines of

Michigan, the Commission noted, Finns were rising and even becoming foremen.[8] Advance was usually slow, however, because the job hierarchy did not favor the newer immigrant arrivals.

The job hierarchy was organized in terms of various nationality groups. In the words of the United States Immigration Commission, "progressive displacement" occurred on the "scale of occupations" when new immigrant arrivals entered the bottom ranks and some of the earlier arrivals moved up into more desirable skilled jobs.[9] From the 1880's this situation meant that the newer immigrants were mainly those from southern and eastern Europe. Coming from the border area between eastern and western Europe, the Finns were among these new arrivals. The older arrivals included the Cornish, Irish, German, and Swedish, who thus had an advantage over Finns.

Consequently, Finnish immigrants became involved in national rivalries in the mines of Michigan, Minnesota, and Montana, the docks of Ohio, the mills of Pennsylvania and Massachusetts, and the lumber camps of the Northwest. Expressing mutual antagonism, they competed with Cornish and Irish workers in the mining towns. Indirectly their hostility appeared, for example, in the ballad deploring the Irishmen's conquest of Finnish maidens. In Maynard, Massachusetts, where the competition for jobs at local mills intensified rivalries, Irishmen were reported to have spit upon Finns in the street. The policies of employers also contributed to the rivalry for jobs between Finns and other nationalities. Because Finns had actively participated in Minnesota's iron strike of 1907, the United States Immigration Commission observed, employers penalized Finnish workers by hiring them last or replacing them with South Europeans. In Butte, Montana, the vice-president of the Anaconda Mining Company justified the discharge of about four hundred Finns on the grounds that, since "Finlanders" were "known trouble makers," his firm did not want many of them working and causing friction with the Irish and Cornish. There was evidence in Michigan's Copper Country that employers encouraged national rivalries to forestall trade unionism and hoped that language barriers would keep workers separate.[10] Whether or not employers deliberately hired according to national quotas, however, the rivalries were sustained by the competition for the limited number of top positions in the job hierarchy.

Although rising in the job hierarchy, Finns found that there were more men seeking to rise than there were job openings. They desired least the plentiful low-paying jobs like tramming, but such higher-paying positions as drill operators and foremen were much fewer in the mines. In spite of their long hours, hard work, and low pay, the trammers held on for a time, hoping to become drill operators, but prospective drillers outnumbered those content to do tramming. So, according to the United States Department of Labor, many trammers became disgusted and quit the mines after waiting in vain for drill work.[11]

Even though they might be earning more in America than in Finland, immigrants were disappointed in their first jobs. They found that economic rewards did not come easily and that milk and honey did not flow everywhere. After over two decades of reporting in America, one newspaper advised prospective immigrants to lay aside too rosy pictures of America and realize that satisfactory employment was not always available. Writing to friends in Finland in 1903 after ten years of working in America, one immigrant observed that "all is not gold that shines" in America because it was difficult to make a livelihood, although to be sure, it was easier than in the Old Country. Another wrote about a strike, bad times, and high living costs, concluding that many were ready to leave Minnesota for Finland, if only they could get their final pay from employers. Two years after leaving Finland, in 1898 a newspaper correspondent recalled working for a Buffalo-to-Chicago railroad company and feeling that he would be able to save much from his daily wage of slightly more than one dollar. When pay day came, however, he received very little after settling accounts.[12] More than once, other immigrants recorded their disappointments and even pointedly stated that they were underpaid. Ordinarily, they reported receiving between one and three dollars a day until wages were inflated by the boom of World War I. Only the exceptional ones who secured positions like foremen and machine operators could report earning more. These disappointing wages were disillusioning to the many who came hoping to earn much money quickly and then return to Finland. If they did return, most did so during their first five years in America.[13] During an economic crisis, like the one in late 1907 and early 1908, hundreds departed without further thought.

If they remained unmarried in their first years in America, moreover, they probably felt freer to leave the country. But single or married, those who stayed in America were much concerned with employment opportunities.

Through letters and newspapers immigrants traded information about employment. They also advised friends and relatives in the Old Country. Writing to his brother in Finland, one immigrant declared that at the moment, in 1883, he did not advise anyone to leave Europe, because bad times prevailed, but when conditions improved in the "promised land" he would send a ticket to his kinsman. He added that it was unwise to burden oneself by bringing a family because a man should be free to concentrate on finding "a good job." A worker also had to find "a good-natured boss" because many had to suffer the devilishness of bosses during hard times.[14] Similarly, immigrants advised each other about good and bad times and whether one ought to move from one community to the next. In newspapers they reported both available jobs and job scarcity and often advised people not to move into areas of unemployment. In so doing, they often tried to be philosophic in their observations. From Pennsylvania one coal miner wrote that at the moment the mines were operating but that mining was like playing cards because the bosses ran mines for a time and then suspended operations, so other people had time for sleeping. Another writer from Waukegan, Illinois, reported the lack of jobs in the wire mills and observed that, although it was good to live in hope, one got tired of hoping too long in vain.[15] When they got tired, workers understandably moved to seek jobs elsewhere.

Besides trading information about jobs through letters and newspapers, immigrants revealed their search for work in other ways. When they raised families, the record of their children's birthplaces showed the various places of parental employment, and frequently all the children of the same family were born in different places. Notices of unpaid bills left by men striking out for new jobs were advertised by boardinghouse operators. Such operators were advised by one writer to circulate pictures of the delinquents. On the lecture platform speakers also reminded their listeners about the constant migrations; one of them announced that he would discuss whether it was advantageous for eastern workmen to move westward.[16] Of course, the immigrants themselves more or less constantly debated the feasibility of moving about, but they did not record such conversations.

The quest for work was a major theme of immigrant writers. They probed the problem of new jobs; they wondered why people moved; they described places seen. One of the first immigrant novels, *Tramps,* described the experiences of two Finns seeking work in the Midwest. Pastor Salomon Ilmonen wrote in 1912 that it was difficult to compile data on his fellow immigrants because they moved so often from place to place in search of work. He noted that thousands of them moved with the fluctuating seasonal work in Michigan and Minnesota. Others moved from mine to mine looking for better pay, and still others in growing numbers moved to farms.[17] Newspaper correspondents, also, reported men moving about as one of their chief themes. Mobility was real, and writers did not have to invent their theme. Since the writers, moreover, were often involved in organized activities, they knew intimately how the migrations affected immigrant life.

The effect of the constant migrations on institutional life was indeed powerful. Societies rose and fell as men moved in and out searching for work. Both seasonal work and unemployment affected them. When single men returned for work in Minneapolis, one correspondent confided that associational life was revived. Reporting on a temperance society in Biwabik, Minnesota, one writer stated that its peak membership was in summer because in winter members left like swallows for work elsewhere. From Marquette, Michigan, another writer looked forward to renewed socialist activity when men returned from their winter jobs in the lumber camps. Societies, however, were affected even more by unemployment than by seasonal migration. If people found steady work in one place, they maintained organized functions on a year-round basis. But when unemployment struck, they moved away. The societies thus had no prospects of renewed activity unless other migrants turned up when jobs became available. The permanent departure of members from a society recalled to a correspondent the saying that there was no eternal city but only the city of the future.[18] To find their future city most immigrants moved seeking work as well as watching for economic advance in other ways.

Looking for economic betterment, Finns first considered the gospel of economic individualism. They discussed it in terms of the proverb which said that everyone was the blacksmith of his own happiness. Discussing some bank-employed Finns who had risen in the economic world, a writer declared that the proverb expressed an eternal truth. It was valid for all time, he said, because the "laws of nature and development" ordained that "every individual must perform industriously in whatever capacity was his lot." To demonstrate such industry, August Edwards' publishing firm in Ashtabula, Ohio, offered the pamphlet called *Guide to Happiness or Everyone Is the Blacksmith of His Own Happiness.* The pamphlet included a statement by the American industrialist, Charles Schwab, that economic advancement came through winning a position by one's own efforts and by working better than others. Likewise, an immigrant newspaper agreed that the proverb could be realized through honesty, courtesy, and hard work.[19] Generally such advocates of the proverb extolled industriousness and thrift, traditional virtues of rural Finland.

Although the individual might be able to create his own happiness, writers also noted his limitations. Though agreeing with the individualistic approach to happiness, one woman maintained that the creation of happiness was subject to divine sufferance. A temperance advocate cautioned that existing circumstances influenced the individual's pursuit of happiness. From New York a socialist correspondent wrote that the proverbial view on happiness was meaningful only to the wealthy. Some workers, he said, might get ahead through servility and slavish toil, but they could not achieve the happiness promised under a reconstructed economic order. Moses Hahl, a socialist satirist, derided those who toiled long hours and saved money to start some business like a store or boarding house. In one of his stories, the entrepreneur left the mine and tried his hand at shopkeeping, farming, and strikebreaking. When finally failure led him to thievery and he landed in jail, his wife exhorted him to remain true to his principles of resisting the socialists who would deny God and redistribute other people's property. According to the socialist, no matter how much the individual worked and saved, his chances of becoming a successful businessman were slim.[20] Yet, of course, there were men who took the chance.

To become a business entrepreneur was the ambition of those who asserted that extreme thrift and industry brought happiness. According to one journal, unemployment depended on one's viewpoint because there was always plenty of work for those really wanting to work. The journal declared that the so-called period of unemployment offered opportunities, especially to those who had saved some money. With such savings anyone could turn agent and sell scores of devices distributed by the journal's publishers. Owning a business brought success, continued the paper, to anyone who was unemployed and tired of hard physical toil.[21] Other writers also assured the immigrants that opportunities knocked at the door. Although there were few Finnish businessmen, it was claimed that private enterprise offered good prospects.

Generally speaking, the advocates of economic individualism were encouraged by the immigrant businessmen who operated various shops for Finnish-speaking customers. Grocery stores were undoubtedly most common among them. In his historical survey of Michigan's Copper Country in 1920, a writer admitted that Finnish businesses were not noted for their luxurious establishments. Although Finns were slow by nature, he felt they were certain of future success by their gradual accumulation of property in the manner of certain entrepreneurs whom he cited. In 1917 another writer had also observed that few Finns had undertaken business ventures and even fewer had succeeded. Among the few successful businessmen he pointed to the self-made man who had departed unschooled and virtually penniless from Finland thirty-three years earlier. After ventures in mining, farming, clerking, and shopkeeping, he shifted to dealing in real estate, grain, and insurance and became the largest stockholder in a bank which he had helped found.[22] Hard work and frugality thus might bring success, according to the advocates of individual endeavor.

But writers felt that education would promote economic success and produce even more successful businessmen. In this vein a journal declared in 1910 that the lack of business and professional success resulted from inadequate education. One writer asserted that in America individual enterprise was closely related to education because knowledge led to material gain. Consequently, to overcome their lack of education Finns endorsed a program of study. Handbooks and self-study guides were especially recommended: for example, in 1914 Mina Walli wrote a cook book which she hoped might help domestic servants improve their position and earn higher wages. Other writers prepared guide books and courses for the study of English. By learning English, Finns might improve their business dealings with others outside the immigrant community. To attain the level of wages earned by other nationalities, a pastor urged his compatriots to study English.[23] More formal study was also accepted by Finns as a means of finding business and professional success.

Full-time study for business and professional reasons was spelled out in various ways. After opening its commercial division, the school of the Synod Lutherans in Hancock declared that training was needed more than ever before to prepare for business.[24] Between the years 1906 and 1921 over one-third of the school's average enrollment was in its commercial department.[25] In Minnesota the Work People's College offered courses in business arithmetic and bookkeeping. In 1912 one of its officials declared that such courses were similar to those taught in any trade school.[26] Besides these two schools, Finns found others, especially Valparaiso University in Indiana from which came a few lawyers, doctors, and engineers. For various reasons immigrant children were better able than their elders to undertake full-time professional study. To encourage study a newspaper featured a column on notable Finns which included young people in the professions. Such youths, it concluded, demonstrated that Finns were able to keep up in the competition for positions.[27] Professional study would as surely bring economic success to the young as thrift, hard work, and self-study would to their elders—so declared those who yearned to escape from the ranks of ordinary pick-and-shovel laborers.

In contrast to the small number of private businessmen and professionals, far greater numbers of immigrants sought speedy economic returns with stock investments. They formed scores of stock companies. As the companies usually sold shares at prices from about one to five dollars, low-paid workers were able to acquire stock. So much interest was shown that one businessman presented a two-day course in the methods of stock selling.[28] The stock companies advertised their need for funds to operate mines, manufacture immigrant inventions, and import products from Finland. Although companies were formed for other purposes, the mining stock companies were most numerous. Enterprises like the mining firms sold shares to all comers, who were promised dividends and rising stock values.

From the formation of the first mining company in 1879 failure marked the stock ventures. In some cases the companies undertook actual mining operations. Investors, however, did not realize their expected returns; the companies failed or else passed into the hands of creditors. Among the companies was the Black Bear Mining Company, which was originally formed under a different name in 1890. It began operations in Colorado, but was forced to reorganize twice under new names until creditors took it over about the time of World War I. Another publicized venture was the Finnish American Mining Company, formed in 1907 to develop mines in Finland. It sold stock widely, but by 1912 its capital was spent and immigrants reportedly lost thousands of dollars.[29] Before they stopped investing in such companies, immigrants had the highest expectations.

Stock promoters continued their assurances that riches were near at hand. Through agents and advertisements they pleaded for renewed confidence. By investing their meager funds as a group, argued one company, individuals found strength. Another declared that the smallest investment would bring riches. If the riches were not forthcoming immediately, at least they promised returns when old age overtook the investors. They assured their public that holdings were almost ready to produce: for example, mine companies promised that a big strike was on the verge of production. The Black Bear Mining Company announced that its offering of stock below face value was the last such opportunity because the opening of its mines would surely raise prices. Its literature declared that the company's mines were worth millions of dollars and that investors need not fear losing their funds, which were in competent hands. Although most investors had lost in stock companies, a new company insisted that it was an exception to the other stock ventures because of its trustworthy leadership.[30] By World War I, however, investors were losing confidence. Critics derided new stock companies and denounced old ones.[31] It was evident that the promoters had been the main gainers.

While promoting speculative stock companies, the immigrants also formed companies and societies for insurance and mutual aid.

In so doing they sought a guarantee of economic relief in the event of sickness, accident, death, or property loss. Accidents were especially likely to happen to those who worked in the mines. On the Vermillion Range of Minnesota accidents were reported as occurring mainly to the Finns and Slovenes who worked underground. In 1900 at Scofield, Utah, a mine explosion took the lives of sixty-three Finnish miners and three years later ninety-four died similarly in Hanna, Wyoming.[32] When such disasters occurred, most immigrants were unprepared for the economic losses entailed. To provide sickness, accident, and funeral benefits local societies were formed in places like Hancock, Ashtabula, and Monessen. On a national basis the Finnish National Temperance Brotherhood gave funeral benefits. On the West Coast a regional organization offered various benefits. In Calumet and elsewhere property owners established fire insurance companies. Benefit societies were also formed for workingmen, and as a result the way was opened for labor organizations.

The mutual benefit associations for workingmen served not only laborers but also shop proprietors and professional men. Their programs emphasized benevolence and education. Chartered in 1890, the Imatra Society of Brooklyn laid the basis for such programs by declaring its purposes of improving the material and spiritual lot of its members. To achieve its ends the society offered lectures, libraries, sick care, and burial benefits.[33] Such early societies did not emphasize class consciousness although they recognized distinctions between rich and poor and between worker and employer. In 1897 the organ of the Finnish American Workingmen's League of Calumet, Michigan, declared that workers should not envy the positions of others, like bankers, for the world needed everyone from the poet to the miner. No matter what position one had, it argued, the individual should strive to do his best and remember that eternal damnation was the lot of the lazy and that blessings awaited the toiler.[34] Not all workers, however, were content to toil beside the bankers, for around the year 1900 scores proclaimed that they would form a society rid of all bankers.

From about 1900 one group announced that it was leaving the vicissitudes of capitalist society for the new Harmony Colony (Sointula) on Malcolm Island near British Columbia in Canada. Rejecting the outside world, the Colony proclaimed the creation of a new classless social order. Under the leadership of the utopian socialist, Matti Kurikka, who came via Australia, the idealistic settlers secured the island covered with virgin forest from the Canadian government. Starting as pioneers, they purposed to create a self-sufficient economic order in which the Golden Rule prevailed and each member lived not for himself but for others. According to the Colony's leader, "dogmatic socialists" wanted to tear down the existing capitalist society and rebuild it. His followers, he said, turned their backs on capitalism, which would disintegrate in its own wretchedness. Instead, they purposed to start an entirely new order in beautiful natural surroundings away from the economic fluctuations of the banking world. The settlers, however, found difficulties in developing the island's forest resources, and dissension arose over finance, discipline, and sex. By about 1905 their efforts had failed and the island was turned over to private development.[35] Numbering in the hundreds, Finns from Canada, Finland, and the United States had thus found only a temporary sanctuary on the island remote from the capitalist world. Through their failure they inspired thousands of others to dream of rebuilding the world.

During the heyday of Harmony socialism, other workingmen turned to the doctrines of class struggle. Among them were men, familiar with the works of Karl Marx, who in time sharpened their class consciousness and rejected the utopian socialism of Matti Kurikka. Their converts included the former temperance advocate, Martin Hendrickson, who first promoted the Harmony Colony and then spurned it for class struggle. When a socialist newspaper was founded in Massachusetts in 1903, its promoters debated the Harmony ideas for months before finally endorsing class struggle.[36] After the formation of the Finnish Socialist Federation in 1906, the class-conscious socialists developed and publicized their views more extensively.

With their American and European comrades, immigrant socialists argued that history imposed upon workers a class mission. Through class struggle workers were to find the way to a classless society and economic abundance. So bad was existing society, said one writer, that workers could not wait for it to adopt idealistic philosophies which would compel the end of oppression and evil. Workers were told to accept struggle and effort under socialist banners. They were urged to seek liberation because no one was free as long as he toiled for someone else who owned the means of production and misappropriated the rewards. Although labor created all value, workers did not receive the full share of the product; the rest was misused and wasted by parasites. If all this were changed, said Moses Hahl, there would be no waste for such things as armies, warships, tombstones, liquor, and expensive caskets. He also declared that bourgeois society was so wrong in every way, and especially in its economic basis, that petty reform was futile. Another writer declared that it was painful for class-minded workers to realize that there were workingmen not fighting for their rightful share of what they created. Hoping to remedy this situation, playwrights endorsed unions and strikes on the socialist stage, showing how in the end awakened workers would be rewarded fully for their efforts.[37] Understandably then, to awaken workers became the socialist mission, and class struggle became the guiding principle.

Socialist class consciousness stirred critics particularly in temperance, religious, and business circles. Utopian socialists also were among the critics: Matti Kurikka kept alive dreams of forming a new social order after the failure of his colony, but derided class-minded socialists for spreading materialism and conflict. Critics generally denounced socialists as disrupters and anarchists whose strike activity and trade unionism made it hard for immigrants to secure employment because employers blacklisted Finns in reprisal. Satirically, one correspondent reported that Finns were blacklisted in order to give them time for erecting socialist halls and making flagstaffs. Especially after the Minnesota iron strike of 1907 and the Michigan copper strike of 1913 and 1914, critics were active in denouncing Finnish strikers and socialists. In 1908 Finnish groups of Eveleth, Minnesota, held a publicized meeting blaming the inability of Finns to secure jobs on the socialist strikers. They stated, moreover, that only a fraction of all immigrants were socialists and that most men wanted to work without belonging to unions. Again during the copper strike, meetings issued similar statements and helped organize anti-socialist leagues to fight the socialists within immigrant ranks. In the spirit of such resolutions churchmen advised newcomers from Finland that to merit respect they ought to stay in whatever job they found and ought not to interfere with existing conditions because, as "revolutionaries" and "anarchists," they faced expulsion from America.[38] Such critics, however, did not succeed in preventing strikes or trade unionism.

From about 1905 the immigrants showed more interest in strikes and trade unions, to some extent because socialists spurred them to action. In some instances Finns formed union groups for themselves such as the Finnish locals of dock workers in Ohio lake ports, which belonged to a national longshoremen's union.[39] Usually, however, they did not isolate themselves and instead joined labor unions in common with workers of other nationalities. In 1895 they were among the striking miners of Michigan, and in the following year some of them joined the fishermen's strike in Oregon. In 1906 miners struck in Rockland, Michigan, where two men were shot. Finnish strikers were blamed for the shooting, but they were eventually absolved. As it attracted attention elsewhere among Finns, the Rockland episode kindled interest in trade unionism and marked the start of their increased participation in strikes.[40] One year later Finns were the most active group in the iron strike directed by the Western Federation of Miners on the Minnesota ranges.[41] In Butte, Montana, miners joined the Federation and became the center of a union dispute in 1912. From about 1910 Michigan Finns in greater numbers joined the Federation which guided the copper strike of 1913 and 1914. By then, employers were singling out Finnish immigrants as prone to unionism and striking.

When the eight-months-long copper strike began in July, 1913, Finns received more prominence than in any other strike. The leaders of the strike used the Finnish socialist hall in Hancock, Michigan, as their headquarters. Their leadership was backed by hundreds of Finns active among the strikers, who numbered perhaps over eight thousand mainly unskilled laborers of different nationalities. On the pages of their daily, published in Hancock, Finnish socialists endorsed the strikers' demands for union recognition, more pay, and improved working conditions. They also spurred strikers to greater efforts and urged the contribution of funds for the families of the strikers. From elsewhere the strikers received editorial support and financial aid, not only from socialists but also from temperance and other groups. But in Hancock the strikers were criticized by the local Lutheran newspaper, which regarded the strike as unwise and especially denounced the socialist role. Other critics made their views known by joining the Citizens' Alliance and sponsoring meetings to end the strike and restrain the socialists. Although after months of striking, the workers failed to secure union recognition, the mine companies announced wage and other concessions both during and after the strike.[42]

Almost as soon as the Industrial Workers of the World appeared in 1905, socialists became concerned with industrial unionism. In 1906 the Finnish Socialist Federation praised the new organization for showing class consciousness, but three years later denounced it for expressing antiparliamentary tendencies. Despite this shift, industrial unionism still attracted support within socialist ranks. After the iron strike of 1907 in Minnesota, it had become attractive to more people. When the strike failed under the Western Federation of Miners, which later became hostile to industrial unionism and returned to the American Federation of Labor, Minnesota workers turned more hopefully to the Industrial Workers of the World as an organization promising to unite all workmen and not to favor a few craft laborers. In 1911 Leo Laukki, then still a member of the Finnish Socialist Federation, aroused socialists by saying that the new unionism meant "action" and for a time he endorsed the disablement of machinery in a strike if it ensured success to workers. Immediately, socialists like Frans Syrjälä denounced such unionism and praised the American Federation of Labor with the argument that, unlike the Industrial Workers of the World, it had made steady improvements in working conditions. Finally the debate ended in 1914 with the expulsion or withdrawal of about three thousand industrial unionists from the Finnish Socialist Federation. The industrial unionists formed their own associations and made their center in Minnesota. In 1916 they took the lead in striking on the iron ranges of Minnesota and in inviting organizers from the Industrial Workers of the World. After three months of conflict, the strike was called off and employers granted wage increases some months later. Although the strike was the high point in their strike leadership, Finnish industrial unionists still continued to organize in hope of eventual success.[43]

As industrial unionism stirred workers during World War I, socialists again were troubled. They saw industrial unionists like

Leo Laukki draw penalties on the ground that the unionists obstructed the war effort. They did not want to invite similar penalties. Foreseeing the possibility of American entry into the war, in February, 1917, eastern socialist editors cautioned socialist newspapers and organizations against giving the government reason to prosecute them for obstructing the war effort.[44] Obviously they could not incite workers to strike action, because they might be accused of impeding war production. When European revolutionists proclaimed that the socialist dream of proletarian class rule was feasible, immigrant socialists faced the decision of accepting or rejecting the view that sooner or later workers would rule. If they accepted and at the same time encouraged strikes, they might be accused of inciting workers to immediate action in America and of thus obstructing the war effort. Subsequently, the Left Wing endorsed the practicality of proletarian rule in Europe and outvoted the Right Wing to secure control of the Finnish Socialist Federation in December, 1920. The Right Wing regrouped its forces as a foreign-language federation within the American Socialist Party. In supporting trade unionism, workers were henceforth split into the Left, Right, and Industrial groups. Before their unity was entirely shattered, however, the socialists hastened workers and farmers into forming coöperatives, so as perhaps to regain the unity lost in 1914.

During the spread of trade unionism, Finns also promoted the coöperative movement among workers and farmers. Their coöperative enterprises included stores, creameries, and boarding houses. In 1920 they even started a coöperative farm in Georgia. As early as the 1880's and 1890's isolated groups set up coöperative organizations to manage boarding houses, threshing machines, and a cannery for Oregon fishermen.[45] During the decade after 1900, coöperative stores were formed in communities scattered through Ohio, Illinois, Massachusetts, Minnesota, and Montana. But it was not until the decade of World War I that most coöperatives were formed. Surveying the enterprises, one editor estimated that there were over one hundred coöperative stores and that in 1918 few had reached their tenth year.[46] In the same year an official of the coöperative wholesale house in Superior, Wisconsin, said that there were almost eighty such stores.[47] These figures differed probably because of different standards in classifying coöperative enterprises.

During the 1920's new ventures increased the number of coöperative stores.

From all ranks the coöperatives received support. As one writer said in 1920, people holding different political views had entertained hopes of salvation in coöperatives. Indeed there was proof of his observation. In 1903 Ohio advocates of prohibition formed a coöperative store in opposition to private grocery men who were against the ban on alcohol. Massachusetts conservatives organized a coöperative store to rival the socialist-sponsored one. In 1907 churchmen of Waukegan, Illinois, formed a coöperative stock company in which stockholders received voting power according to the number of their shares. About ten years later socialists formed a rival store which adopted the traditional coöperative custom of allowing one vote to each member irrespective of the amount of his stock.[48] Although others helped initiate coöperatives, the socialists gave them the major impetus.

In the socialist view coöperatives helped to liberate workers and farmers from capitalism. Socialists did not regard coöperatives as investments for speculative purpose; on the contrary suggestions were made that coöperatives became too bourgeois in urging patrons to extreme thrift. Socialist editors printed a warning that coöperatives should not copy ordinary stock companies in paying large dividends lest individual greed replace higher purposes. Unlike the individualistic ambitions of other stock companies and private businessmen, they stressed common economic purposes. Defining their aims, one official said that they did not want to become capitalists, but rather wanted to break away from capitalism by teaching the people how to operate their own institutions. As long as industrial capitalism remained, coöperatives were thus regarded as aids in the class struggle. In this spirit during the copper strike coöperatives were formed among the strikers. Through coöperatives there was hope of removing the middlemen and ending their profits. Pamphleteers, for instance, argued that a coöperative bakery would transfer all benefits to the consumer. In line with the desire to replace middlemen one writer said that a coöperative boarding house had replaced high-priced private eating places.[49] With their coöperative approach socialists thus tapped sentiments common among immigrants who desired to escape from industrial capitalism. While socialists were promoting coöperatives, thousands left industry for farms.

Then the new farmers built coöperatives and gave added impetus to the movement for liberation from industrial capitalism.

Almost as soon as immigrants had found industrial work in America, "land fever" began to draw many from the shops and mines. Leaving the strike-ridden mines of Minnesota in 1907, they set up farms in the hinterland of the iron ranges. Newspaper correspondents often reported the landward movement from the mines and mills. One correspondent stated that "land fever" had beset Finns in the mining town of Red Lodge, Montana. From Glassport, Pennsylvania, another reported that the "Wisconsin fever" or "potato fever" drew his countrymen westward in search of farms. After a steel mill closed in Youngstown, Ohio, others were reported seeking farms in New York. From Kearsarge, Michigan, mine workers revealed plans to leave for farms.[50] Far and wide such reports revealed the Finns' desire to leave the ranks of industrial wage earners.

Publicists and land agents hailed farming as the panacea for the ills which beset industrial workers. They liked to emphasize that farmers were independent and well-fed according to the proverb, "If one has land, surely the land will feed him." Reporting the loss of lives by Finnish miners in 1887, one paper observed that the individual was happier if he could work on his own land. Another declared that the farmer was his own master in not being dependent on capitalists. An editorial writer urged the poor to depart landward and secure independence from the insecurities of wage earning. Besides independence, farmers were promised health and peace of mind. By moving to the land, according to one writer, workers who had lost their health in industry would regain it. Another advised those seeking nature away from the hustle, crime, and poverty of cities to build a "Garden of Eden" away from "Babel." Consequently, real estate agents expressed their willingness to help immigrants become healthy and happy, for "When God wanted to make man completely happy, He put him on a piece of land."[51]

But landward-bound workers received warnings, especially from those skeptical of misleading land offers. In 1918 one publisher declared that land-selling was the easiest field for speculators, who sold worthless lands to their fellow immigrants. Although favoring the landward movement, newspaper editors warned against agents who sold land under false pretenses. Deluded land buyers in Florida and elsewhere reported their experiences and denounced the land agents. Socialists warned that farmers did not escape from capitalism. Yet farming proved attractive to twenty socialist newspaper workers who bought mortgaged farms to quiet their nerves.[52] Even if they found some truth in these warnings, readers continued to buy farms in increasing numbers, particularly after World War I.

After trying to master industrial life, thousands moved to farms. On arrival in America, few went directly to the land; those who did took homesteads in Minnesota and the Dakotas. But most immigrants first entered industry. Even if they had wanted farms, they lacked funds to acquire them until they could save enough from their earnings as wage earners. Listed for the first time in the United States census of 1920, Finnish immigrants totalled 14,988 farm operators. Over two-thirds of the farm operators lived in Michigan, Minnesota, and Wisconsin, where they occupied mainly the cutover lands. Others lived in the Dakotas, Washington, Oregon, and in the abandoned farm areas of New England and New York. In the same census, it was reported that almost half of all foreign-born Finns lived in rural areas.[53] Farming really had become a refuge to thousands.

Whether or not they became farmers, Finnish immigrants did not cease their quest for economic salvation. They moved from job to job, mine to farm, stock company to coöperative, and even from America to Finland. During their first five years in America, they were undoubtedly most free to move about and to leave America, as it took time to sink roots. When they finally settled down, married, and organized institutions, they found more reasons than before to reconsider any plan for further migration. Nonetheless, the bread and butter question remained ever paramount to most Finnish Americans.

CHAPTER V

# LOVE

*Conditions are still undeveloped in the west, Finnish settlements are mobile, so that only in a few major centers have Finns united to form congregations, temperance societies, workingmen's associations, and similar organizations in order to achieve spiritual bonds. Most of them are still 'wild'; the saloon their home, cards their books, vulgarity their spiritual nourishment.*

TIEDON HENKI [1]

Finnish immigrants did not reject the bonds of love in America. In two different ways they developed their ties of affection. Love united romantically men and women and created family life. It also brought together likeminded friends and strangers into fraternal relationships. As most immigrants were single on their arrival in America, they had no family life until they married. When they did marry, men and women found that the family in America had fewer disciplinary, recreational, and economic functions than their parental homes in rural Finland. Both single and married immigrants found that recreation was less and less dependent upon the home. Instead, they developed fraternal bonds outside the family to organize and discipline themselves during leisure hours. So even if immigrants married, their affections extended beyond the family.

Most immigrants arrived eligible for marriage, since the unmarried represented 75 percent of the passport applicants in Finland between 1901 and 1920, and both men and women belonged to the most eligible age groups.[2] The age group from sixteen to thirty years included 69 percent of the passport applicants, and those in their thirties were another 13 percent.[3] No wonder then that marital matters concerned the immigrants.

Although so many arrived eligible for marriage, the rate of marriage was undoubtedly slowed by the uneven sex ratio. During the years from 1893 to 1920 women represented 39 percent of all passport applicants in Finland, but not all of these came to America.[4] American figures indicate that during the fiscal years from 1901 to 1920 35 percent of the arrivals from Finland were women. The percentage of women arrivals was smaller in the first years of emigration and increased thereafter to reduce the ratio of men to women.[5] Census figures show that among the foreign-born Finns there were 181.9 males to every 100 females in 1900, 156.4 to every 100 in 1910, and 132.2 to every 100 in 1920. Depending on employment conditions, the ratios varied in different sections of the country. In 1910 the ratio of men to women was highest in the western states because at first the newly developing lumber and mine areas had attracted mainly men. The two sexes were most nearly equal in number in New England. Of the six geographical divisions into which the country was divided, only the mid-Atlantic group of New York, New Jersey, and Pennsylvania had more women than men and, hence, the lowest ratio of men to women.[6] This exception occurred because women sought domestic employment in New York City, and women generally outnumbered men in cities. Because of this uneven distribution of the sexes men and women had difficulties in meeting each other.

Yet men and women found ways of coming together to raise families. According to the federal census of 1910, almost 40 percent of all persons of Finnish stock had been born in America. In the ensuing decade the American-born Finns increased in numbers faster than before, so that they represented over 49 percent in 1920.[7] Immigrant surveys also revealed the presence of children. In their census of 1898 immigrant editors reported on children in communities from the Atlantic to the Pacific: for instance, Clatskanie, Oregon, had 191 children, 62 women, and 97 men. In 1897 the foreign-born of Ashtabula, Ohio, numbered 439 men, 325 women, and 98 children; there also were 440 children born in America. According to a tally made in 1907, the Finns of Ishpeming, Michigan, numbered 1,134 children, 604 women of whom 447 were married, and 1,220 men of whom 509 were married.[8] Quite obviously, marriages were taking place, but under circumstances different from those of long-established rural communities.

Immigrants who married tended to forget the social and economic distinctions of a landed society because they were landless workers. Hence, they felt no compulsion to observe the values of a land-owning class which insisted that the marital relationship should be based on social, property, and other considerations. No longer did they find sense in the proverb, "Human beings marry each other; servants and hired men mate with each other." They married without direction from elders or from parents with farms who insisted that marriage partners be chosen for their frugality and experience in domestic arts or for their ability to take over the parental lands. If they considered the economic aspects of marriage, the main emphasis was on the man's wage-earning capacity and the woman's ability to budget money. They joked, for instance, that "Love was too fine for the workman" and "They would marry when potatoes were fifteen cents a bushel." [9] As laborers they had earned little cash beyond their keep in Finland, but they worked mainly for cash in America. So they were freer to arrange their economic affairs and support families. This fact was pointed out by a pastor who declared in 1904 that young men and women could enter marriage more easily and confidently in America than in Finland. In America, he said, they secured economic competence to begin families much sooner than in Finland.[10] Young people were therefore freer to court as romantic personalities.

In America immigrants also found themselves freer to marry because of the absence of a State Church. Since the state could not compel anyone to join a church, those wanting to marry were free from the requirement that a church must announce bans and perform marriage rites. Then too, they found it no barrier to marriage if they were not confirmed or had missed communion. Instead, they dealt with civil authorities concerned mainly with the age requirements for prospective husbands and wives. Consequently, immigrant editors felt it newsworthy to point out that marriages were performed by justices of the peace, police officials, and English-speaking pastors rather than by Finnish pastors. Very few immigrants, however, agreed with Matti Kurikka that natural law gave women the right of motherhood without benefit of marriage ceremonies. Many agreed with the playwright who stated that clergymen added nothing to the wedding, which might better be performed by civil authority because marriage was rightfully based only upon the personal desires of two persons. As many others, or more, favored church marriages which were performed only at the request of those immediately concerned. Regarding the family as the divine basis of society, they believed that clergymen should bless and make holy the ties between husband and wife.[11] In the main, immigrants agreed that mutual love and consent rather than the demands of outside agencies were basic to the marital relationship.

Because immigrant women tended to acquire a status equal to that of men, they entered marriage in America more nearly as equals of men than if they had been in Finland. They had greater freedom to choose marriage partners in America, as much because of the immigrant sex ratio as because of the absence of coercive paternal authority.[12] As most women came unmarried to America, they were forced to support themselves mainly by domestic employment. At least until they married and were tied down by family duties, thousands of former dairy maids and farm servants, who had earned little cash, if any, in Finland, became independent economically and socially in America. If they did not seek employment after marriage, women still found opportunity to leave their homes for participation in organized activities. Both secular and religious spokesmen recognized that women were able to match men in such activities. According to one speaker, since they helped create and rear future generations, women had the right to take part with men in economic and political affairs.[13] Consequently, the view developed that harmony in both homes and organizations properly depended less upon masculine domineering and more upon feminine ability to influence people.

Organizations increasingly opened their doors to women on the same basis as to men. Churches began to accord women the same voting and other rights held by men. After more than a decade of existence, Synod Lutherans gave women equality with men in 1908 and National Lutherans gave them voting rights in 1909.[14] Earlier they had accepted women in such capacities as Sunday school teachers and organizers of sewing circles. Temperance groups declared that women had an important role in the crusade against liquor. As one writer said, women had once been considered only as men's playthings; now women were not only rearing their children but also learning to participate in social and political affairs once limited to men. Other writers were more specific and said that wives had a special role in helping their husbands stay away from saloons.[15] Workingmen's groups also broadened their views. In 1897 a labor paper agreed that women perhaps should vote in school elections and in later years socialist clubs supported woman suffrage.[16] Other groups also endorsed suffrage and various new roles for women.

That immigrant courtship occurred in new circumstances was shown, for example, by the romantic advertisements of men seeking correspondence with unattached women. Passionate, indeed, was this correspondence which led to the exchanging of visits. Young women joked in Erie, Pennsylvania, that if they went to Maine, men would surely meet them even with a wheelbarrow.[17] Thousands of men paid to advertise their romantic aspirations in the immigrant press. Even groups of men numbering from ten to fifty signed joint advertisements directed toward finding lady correspondents interested in marriage. Whether or not they advertised in groups, men gave their sentiments in verse and prose. One man wanted correspondence with an immigrant girl whom he had known in Finland and also invited letters from others of the "finer sex." Seven men declared that they were in the best years of manhood, unfaded by factory life, filled with the "everlasting gifts of Amor," and anxious for marriage. Five men wanted wives who could cook and sew and, as they themselves had no riches, none were required from their future wives. Still others advertised for wives without wealth but with "bushels of love."[18] There was no record kept, however, of the marriages contracted through such advertising.

Although a few advertised like the men, women more often used newspaper columns publishing letters on love matters, especially in the *Siirtolainen* ("Immigrant") of Kaleva, Michigan, and the *New Yorkin Uutiset* ("New York News") of Brooklyn, New York. The latter paper was nicknamed the "Marital News" because it frequently devoted one page in an issue of six or eight pages to such letters.[19] On its pages, mainly women asked and gave advice concerning love and passion. One woman writer advised another to enter a nunnery if she feared sex instincts but, as for herself, she was no exception to natural law in her desires. Another writer warned domestic servants against having love affairs with the sons of the millionaire families for whom they worked. Still another defended the view that marriages should be based only upon love. Other letter writers described their romances.[20] For all such writers it was tragedy, needless to say, when love and passion were crushed.

Besides printing letters, publishers gave additional space to the romantic theme by reprinting stories of love and romantic adventure as paper-bound booklets or as serials in newspapers. A woman published her own novel, *Broken Youth or Wealth Conquered Love,* in which a son's happiness was destroyed when his mother insisted that he should not marry his poor sweetheart.[21] The romantic titles, such as *The Power of Love,* however, were usually reprints from sources in Finland or translations from American and European sources.[22] The romantic theme was especially strong in the titles issued by August Edwards, an immigrant publisher in Ashtabula. He listed works like *How Matt Won Lisa, A Way to Become a Bride in a Short Time, One Hundred Degrees of Love,* and *The Great Secret on How to Win the Love of Every Man and How to Become a Bride in Four Weeks.*[23] Such publishers also issued works on the physical or passionate basis of love.

In verse, song, and prose immigrants recognized the physical aspects of love. For the married and unmarried, publishers issued works on sex which explained in scientific terms sexual functions and stressed the importance of the sex drive in human behavior. They also explained contraception and counseled happy marital relationships. Antero Tanner became a publisher when he issued his own books on marriage and birth control, including one edition banned in Finland.[24] Newspaper publishers in New York, Fitchburg, Ashtabula, Kaleva, and Hancock sold imported books on sex as well as publishing their own titles like *Sex and Marriage* and separate volumes on the sexual drive of men and women. Although such works warned against illicit sexual relations, they declared that sex was nothing of which to be ashamed. As the editor of one work said, sex was divine and no more shameful than the desire to eat, for sex had as its purpose the continuing of the human race, but even if there were no issue the sexual partners were not necessarily damned.[25] Consequently, frankness about sex was recognized more and more in discussions of love and marriage.

Although ribaldry among men had long dealt with sex, physical love increasingly became a fitting subject for mixed audiences. To be sure, in Finland both sexes showed a growing interest in books on love and sex. But rural areas were not noted for buying literature, to say nothing of the romantic novels which urban youths acquired readily. Leaving the rural areas, immigrants thus discovered, really for the first time, the suitability of love as a public subject of consideration for both sexes. Their discovery came through poets, songsters, and novelists who wrote of romantic sentiments, passionate love, and physical attractiveness. The physical was emphasized humorously, for example, in the boudoir scene in which the lover discovered that his lady was not endowed with fair hair, bright eyes, and beautiful body. One poet placed the scene on the wedding night when the stunned bridegroom found that his bride wore a wig and false teeth and paint. Another poet merely warned the lumberjack to scrutinize more closely his lady friends of the street lest he wake up in some hotel room to find that his chosen one wore false hair and teeth as well as artificial aids for a well-filled bosom.[26] Although men were not neglected in such verses, women probably were accorded the greater attention.

Since romantic love emphasized mutual sex love, writers increasingly conceded to women a role which had been previously regarded as improper or non-existent. In part, they raised the feminine issue to disprove the view that women were more passive and subordinate than men; they rejected the older idea that women, save for prostitutes, lacked sexual initiative. The new books on such matters suggested that women properly were not so passive. Among such publications was a translation of a work co-authored by Bernarr MacFadden, which said that sexual ignorance developed unhealthy bodies for women. Women, it declared, should love physical beauty and reject the idea that body functions were shameful; it was hypocritical to frown upon the lady whose skirts were lifted by windy gusts. In her novel on prostitution a writer suggested that the social evil was not the fault of seductive women, but of brutish males. Another woman writer who was a socialist declared that social and economic conditions brought supremacy to men and forced women to earn their livelihood through prostitution.[27] In other words, these writers wanted the same standards of sexual behavior for both men and women.

Understandably then, immigrants came to base marriage more and more on mutual love, equality, and compatibility. This meant

*Finns predominated in this group of mine workers in Negaunee, Michigan*

*Before they married, women often worked as domestics in New York City*

Incorporated under the Laws of State of Minnesota

Finnish-American Mining Company,

This Certifies that ... is the owner of ... Shares of the Capital Stock of

Finnish-American Mining Company,

transferable only on the books of the Company by the holder hereof in person or by Attorney upon surrender of this Certificate properly endorsed.

In Witness Whereof, the said Company has caused this Certificate to be signed by its duly authorized officers and to be sealed with the Seal of the Company

*Immigrants bought the stock of mining companies located not only in America but also in Finland*

*Immigrant farmers built hay barns in Old-Country style at Nisula, Michigan*

that married women were regarded less and less as subordinates designed just to wait upon men and to raise children. Instead, marriage was seen as raising men and women to higher relationships. More than once, it was said that God made wife and husband into lifetime companions to treat each other with love and equal regard. The future wife, hence, should properly attend school to attain intellectual equality with her husband. Love, rather than riches, said one writer, made a happy family. No longer were women to be slaves of men. Marriage simply was meant to be the holy union of two young persons wanting to enjoy life together.[28] Besides, in America marriage seemed more romantic because the couple felt less obligated to observe the demands of outsiders than in Finland.[29]

At the same time immigrants tempered their view of marriage with reality. They were disturbed partly by the fact that some men came without their wives and children from Finland, and instead of sending for them, remarried in America.[30] Many husbands and wives who were undoubtedly hard pressed to support their children could recall the proverb which said, "When poverty enters the door, love goes out by the window." Churchmen worried that marriages performed by others than pastors were weak. Temperance advocates were disturbed by the fact that men succumbed to drink and forgot their family responsibilities. Socialists attributed the breakup of homes to the same economic insecurity which created prostitution, intemperance, and child labor.[31] Undoubtedly, because of their rural backgrounds, these different spokesmen were disturbed by what they regarded as weakening family ties. They had grown up in an atmosphere which expected the rural home to satisfy the economic and recreational needs of its members under the moral guidance of the church. But it was different in America, where people did not find recreation and economic self-sufficiency at home.

Finding leisure activities away from home shocked immigrants with particular force. Both the married and unmarried found that the control of the home and church over leisure activities was weakened, leaving the individual alone to decide how to spend his leisure time. But the individual immigrant was not always prepared because, as Finnish officials pointed out, those who left Finland had often been under the confining supervision of "patriarchal circumstances."[32] Another observer contended that immigrant youths equated freedom with departure from the ways of their fathers. For instance, youths came to address their parents with the informal rather than the formal personal pronoun and, hence, showed less parental respect. Instead of remembering the great holidays of Finland, he said, they now celebrated with saloon dances and drinking parties.[33] In other words, immigrants were released from established discipline in using their free time.

Saloons became the chief centers of leisure activity outside the home. Concern was felt for immigrants from the rural areas of Finland, who were not used to the commercial drinking places found only in the towns. Temperance spokesmen early in their work saw a connection between intemperance and the lack of family life. The reformed drunkard who had neglected his family left behind in Finland served as an object lesson for the writer urging men to mend their ways.[34] In so doing, the writer emphasized the fact that immigrant men faced problems in using leisure time. During the early years when men came alone to the newly-developed industrial areas, they had no home life. Consequently, men in the mining towns of Minnesota sought saloons for entertainment and prostitutes as substitutes for home and family. Such primitive mining communities and lucrative hard manual labor were correlated with "equally intense and vicious forms of amusement."[35] Early Finnish arrivals were no exception to this pattern in the mining towns.

In fact and fiction the married as well as the single found occasion to visit saloons. In fifteen iron towns of Minnesota the United States Immigration Commission singled out the Finnish and Slovenian immigrants as the heaviest drinkers. Finnish writers recalled that their fellow men were known for hard drinking when they first settled in America. A pastor declared that during their early years in Pennsylvania Finns spent their leisure by drinking, fighting, and playing cards. In Ashtabula, one writer reported that the men left the saloons only long enough to do their day's work.[36] Moreover, such observers associated drinking with disorder.

Accordingly, Finns became legendary for their fights and *puukkot,* or hunting knives. Recalling the early days, one temperance writer declared that all sorts of stories were circulated, but that there was little good to relate. He cited the example of the town in which officials forbade anyone from lodging Finns, who were much feared when drunk. In 1915 another writer recalled that in the early days his compatriots were so poorly regarded that, if one of them lost his life in a fight, authorities did not investigate because they assumed that self-defense had led to his death. Noting the legendary fighting powers of the Finns, one pastor repeated his father's story of the Finn who rose to battle for fellow countrymen in a saloon. The hero drove out his foes by using a chair with the same energy that he had used in bayoneting Turks in one of the Russo-Turkish wars until his generals stopped him.[37] Memories and legends, however, did not alone sustain the fighting Finn.

Reports of fights appeared in actual contemporary accounts. In 1890 one Finn wrote in his "America letter" that where he lived the walls shook during vigorous fights among his fellow countrymen. A correspondent from Vinal Haven, Maine, was not the only one to report drunken men arrested for displaying knives in public places. From Brooklyn one reporter emphasized that again another Finn was beaten and knifed; he explained that the men filled the saloons not only on weekends but also on weekdays. Another reported from Newberry, Michigan, the arrest of a drunken man for fighting and using an illegal weapon; he wondered whether the county jail was made only for Finns. An Ohio newspaper told its readers about two men who were jailed for hitting a streetcar conductor with a whiskey bottle and who had been ousted from the car only after all the other occupants rose to do battle. Reporting a Sunday fight, an American newspaper asked if Finns had souls.[38] In fact and in fiction saloon life and fighting certainly showed the lack of disciplined behavior.

To instill discipline Finns evoked the sense of remorse and guilt. They stressed morality and social ethics in explaining misbehavior and its cure. Among churchmen, misbehavior was attributed to man's unbridled passion and innate sin. According to temperance advocates, social evil came from inward weakness as well as from an unhealthy environment. Socialists declared that even the most angelic succumbed in unhealthy economic circumstances. To avoid evil, they all declared, each individual must accept the moral restraints of organized activities. Like a parent the organization would then supervise his leisure time.

In disciplining themselves Finns also emphasized fraternal love. To do so was not out of place because their religious experiences had long stressed the value of love. To be sure, among human relationships based upon love, Christian spokesmen placed marriage high. But they differed about whether the various forms of love revealed the Divine or the human personality.[39] In part, at least, the romantic view of marriage emphasized the development of human personality and its potentialities. As Christian love also commanded one to love his neighbor, such emphasis on personality merged with the view that the fellowship of men of good will revealed the world's potential goodness. Men's goodness in the world, hence, could be discovered only by each man helping the other to reveal his personality. In short, neighborly love became the fraternal bond by which men and women developed each other's character. This love was shown in various ways. Laestadians proclaimed that ecstatic intimate union with each other was the best way to purge sins. To help resist common temptations Lutheran churchmen employed the symbol of brotherhood in organizing against intemperance; at one of their meetings a commentator said that he felt as though he were among the children of one big family.[40] Members of mutual benefit societies also addressed each other in the family spirit. Deploring economic obstacles to personal development, socialists united in behalf of comradely endeavor. No matter in what form the fraternal spirit appeared, however, organizations tried to develop especially those aspects of human character needed outside home life.

In the role of parents organizations offered substitutes for the private home. They supplemented the services of private proprietors by organizing coöperative rooming and boarding houses mainly for single men. The *poikatalot* ("boys' houses"), which Leo Laukki called monasteries, served until the men wanted to marry. Women also had coöperative rooming houses, and families owned and operated apartment houses on a coöperative basis. Generally, however, Finns did not concentrate on providing such residences. Instead they maintained many more "homes" in the form of churches and halls.

All in all, Finns maintained hundreds of buildings to provide leisure activities. Church, temperance, socialist, and other groups valued their buildings in the thousands of dollars. In virtually no community were immigrants content with one building. They wanted to own a building for each particular purpose. If dissension arose within an organization, it was not uncommon for courts to settle disputes over building ownership; the losing faction then withdrew to maintain its own new building. If groups lacked buildings, they rented rooms or met in private homes. But they preferred to own buildings which made possible more varied activities like athletics, dances, plays, lectures, libraries, restaurants, meetings, and concerts. When they assembled, business meetings, church services, and evening programs were most common.

To present their chief attractions the organizations drew on varied talents from among their supporters. Churches used pastors, preachers, teachers, organists, sextons, and choirs for their services. Temperance, socialist, and other societies employed different talents for their evening entertainments (*iltamat*) even though they also had the counterpart of the pastor in their speaker. The variety of talents was shown, for example, in Quincy, Massachusetts, by the temperance society which acquired in 1912 its own new hall seating five hundred persons. In 1913 its programs included 95 speeches, 92 poems, 103 songs, 24 choral numbers, 26 narrations, 11 tales, 18 performances with piano, violin, and mandolin, and 26 readings of the handwritten "fist paper." During the year it also had three family nights and twenty evenings for drama. Its sewing club held three bazaars and thirteen other entertainment nights.[41] By offering such varied programs, organizations hoped to keep their audiences satisfied and disciplined.

Although the programs and entertainments themselves proved attractive, men and women also went to the halls and churches for courtship. Such gatherings allowed young women to display their attractiveness to the men, who often outnumbered them. So much courtship went on that speakers were distracted; once Martin Hendrickson advised the men and women of his audience to find more suitable places "for continuing the human race."[42] There was more fact than fiction in the stories about the ardent suitor wishing to accompany his lady after an evening's entertainment and in the anecdotes about men and women who were not content to meet at one hall but also visited the halls of rival groups. To assure a quorum for a meeting in New Rochelle, New York, one correspondent told the women to invite their male friends in order to accomplish two purposes at one time.[43] Courtship existed, however, only as a byproduct because, of course, organizations did not organize, at least not ostensibly, to stimulate it.

Organizations were concerned with public ethics as well as private ethics. Public behavior in dancing, strikebreaking, or drinking, was specifically a focus of attention. Churches stressed moral guilt and responsibility; temperance societies called for the pledge of abstinence; socialists emphasized loyalty to class consciousness. They all were concerned lest low private morals endanger the rest of organized society. Discipline became doubly important when individuals lacked the counsel and restraint of family life.

Finns first sought moral discipline mainly in three Lutheran organizations. In general, the Lutherans agreed that sin was innate in man and that spiritual rebirth would direct him away from evil. As they had doctrinal differences, the church groups also differed somewhat in their methods of awakening a sense of moral guilt and regeneration. But they all imposed membership qualifications and maintained discipline by expelling the erring member, if necessary.

Although split into sects, Apostolic Lutherans generally sought repentance for sin through the Bible, simple ritual, and a minimum of church organization. They believed that the Lord's message was so clear in the Bible that even laymen were qualified to preside at services. Through chants and hymns they aroused their sense of guilt and rebirth. To help each other find the presence of Christ they were apt to rise, confess sins, and clasp hands while frenzied dancing overcame them. It was even reported that during these services windows were sometimes broken. Apostolic Lutherans insisted upon simplicity, for satanic temptation presumably had more opportunity in elaborate rites and rigid church organization. Worldly temptations in weekday life were also barred for the same reason. But the sects differed in their evangelical approach; some believed that the saving grace of Christ's sacrifice did not require detailed laws for Christian living; others prescribed rules to fight man's sinful nature, which was disclosed at the slightest relaxation. In varying degrees the sects, accordingly, dictated the manner of dress and adornment in homes. Some even forbade the use of curtains and the taking of photographs. In

1916 the Big Meeting session declared that there was no divine warrant for life insurance although it had desirable economic purposes; such insurance, it said, often led people to commit arson, murder, and other wrongs. In the Apostolic Lutheran view, extreme remorse, abstinence, and repentance could best help believers to resist earthly temptations.[44]

According to the Lutheran Synod or Finnish Evangelical Lutheran Church, intellectual rebirth brought religious salvation. Transferring sacraments, services, and doctrines of the Finnish State Church, the Synod did not stir inner religious awakening, but persuaded immigrants to resume old church ties. Its appeal was intellectual and so it stressed the role of learned clergymen. Consequently, it deplored the immigrants' accepting untrained clergymen so readily. Presenting its case, one pastor said the shepherd needed more knowledge than his flock. Through clerical guidance, Bible study, and prayer the faithful then acquired "right knowledge." The faithful, moreover, respected church and secular authority, for it was all divine in origin. They learned to do the right thing during their short earthly stay: for example, one did not read newspapers which gave "wrong knowledge" serving Satan. Through evangelicalism the believer learned to seek the presence of Christ whose death had atoned for man's sin. But he usually was too weak to reform anyone except himself. If higher powers did not change the individual's mind, enlightenment could not reform those defending "evangelicalism of the flesh." Although outward conditions might induce drinking, one pastor declared that evil was *a priori* within the individual and without inward reform any improvement in outward conditions was futile. But Synod supporters conceded that their contemporaries properly emphasized social issues which went together with religion and that even socialists, who erred in regard to human sin, worked like churchmen for all humanity. According to a pastor, his fellow clergymen needed more study in economics and sociology and their church more zeal in interpreting social matters in the press.[45] Except for temperance work, however, the Synod did not identify itself with any major reform to combat social problems. Instead, it continued to give weight to inner moral reform.

In a sense, the Finnish National Evangelical Lutherans combined characteristics of both the Apostolic and Synod Lutherans.

Like the Synod Lutherans, they used trained clergymen and formal church organization. Twice they set up a seminary for training clergymen, but they also welcomed lay preachers. Although on somewhat different grounds from the Apostolic Lutherans, they disliked a State Church and did not feel that formal training was the most important qualification for pastors. As their president said in 1903, the important element was that clergymen, like laymen, should be qualified not by learning but by rebirth and understanding of Christ's evangelical message. The National Lutherans also felt that the Apostolic Lutherans had little appreciation for the evangelical message in their rebirth, but instead overemphasized pietism. They also felt that the Synod Lutherans had pietistic leanings. Unlike the Apostolic and Synod Lutherans, the National Lutherans felt to some degree "saved" by their Christlike rebirth, and some even felt qualified to reform society and to combat social ills like intemperance. In 1903 their annual meeting declared neutrality towards socialism but authorized its pastors to participate in all good social causes.[46] Such participation in earthly reform did not deny original sin, because man had partly purged himself of sin in rebirth and was acting as though Christ had returned to earth. In other words, he could bestow the bounties of Christ's love for mankind. In this regard they were close to the Unitarians and Christian Socialists who felt themselves strongly enough reformed to undertake the reformation of their fellow men and society. One Congregational pastor even found Biblical sanction for socialism, which he differentiated from the doctrines of those socialists who rejected Christ.[47] And so, churchmen ended by finding a place for reforms in a period which abounded with concern for social problems.

From religious quarters came the first major impetus for temperance reform. Synod Lutherans supported the Finnish National Temperance Brotherhood, which became the leading group in the crusade. Their close relationship was endorsed by persons who declared that temperance needed religious inspiration. To provide such inspiration an essay contest was held on Christianity and its connection with temperance. In its publications the Brotherhood stressed that mere changes in the economic environment would not reform man because true reformation came from mastering his innate corruption. To point this out, for instance, a local of the

Brotherhood asked in anecdotal form whether it was the fault of society that one failed to find a husband. Defending the organization, one writer declared that if temperance were promoted for "outside reasons" rather than from one's inward submission to a high ideal, there was no merit in the cause.[48] At the same time, however, intemperance was related in varying degrees to economic conditions.

Temperance advocates failed to associate intemperance with sheer moral weakness. Writers pointed out the social significance of excessive drinking and its relation to prostitution, low wages, and mental illness. A playwright exploited the common theme of families suffering from the lack of money because men had spent their wages in saloons. Writers also suggested that men used drink as a means of forgetting their economic and other difficulties. When alcohol itself, rather than innate human sin, was partly blamed for such social consequences, temperance spokesmen spread information on how alcohol abused human bodies. One doctor declared that "poisonous alcohol" made a man into a robber, scoundrel, fighter, and murderer who forgot his earlier ideals. Then there were temperance groups that rejected, outright, clerical explanations of intemperance mainly, if not solely, in terms of innate sin. Debating the merits of the New York association which withdrew from the Finnish National Temperance Brotherhood, one critic declared that the parent organization had been too restrictive and dogmatic because of the "black frocked men."[49] But all temperance groups agreed that their members should abstain from alcohol.

Temperance societies disciplined their members by insisting upon abstinence. They entertained and instructed everyone they could to keep away from saloons. Their instrument of discipline was the pledge. Upon admission with appropriate rites, the new member pledged to abstain from using intoxicants, and in some associations he promised to refrain also from cardplaying, dancing, or even strikebreaking. Then the associations sent investigators who checked on members and to everybody's dismay reported violations. Those reported often renewed the pledge remorsefully, only to succumb again. In 1911 the Finnish National Temperance Brotherhood reported that of its members 404 broke the pledge, 631 failed to pay dues, and 256 were expelled for other reasons.[50]

Very early in its existence the Brotherhood had concerned itself with restoring to membership those who broke the pledge. In 1890 when a member asked how many times a repeating violator could be taken back he was told that more care should be taken in passing on applications for readmission.[51] Temperance societies, in general, forgave the confessing transgressor because the confessional served to instill the fear of drink in other members just as the confession of sin stirred the religious community. As religious communicants were divided on the question of earthly temptations, so, too, temperance advocates differed.

As it first gave major impetus to the temperance cause, the Finnish National Temperance Brotherhood first raised the issue of extending the ban on alcohol to other fleshly temptations. Its associations denounced dancing, cardplaying, and dramatic performances, although later on they became more lenient. In 1898 one writer condemned plays for teaching murder, theft, adultery, and "terrible love adventures." But by 1913 another writer conceded that plays could present serious and worthwhile subjects. In spite of the dangers, he said, temperance societies continued to build halls for presenting plays while they neglected to erect churches. The Brotherhood associations were probably stronger in denouncing dancing, which in their eyes brought damnation and destroyed chastity. From the very beginning in 1888, they were troubled over dancing. At their first national festival, a pastor recalled that young people had almost spoiled the affair by dancing but were soon stopped by the more serious members. Later the Brotherhood altered its by-laws to ban dancing. As a result, in the 1890's its action led to the expulsion or voluntary withdrawal of local societies opposing the ban. Independent societies often sanctioned dancing: one, for example, permitted members to dance in saloon rooms provided the occasion was for the benefit of some philanthropic group. By 1913 the Brotherhood altered its by-laws: it still forbade dancing to local societies, but permitted them to rent their halls to dance groups, hoping that no one would abuse the right to rent.[52] These concessions were undoubtedly made to regain supporters for the Brotherhood, which had been growing weaker in membership.

Becoming articulate, socialists also concerned themselves with temperance and morality. At its convention in 1906 the Finnish

Socialist Federation endorsed personal temperance and total prohibition except for medical and industrial uses. Some speakers decleared that drunkenness had social causes, for the poor had no other pleasures. Others approved of moderate drinking. Later in debating the role of temperance, socialists increasingly stressed the idea that prohibition was ineffective in ending the degradation of workers, and at the next convention in 1909 the Federation did not endorse prohibition, although disapproving of the degrading effect of intemperance on workers.[53] Instead, it placed emphasis upon the economic measures which would remake society to ensure a more abundant life for workers. In later years temperance drew even less attention from socialists.

According to the socialists, moral rebirth did not come from mere moral precept. This view was reflected in the remark that human genes do not transmit the sins of one's elders, because a person's moral nature corresponds with the character of his environmental and developmental possibilities. If the environment failed to satisfy physical needs adequately, moral teaching was not enough in the presence of physical temptation. Because the desire to live was strong, even in the face of moral teaching, inadequate incomes forced people to become thieves, murderers, harlots, and scoundrels. True moral rebirth came by rebuilding society, reshaping economic conditions, and removing class lines. At the present time, socialists declared, upper-class morality prevailed and justified the ambitions and privileges of the owning class in order to keep workers content with their menial status and economic deprivation. To deny the morality of physical need merely kept workers from creating adequate means of satisfying their legitimate desires. So for the present socialists emphasized moral affirmation in the spirit of class struggle to demand and create a classless economy of abundance.[54]

To develop the new morality socialists imposed party discipline. Like the temperance and religious groups, they offered the confessional to the accused, who could defend himself against charges of transgression and, if guilty, promise to submit to further party discipline in order to regain good standing. Committees especially studied charges against members accused of strikebreaking and revising party doctrine and practice. In 1913 and 1914, for instance, revisionism was charged against hundreds who were expelled for promoting industrial unionism. Socialists also continually checked the qualifications of their speakers. At one meeting a delegate declared that women were unable to agitate because they could not carry as large cases of books as men could on lecture tours. Correspondents debated whether speakers should use fountain pens or wear overalls and red neckties. Besides submitting to such scrutiny, everyone paid dues, read party newspapers, attended classes, and, if possible, joined trade unions. Then too, they were reminded that attendance was imperative at the socialist halls, even if there was no dancing, for there at first hand, speakers, actors, singers, and poets could instill moral discipline.[55]

Although discipline was developed, critics within socialist ranks complained that it was neglected in the time-consuming efforts to finance and maintain halls worth thousands of dollars. In 1910 one critic wondered whether socialists maintained halls for principles or for making money. Socialist locals, he declared, promoted money-raising activities like dances and neglected lectures which were often more rewarding both intellectually and financially. Developing this criticism, radical socialists or industrial unionists described the prevailing activities as "hall socialism." According to them, socialists found it hard to influence workers, especially young ones, without providing entertainment, plays, and similar activities. Hall socialists, they argued, neglected the real aim of discussing, promoting, and participating in the American socialist movement. The radical socialists proposed less hall activity and more trade unionism as the best way of developing moral discipline.[56]

To develop moral discipline various organizations resorted to physical culture. Temperance and socialist groups declared that healthy bodies meant healthy minds. As a temperance advocate said, physical and mental health were mutual. Another believed that physical exercise led a person to "nature's bosom" and strengthened his character, fraternalism, decisiveness, and idealism. A socialist writer agreed that gymnastics and athletics promoted coöperation between people, while a fellow scribe stated that character was developed through exercise. Still others urged workers to develop their own ideal physical culture for class conscious purposes.[57] If mind and body were well trained as a consequence of such exercise, surely moral discipline would gain.

From about 1900, gymnastic and athletic activities were increasingly organized, especially by temperance and socialist groups.

Independent athletic clubs were also formed, but since few if any had their own rooms, they gravitated towards organizations with rooms available for practice. As long as there were plenty of single men and the second generation was interested, gymnastics and athletics flourished. To encourage sheer physical development and group participation, gymnastic performances like pyramid building were arranged. By 1910 competitions were sponsored for individual athletes. In the East, track competitions were spurred by the American appearances of Finland's Olympic champion, Hannes Kolehmainen. In the Midwest, wrestling publicized physical culture.

According to one journal in 1910, so much interest was shown in wrestling that people forgot other gymnastics. It criticized Americans for not appreciating wrestling as pure exercise to develop beautiful physique. Since sheer physical power was at stake, the journal frowned upon Americans for generally preferring catch-as-catch-can wrestling in which opponents seized each other's bodies at any place. Instead, it approved the Finns for taking up Greco-Roman wrestling—a genre requiring more coördinated body control since opponents could grasp each other only above the waist.[58] Wrestlers like Karl Lehto engaged in matches with all comers and made the sports pages of Finnish and American newspapers. By World War I wrestling had reached its peak popularity.

Physical culture was also developed through the practice of natural medicine. In part, natural medicine received impetus from the view that genetic inheritance was not insurmountable. This was shown in the advertisement of a translated guide by Bernarr MacFadden, that said anyone could develop health, vigor, and beauty through physical culture whatever his inherited physical endowments.[59] The "new medicine" also interested those who assumed that urban life produced artificiality and impurity. Patent medicines hence were in disfavor. As one religious writer said, massages, baths, and exercises were far superior to patent medicines.[60] Then too, natural medicine drew on the immigrant rural background with its *sauna* or steambath and home remedies. According to proverb, "Where the sun shines, the doctor has no business," and "If the bath house and brandy cannot help a man, death is near at hand." So natural medicine won favor by its emphasis on bathing.

To justify baths the advocates of natural medicine explained that unnatural elements required removal from sick bodies. Dieting, fasting, exercising, massaging, and "sun, air, sand, steam, water, and other baths" sufficed in the view of one natural doctor. Book dealers imported the works of Louis Kuhne, whose name became synonymous with bathing. According to the German writer, all diseases were manifestations of only one disease which was "the foreign element" in the body. Those having a sufficiently strong will to live were assured recovery by various baths and dieting, without resort to medicines or surgery.[61] And so, natural medicine found support among immigrants who became masseurs and masseuses, and even medical practitioners with their own sanitariums in Minnesota and elsewhere. Then, too, there were those who sought natural cures at home through guides issued by the exponents of the new medicine. As in Finland, some also practiced bloodletting in the bath houses. They all declared the need to purge unnatural impurities from innocent bodies in the search for healthy minds.

In seeking moral discipline, each rival immigrant group argued over who was most successful, and each was sure that its competitor was morally unworthy. More than once Finns went to court about their reputations and behavior. In the newspapers they excoriated each other for alleged moral shortcomings. These charges and countercharges were true, in so far as most groups had some members who were drunk, who had committed adultery, or who had done something else which was regarded as reprehensible.

Competing groups assumed the worst about the objectives and methods of each other. In particular, those who were first in forming organizations resented the latecomers who developed new associations. Churchmen and temperance advocates denounced socialist newcomers as agitators who disrupted communities and spread spiritual poison. Critics also characterized socialists as anarchists and bomb throwers who committed hooligan-like acts. In reply, socialists stated that their critics were reactionaries, who had neglected to keep up with the time and so continued to serve as scabs, gunmen, and company tools during labor strikes. As first-comers, Synod Lutheran clergymen deplored the appearance of ambitious lay rivals. According to one churchman, adventurers came from Finland to create dissension and to mislead immigrants away from orderly religious activity. An editor who supported a new church organization which attracted lay preachers argued that the misbehavior of a Synod pastor simply confirmed his view of the rottenness of the entire Synod.[62] Likewise, other rivals concluded that the personal behavior of their foes showed the unworthiness of the groups under criticism.

Rivals especially tried to show that their opponents lacked honorable motives and were impelled by self-interest rather than by principles. They were sure that their foes worked as leaders of organizations to avoid honest physical labor. One Synod Lutheran observed that digging ditches was more honorable work for a layman who had once aspired to become a cleric but had been expelled from his congregation for drinking and sexual indiscretions. Another Synod Lutheran suspected that a rival church group neglected the work of God to organize money-raising activities on Sunday. Synod Lutherans also described editors who criticized them as men who did not like physical labor. In reply, one of the editors under attack stated that he worked honorably to support his family, which was something a certain Synod clergyman could not say. He also dismissed charges that he did not deserve payment for work done at the request of a temperance group; moreover, he attributed such charges to temperance men who wanted the job of publishing for the group. Later when socialists appeared, the newcomers claimed that clergymen included bankrupt fortune seekers who had come to fill their pockets by organizing congregations. To qualify as a preacher was easy, said a socialist writer, since a painter could receive his "call" merely by falling from a ladder. Such charges were answered by critics who suspected socialist spokesmen of misusing funds for personal gain and mouthing high ideals as a cloak for their greediness.[63] In other words, the various rivals suggested that their opponents were hypocrites seeking an easy livelihood to avoid physical toil.

As part of their charges of hypocrisy, rivals pointed to alleged evidences of financial dishonesty and disrespect for property rights. When one pastor fled his congregation, a critical editor cited his failure to pay personal debts. Since they stressed economic change, socialists drew the criticism that they wanted to divide and misappropriate the property of other people. Reporting the arrest of two women for theft, a correspondent deplored their misbehavior and noted that the women were socialists. In Fitchburg a rival newspaper alleged that advertisers boycotted the local socialist paper because of the shameful actions encouraged by socialists. Local storekeepers, it declared, were forced to hire more employees in order to watch socialist patrons. From Minnesota one correspondent replied to such allegations by citing the critic who was arrested and fined for attempted theft in a paint store. He observed that the critic was always accusing socialists of wanting to level property ownership, but now the critic himself was seeking to redistribute property.[64] Immigrants, however, were probably less stirred by such charges than by those involving sex and drink.

The competing groups accused each other of sexual misbehavior. Before socialists appeared, on more than one occasion the sexual behavior of religious spokesmen stirred debate. Critics later declared that socialists threatened the sanctity of marriage, and socialists replied that clergymen seduced women at every opportunity. In denouncing socialists one critic argued that his charges were proved by the Harmony Colony of the utopian socialists, who had quarreled over whether wives should be held in common. Reporting the alleged rape committed by a socialist, one critical editor stated that his paper again had occasion to report a crime done by a member of a group which sanctioned the acts of its membership. From Brooklyn a pastor was reported as writing to American newspapers that the local socialists promoted free love, immoral dances, and anarchism. In giving the report, the correspondent reminded readers that the pastor himself had been ousted from one congregation for his philandering. Earlier another correspondent had emphasized that the same pastor was ousted for seeking not spiritual, but physical, contact with the ladies of his congregation. Taking note of the continued charges against him, the pastor advertised for proof that he drank, misappropriated funds, and committed adultery.[65] Sexual indiscretions, however, were not the only alleged evidence of moral bankruptcy.

Reinforcing their accusations, rivals exchanged charges and countercharges about each other's addiction to drink. In the pre-socialist period, church rivals publicized each other's supposed liking for drink. Synod Lutherans reported that one would-be pastor had been arrested and jailed many times for drunkenness. A critic reported that an editor, friend of the Synod Lutherans, was sus-

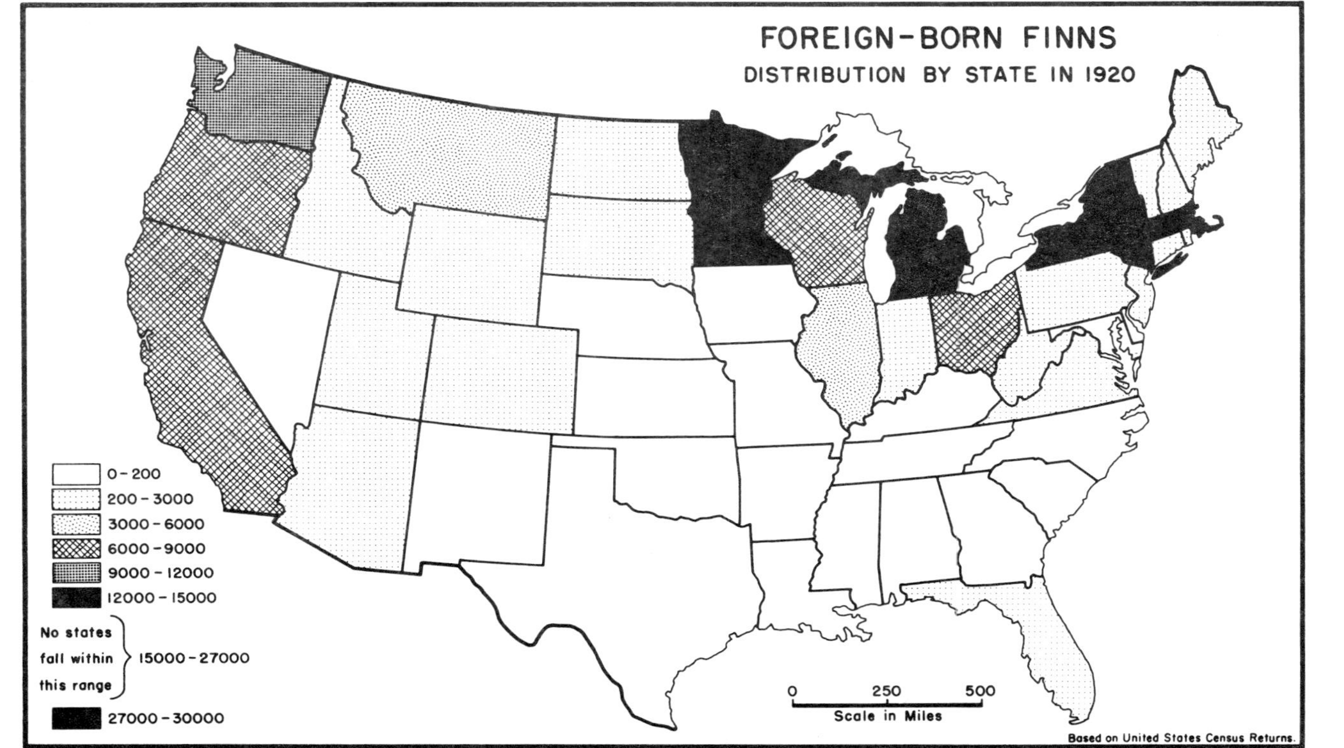


*Map of the United States showing the distribution of Finns*

*Immigrant halls and churches ranged*

*Temperance hall in Crystal Falls, Michigan*

*The Synod Lutheran church and parsonage in Monessen, Pennsylvania*

*from the modest to the pretentious*

*Temperance hall in Ashtabula, Ohio*

*Socialist hall in New York City*

*When immigrants of different persuasions organized their leisure time, they offered substitutes for saloon life*

SUURI! VALTAVA!

Suomalaisten Republikaanien

# Kokous

pidetään

## Hancockissa

Germaniahaalissa

## Tiistai-iltana Lokak. 9 p.

kello 8 i. p.

Kokouksessa tulevat puhujina esiintymään:

J. H. Jasberg, J. E. Saari, C. A. Wright, W. Frank James, Jos. Wills, L. H. Richardson, Fred. Karinen, C. J. Wickström.

Quincyn Torvisoittokunta!

SUOMEN SÄVEL ja SUOMEN KAIKU LAULUSEURAT!

**Kokous on tärkeä**

ja suuri merkitys on pantawa siihen, että suomalaiset kokoontuwat miehissä. Wilkasta osanottoa toiwotaan Calumetista, Bostonista, Arcadiasta, Atlanticista, Dollar Baysta, Houghtonista y. m.

## Ylimääräinen juna Calumetista

lähtee puoli 8 samana iltana ja palaa kokouksen loputtua takaisin Calumetiin. Matkapiletin hinta on 50 senttiä. Asemalla ollaan wastaanottamassa!

*Handbill issued by the Finnish Republican club of Hancock, Michigan, in 1900*

*Temperance summer festival in Crystal Falls, Michigan*

*Socialists parading in Monessen, Pennsylvania*

*Folk dancers of a nationalistic society in Chicago*

*Socialist brass band in Monessen, Pennsylvania*

*Temperance society's presentation of a play by Alexis Kivi in Crystal Falls, Michigan*

*Gymnastic group sponsored by the socialist club in Glassport, Pennsylvania*

*Sewing circle associated with the Synod Lutheran church in Monessen, Pennsylvania*

*Synod Lutheran confirmation class in Monessen, Pennsylvania*

pected of being drunk at funeral services. According to their critics, socialists encouraged drinking. In Newark, New Jersey, one correspondent labeled the socialist center a "beer hall" where drunken men and women spent nights together. At the socialist convention of 1906, a critic declared that half the delegates spent their time in saloons while speakers denounced temperance work. In reply socialists charged that temperance workers broke their pledges of abstinence at every opportunity. One correspondent attributed an application for a saloon license from a temperance advocate to his seventeen years of crusading. Another testified that clergymen were latecomers in the crusade and that with no one else did he have to debate as hard about the merits of temperance.[66] Since saloons did attract immigrants, no doubt such charges of intemperance seemed meaningful warnings to the promoters of organized discipline.

Lacking the moral restraints of home life, immigrants had found in various ways new parents in organizations which provided discipline and recreation. This meant that fraternal love united them more and more as members of the organizations. To be sure, marital love was still important, but it became more the romantic concern of just two persons when marriage lost economic and social functions. As a less home-centered life emerged, associations reflected common interests which did not depend upon family connections. They particularly found reason to provide discipline during leisure time.

CHAPTER VI

# STATE

*Elections were coming and there was enough to converse about just on how we would vote. In the dryhouse the men had a sharp debate. The Republican, Socialist, and Prohibition parties campaigned as if it was election day.*

RAITTIUS-KALENTERI WUODELLE 1910 [1]

Since naturalization took time, Finnish Americans only gradually secured voting rights. Most of them arrived without electoral experience, because few people had shared political power in Finland before the reforms of 1906. As political wards before acquiring rights of suffrage, the immigrants felt themselves objects of state paternalism and discipline just as they had been in Finland. But they also found themselves politically freer in certain ways, although American agencies of government imposed restrictions during World War I. Undoubtedly, the ballot box was not the first concern of most new arrivals. Instead, immigrants probably appreciated more the laws and officials that helped them master their new life and its problems.

Until electoral reform occurred in 1906, few persons shared in the powers of governing Finland. Besides, until 1918 such powers were limited by the Russian Tsar, who as Grand Duke was represented by his governor-general in the Grand Duchy of Finland. Administration was by the Senate, which consisted of Finnish citizens, except for erstwhile Russian members, after about 1900. The Diet was composed of four estates, the nobility, the clergy, the burghers, and the peasants. Although the peasant estate drew on the most numerous part of the population, it had no more power than any other estate. Then too, its electorate was considered inferior because the peasants were the only voters unable to select their representatives directly; instead they chose electors who named the members of the peasant estate. In short, the government was not organized on a popular basis.

Before electoral reforms were made, relatively few male adults voted, since property qualifications limited the right of suffrage. Towards the end of the nineteenth century 70 percent of the population did not qualify for membership in the four estates, mainly because they had no property. They represented the landless element that had increased so rapidly in the preceding decades. In 1900 the male taxpayers who were eligible to vote numbered about 23,000, or less than 7 percent of the urban population, and 102,000, or over 4 percent of the rural population. As landowners were now about one-fourth of the rural households, the heads of the other households were excluded from parliamentary representation. The noble owners of landed estates perpetuated themselves through primogeniture. Property qualifications excluded most urban workers from voting for the burgher estate; in Helsinki over 86 percent of the factory workers were unable to vote.[2] Since property ruled at the ballot box, most people were subject to the paternal guardianship of the propertied classes.

In spite of the fact that new social groups had developed outside the four estates, suffrage was not extended to them without struggle. Electoral reform was opposed especially by the burghers and nobles who came mainly from the upper-class Swedish-speaking minority. The clerical and peasant estates were more disposed to reform the suffrage as well as to recognize other prerogatives for the Finnish-speaking majority. In response to the public demonstrations of 1905, the estates were finally abolished in 1906 and universal suffrage was given to all men and women who were twenty-four years old and older, except for those disqualified under certain conditions. At once, the qualified voters increased ten-fold. But voting rights were not changed for electing local officials. Even as late as 1915 urban officials were elected by voters who could each cast as many as twenty-five votes if they had sufficient income. Electoral reforms came too late, however, for many immigrants to have voting experience before reaching America.

Although upon arrival in America they lacked citizenship and were political wards, immigrants were in a sense freer than they had been in Finland. As there was no State Church in America, they associated freedom with the oportunity to determine the extent of their church obligations, if any, without fear of penalty. According to a visiting baroness in 1888, the immigrants often equated freedom with license. Partly because of language barriers, she said, they lacked proper religious information to decide political and social issues as they were not "brought up for such freedom" in Finland.[3] Religious and temperance crusaders felt that freedom of decision was misused to allow anyone to remain outside churches and to enter saloons. Aware that newspapers were frequently critical of churchmen, they accused journalists of equating freedom with irresponsibility.[4] In other words, they complained that this freedom resulted from the failure of the government to enforce certain moral obligations. Indeed they had reason for complaint, because the state did not compel anyone to pay tithes for the upkeep of clergymen as state employees. Those within and without the churches had no fear of losing their only cow for failure to pay tithes. Nor could any church impose conditions before marriages were permitted and passports were issued. Although grudgingly recognized by some, freedom from a State Church was finally accepted as one of the very real and inescapable results of leaving Finland.

In terms of social equality immigrants found more freedom because in America the political system stressed class and property distinctions less than in Finland. A man was called "mister" irrespective of his economic status and occupation. To be sure not everyone readily gave up title consciousness. Although immigrants talked much about equality, according to one correspondent, there were still those who regarded the titled shaggy ass more highly than the untitled purebred horse.[5] But at the same time, with or without titles, immigrants observed a less static class structure than in Finland. As one editorial writer declared, there were no fixed classes and no one had such a low status that he could not rise higher. In fact, he said, the only respected upper class was that of the workers, and even wealthy sons became doctors and lawyers to show their worthiness. Of course, another writer conceded, immigrants found a classless equality which was hitherto unknown to them, but then they found new class lines created by the possession of money.[6] In spite of the new distinctions, however, he recognized that class lines were more rigid in Finland, where the political system reinforced them. It was a continuous struggle to remove economic and social distinctions in Finland and legislation was required to permit people to move about freely and engage in economic activities which were once outside their class. Census enumerators categorized the population according to occupation and land ownership in terms commonly used to denote social status. The four estates were mutually exclusive and gave few openings to outsiders. In America, although differences existed between workers and employers and between those with and without land, political usage did not rigidify them and make class mobility entirely impossible.

During the early 1900's immigrants also felt freer in terms of political rights in America. An editor repeated the view that his readers were obligated to vote in American elections, since they had secured suffrage rights often in "freer circumstances" than in Finland.[7] Another newspaper writer observed that, unlike America, Finland regarded a man as "underage" as long as he failed to acquire the land which brought voting rights.[8] Between the years 1899 and 1905 immigrants found that they were freer to use other rights which were restricted in Finland by the Russian governor-general, who tried to stem the reform and nationalist movements. Whether or not they held public office, Finnish citizens faced censorship of publications and restraints against assembling. If they did not seek voluntary exile, scores were fined or imprisoned for displeasing the authorities, and young men faced conscription by the Russian Army. Consequently, hundreds had special reason to seek asylum in America, and those who had already left felt thankful that they were not then in Finland. Immigrants were especially pleased that until World War I they could publish free of censorship in America, and no doubt their concern with the repression in Finland made them more appreciative of their newspapers. Exiles also had no censorship troubles in America: Eero Erkko, an exiled publisher, issued an American edition of a journal which included several articles failing to pass Russian censorship.[9] When political conditions eased in Finland, such exiles often left America. But as long as repression continued in Finland, immigrants had special reasons to feel politically freer in America.

Although they were freer in America, immigrants again discovered the power of the state. They saw it personified by the officials who inspected them at Ellis Island, the policemen who arrested the rowdy and drunken from their midst, and the postal clerks who transmitted their money orders to Finland. As owners of houses, shops, and farms, they met the tax collector. Developing their organizations, they made use of the law. They learned to incorporate their associations. In response to attacks on it, one temperance organization incorporated and then reported that it now had the "protection of the laws of the United States." Another temperance organization employed the services of a lawyer to settle disputes and to advise on other matters. Organizations had frequent occasion to resort to lawyers, courts, and sheriffs in settling disputes over the ownership of halls and church buildings. In 1905, for instance, in Fitchburg, Massachusetts, after the disputants tried to exclude each other from a building by various means such as changing locks on the doors, the possession of the meeting place was settled by a court.[10] Immigrants learned early to use the state's police power to their advantage.

Upon entering developing industrial and agricultural areas, Finns saw in process the actual introduction of organized government. In the 1880's immigrant farmers gave a Finnish name, Savo, to a new township in South Dakota. During the 1890's and the following decade other immigrants saw and even helped the organizing of mining towns in Michigan and Minnesota. For instance, in 1906 South Range, Michigan, was incorporated as a town and its first council included representatives of the Finnish Americans, who were the majority of the local population totalling about 1,100. As such mining towns were noted for disorganization and pioneer vices, various citizens gave impetus to political moves seeking law and order. One judge, announcing that Eveleth, Minnesota, was no longer a frontier where it was proper to carry guns and knives, started to enforce the law by collecting a fine from a "Finlander" for drunken behavior and displaying a knife. Eveleth as well as other iron towns in Minnesota undertook political and other means to meet the challenges of intemperance, prostitution, and gambling. In 1907 Finnish temperance members helped the Eveleth Civic League begin its crusade. At the same time, such endeavors snowballed to secure pavements, public works, and other local conveniences supported by taxation.[11] Consequently, immigrants could see that political power was useful beyond maintaining laws on saloons. That the imposition of taxes could secure positive advantages such as public works suggested the relationship of politics and economics.

As in their Old Country, so too in America, immigrants found that economic advantage was related to political power. This fact was shown in the iron towns of Minnesota by the long struggle between the companies, wanting to increase their profits, and the local public, seeking higher taxes from the companies to pay for public works.[12] In the county of Houghton, Michigan, copper companies owned most of the land and dominated the supervisors who assessed all property and authorized all expenditures.[13] The role of these supervisors was scrutinized by Finnish strikers during the copper strike of 1913 and 1914. If others found reason to seek political advantage for economic purposes, immigrants tried to do likewise. In Ashtabula, Ohio, an immigrant contractor drew business by building roads for the city. Unemployed men sought town jobs in various places. Finnish-American voters of Ishpeming, Michigan, were urged to elect one of their compatriots as city treasurer because he could not engage in hard physical labor after accidentally losing a leg.[14] Those disgusted with industrial employment looked for government land, and the immigrant press did not fail to explain how to acquire homesteads. Then, reading their newspapers further, they learned about the economic role of government in terms of tariff legislation and trust control. Certainly, they did not have far to look for the relationship of economics and government.

The power of the state also confronted Finns who were labor organizers. Socialists, strikers, and trade unionists faced public officials in conflicts which involved particularly rights of assembly and free speech. In 1906 Finnish strikers were accused of killing two men in Rockland, Michigan, but later two of the indicted workers were acquitted and charges were dropped against the others. The work of their champions in keeping the case open led a temperance writer to say that workers must elect the right kind of officials to protect them. During the ensuing years, occasionally with conscious purpose to test the protection afforded by officialdom, labor organizers carried red banners and spoke in public places. In 1907 paraders started a court fight of several years after being arrested for carrying red banners to challenge a local ordinance in Hancock, Michigan. As the sponsors had anticipated trouble, paraders had been advised against resisting arrest and carrying anything which might be labeled as weapons. In the same year the red banners of Minnesota Finns aroused American newspapers to suggest the deportation of that "red rag bunch." Fearful of the spread of socialism, local businessmen also in 1907 persuaded a Finnish speaker not to hold a meeting in Crystal Falls, Michigan. Two years later in the same place another socialist organizer, the third such person trying to speak publicly, was run out of town by men who reportedly included the mayor and who made disrespectful remarks about constitutional rights.[15] Such incidents also occurred in other states from coast to coast.

Of all the labor episodes involving officialdom, the copper strike of 1913 and 1914 probably most stirred Finnish Americans. As active participants, they faced federal, state, and local officials. Injunctions were issued; arrests were made; penalties were imposed. Such actions were supported by over 4,300 men who included deputies under arms and militiamen with drawn bayonets.[16] In fact, the entire National Guard of Michigan was called out. Trying to settle the strike, various state and federal officials investigated, offered mediation, and heard strikers plead their case. Among such officials were congressmen who conducted an official inquiry. Since their inquiry occurred in the midst of charges about lawless strikers, an interpreter emphasized that the majority of the Finnish-American witnesses, who numbered over eighty and supported the strike, were citizens of the United States. When company attorneys asked these witnesses whether or not they were members of a socialist organization, the committee chairman agreed with the labor counsel that the committee had no right to ask whether or not they were Socialists, Republicans, or Democrats.[17] Instead, the witnesses preferred to deal solely with the economic merits of their cause. Although in such hearings strikers wooed federal authorities, no action came from Washington to override local and state officials in dealing with the strike.

During World War I Finns had particular reason to sense the power of government. Officials and private agencies in a rising crescendo exhorted immigrants to Americanize and demonstrate loyalty for the United States. In 1918 President Woodrow Wilson proclaimed Fourth of July as a special loyalty day for the foreign-born, and he invited representatives of different nationalities, including the Finnish, to meet with him. The Committee on Public Information had a Finnish department which explained official policies to solicit backing from immigrant editors.[18] To secure mailing rights newspaper publishers had to meet the loyalty standards of postal officials and to file translations of their war reports. Various agencies made insistent appeals that immigrants should buy Liberty Bonds and support Red Cross activities. After the United States entered the war, the military services inducted both foreign and native-born Finnish Americans totalling an estimated 10,000, probably an exaggerated figure.[19] When officials solicited support for the war and scrutinized immigrant activities in such ways, labor organizers, above all, felt the hand of government.

As socialists had long doubted the wisdom of war and called for a new social order, government agents scanned their activities. In Fitchburg, Massachusetts, the local socialist newspaper drew official attention, no doubt for making statements like the one made in 1914 to the effect that patriotism camouflaged rapacious capitalists who profited by building warships for the United States government. During 1918 offices of the newspaper were searched by agents of the War Department, but no charges were made. On the West Coast four editors of another socialist newspaper were arrested partly because of their possession of an antiwar book published in 1910.[20] Although socialists incurred such official disfavor, supporters of the Industrial Workers of the World fared even worse.

Critical like the socialists, followers of the Industrial Workers of the World received blame for antiwar sentiments. Such views were intimated, for example, by the industrial unionist who wrote from prison that capitalists found more than one way, like the payroll deductions for war bonds, to take money away from workers. Such views aroused officials, who continued to investigate and discourage the activities of the industrial unionists. In Ashtabula, Ohio, federal agents raided the hall of the industrial unionists and confiscated and burned literature, including a book printed in German script, but they found no positive evidence to arrest anyone. Other unionists were less fortunate, and scores were arrested particularly in Minnesota. In 1918 five of them were convicted in Chicago by the federal court, which tried about one hundred leading industrial unionists of different nationalities. The charges against them included obstruction of the war effort by inciting men to resist registering for the draft. This charge was seemingly given substance because, out of ignorance or even by willful design, hundreds of Finns had failed to register for the draft in Minnesota. On one occasion an immigrant returned his first papers, which were issued upon applying for citizenship, because he felt that such action exempted him from the draft, but instead an angry mob lynched him. Resistance to the war was also attributed to the industrial unionists of Marquette, Michigan, where one person was fined for ridiculing the Red Cross.[21] No doubt, the imposition of such penalties served as warnings to other immigrants.

Responding to the demands of federal officials, various individuals and groups took special pains to demonstrate loyalty. In April, 1917, a writer advised that, since the United States had entered the war, it was best to obey the laws and "keep your mouth shut." Another urged his compatriots to assemble at a summer festival and convey their sentiments of loyalty in letters to those "honored men, who are in the people's government." Accordingly, scores of societies sent resolutions to officials in Washington. But resolutions were not enough in the view of a lawyer who urged businessmen to take the lead in holding public meetings. Others agreed with him and sponsored rallies and parades to sell Liberty Bonds and to help the Red Cross. To spur these demonstrations on a nationwide basis the Lincoln Loyalty League was formed by persons who took part in various religious, temperance, fraternal, and business groups. At the meeting which laid the basis for the new association, the sponsors told the American press, socialists and industrial unionists were denounced as disloyal. Helping the new association was Oscar Larson, who declared that except for the "ultra-radical class-conscious Socialist element" Finns were as loyal and as patriotic as any other foreign-born Americans.[22] Following such professions of loyalty Finns were often advised to prove their devotion to the United States by becoming American citizens.

Finding such evidences of governmental power, immigrants were aroused politically. Above all, they tried to become citizens. As most probably did not arrive determined to stay indefinitely in America, they first had to decide to remain and then to seek citizenship. But moving often in search of work, they could not always fulfill proper requirements for speedy naturalization. Most of all, language difficulties precluded early naturalization, for the English and Finnish languages were so dissimilar that learning the new language was no easy matter. Consequently, Finns organized to overcome the language barrier.

To secure citizenship and voting rights Finnish Americans used their own organizations, attended public night schools, and received assistance from different agencies promoting citizenship. Even women sought suffrage for themselves through special efforts; their representatives were among those parading in Washington on the day before President Wilson's inauguration.[23] Generally, however, immigrant groups concentrated on teaching English and citizenship. Such activities probably appealed more to men than women because alien wives acquired citizenship through their husbands. Organizations had special committees which promoted naturalization and conducted English classes. They even had correspondence courses in English. Besides these efforts, agencies provided appropriate literature to the prospective citizens.[24] Publishers issued pamphlets explaining how to obtain citizenship and supplying correct answers to questions frequently asked at naturalization proceedings. Most of all, they printed dictionaries and grammars. Although no one measured the effectiveness of these various aids, probably as many persons, if not more, learned English through shoptalk at their places of work and business because physical exhaustion did not encourage regular sustained study at night. At any rate, thousands qualified for citizenship.

According to the censuses of 1910 and 1920, the percentage of citizens among Finns was below the average for all the foreign-born in America, and even lower in comparison with other North European immigrants. In 1910, 45.6 percent of all foreign-born males, aged twenty-one years and older, were naturalized while the comparable figure for the Finns was 30.6 percent. By 1920 in the same age group 47.8 percent of all foreign-born men and 39.2 percent of the Finnish men were citizens. Parenthetically, in 1920 the naturalized represented relatively more of the women than the men from Finland. In comparison with the foreign-born from North Europe, the Finns were far outdistanced. In 1910 the percentages of citizens for each immigrant group from ten countries of North Europe were almost, or more than, double the figure for the Finns.[25] This was understandable, however, because the Finns as latecomers to America had not had as much time as other immigrant groups to acquire citizenship.

But in comparison with the so-called "newer immigrants," mainly from eastern and southern Europe, Finns were active in setting the pace for acquiring citizenship. According to the census of 1910, Finns headed all the immigrant groups listed as recent arrivals from Europe in becoming naturalized. Studying the citizenship of over 68,000 immigrants of different nationalities, the United States Immigration Commission drew a similar line between old and new arrivals from Europe. It reported that the "Finnish race" was almost in second place among the recent arrivals in securing citizenship or acquiring first papers. It put the Finns in first place with the Swedes and the Irish, who were among the older arrivals, in showing the greatest interest in seeking citizenship as soon as as they became eligible for it. Others also singled out the Finns, partly in response to the view that socialists were exceedingly anxious to become citizens. In 1914 a federal labor investigator said that most of the alien Finnish witnesses appearing at one session of the congressional committee on the copper strike could not be socialists, because it was well known that socialists became naturalized as speedily as possible to obtain voting rights. Such a view no doubt gained substance from the publicity created by the efforts to deny citizenship to socialists on more than one occasion. In 1908 a federal attorney sought to prevent the naturalization of Finnish socialists by classifying them as "Mongolians" and, hence ineligible for citizenship. On the other hand, there were reports showing that Finns were also slow to become naturalized. One such report declared that only about fifty persons were able to vote in an immigrant community of fifteen hundred in Massachusetts. Studying the largest iron company which employed mainly immigrants in Minnesota, a federal investigator concluded that the general impression was not borne out in regarding Finns as second to the Scandinavians in promptness to become citizens.[26] Although these reports tempered views in regard to the Finns, official reports placed them ahead of most recent immigrant arrivals in seeking citizenship on a nationwide basis.

From about 1890 Finns who had become naturalized started to

fill a scattering of local offices, such as those of town clerk, road commissioner, and school director. Gradually they became city mayors and councilmen and county supervisors, treasurers, and prosecutors, most commonly in rural areas and small towns which had sizable Finnish populations.[27] So it was possible for Finns to fill all offices on the town council of Oulu, Wisconsin, and in the same state local official records were reportedly written in the Finnish language.[28] As time passed, immigrants or their children secured state offices. At one time or another they held seats in the legislatures of such states as Oregon, Minnesota, and Montana. In 1920 their first congressman, Oscar Larson, was elected and sent to Washington from St. Louis County, Minnesota. Coming at the age of five years to America, Larson finished his schooling in law and was a county prosecutor in Michigan before moving to Minnesota where he rebuilt his political career.[29] Finnish Americans, however, usually did not hold many important political offices. Instead, they were better known for their support of the Republican, Socialist, and Prohibition parties.

Disappointed by their limited political success, nationalists encouraged their compatriots to enter politics and advance as an ethnic group. As in employment, so too in politics, rivalries occurred between different nationalities. In 1892 one newspaper complained that Swedes monopolized local offices in Ishpeming, Michigan, and that, after long last, Finns should receive offices. Four years later another newspaper stated that, although by law the Finns and Irish were equal, the former were unrepresented on the Republican ticket in Hancock, Michigan, and it urged readers to use the threat of voting for Democrats to secure redress. To remedy such situations still another newspaper endorsed the formation of political clubs and argued that its readers should act as an ethnic group to secure political prominence. One such club was formed in Maynard, Massachusetts, where Finns resented Irishmen who held local offices. Ordinarily, Finnish Americans were a minority in local elections and could scarcely hope to win except by allying themselves with existing political parties and, particularly, with the winning party. Aware of the Republican success in Michigan, Oscar Larson in 1904 encouraged his countrymen to vote for Republicans in the local election at Calumet, Michigan, to pave the way for future Finnish political victories even though they had failed to have a representative on the ticket.[30] Such attempts to advance politically were not surprising since they supported a party which emphasized getting ahead.

Before 1920 Finnish Americans campaigned mainly for the Republicans. Of course, Democrats received some votes and editorial support: for instance, in 1900 one newspaper changed owners and in doing so shifted its editorial support from the Republicans to the Democrats. However, such instances were the exception rather than the rule. As early as 1888 immigrants formed Republican clubs and in 1900 the future congressman, Oscar Larson, took the circuit to oppose the Democrats. Such individuals were anxious to get ahead politically by supporting the winning party, which could make or break the political fortunes of ambitious new politicians. For example, an editor who campaigned among farmers for the victorious Republicans in 1896 was rewarded with an appointment to a customs office in Minnesota.[31] Then, too, Republicans represented economic individualism which appealed to the immigrants anxious to get ahead as businessmen and professionals. Such immigrants stood out among the first Finnish officeholders elected on the Republican ticket.[32] Workers, too, supported the Republican Party in terms of getting ahead but for a different reason. Being part of an often insecure, unskilled labor force, they responded politically to fluctuations in employment conditions. Remembering Grover Cleveland's second administration, they refused to absolve Democrats from the onus of unemployment and instead accepted the "full dinner pail" argument of the Republicans. Just before President William McKinley's inauguration in 1897, one of the earliest immigrant workingmen's papers, anticipating enough work and good wages, greeted him as inspiring confidence and making it unnecessary to speak any more about a "Democrat era."[33] Since workers were more numerous than entrepreneurs among the voters, the "dinner pail" argument obviously received most emphasis.

From the 1890's newspaper writers made sure that their readers did not fail to associate the Democrats with unemployment. When the election returns were announced in 1896, one editor rejoiced that the Democrats had not won, for surely then rebellious unemployed workers would have marched upon Washington. In 1900 another newspaper writer recalled the bad times of the Democrats and expressed confidence that business life was flowering under the Republicans. Four years later still another writer declared that industrialists simply could not trust the Democrats, who brought bad times.[34] As late as the decade of World War I, newspapers continued to correlate Republican success with full employment. By this time, however, there were editors and readers who felt uneasy and even rejected party regularity. Instead, they shifted to the Progressive banner of Theodore Roosevelt, who had bolted the Republican Party in 1912. Oscar Larson was one of those who campaigned for the Republican-nurtured offspring, and the newspaper with which he was associated supported the new cause. Various newspaper writers and editors expected economic improvement from the reform proposals of Theodore Roosevelt and the new party, rather than relying upon private industrialists to maintain economic well-being under the Republican Party.[35] But this break was largely temporary because ex-Progressives were returning to the fold by 1920, and their return was marked by the election of Larson as a Republican congressman.

Although Republicans continued to draw support from Finnish Americans, temperance advocates tried to break away to support the Prohibition Party. Some, however, preferred to work for prohibition through the Anti-Saloon League, which solicited temperance pledges from candidates of existing parties. Consequently, debates ensued whether the Party or the League had done most to secure prohibition laws from legislatures. The Finnish National Temperance Brotherhood, moreover, debated the propriety of requiring temperance advocates to support a particular party. No doubt it was aware that its members included Republicans who were unwilling to advocate changing party allegiance. In 1903 it endorsed the Prohibition Party but left local societies free to decide on their particular course of political action. By 1910 it was again stirred over political policy and decided that local conditions determined whether it was best to work through the Party or the League, both of which promoted prohibition laws. Subsequently, the Brotherhood intensified its campaigning for prohibition laws and temporarily was closer to the Prohibition Party around the time of World War I. When prohibition laws were enacted during the war decade, temperance advocates made renewed demands for their own political organizations to serve as watchdogs in the enforcement of the laws.[36]

According to the prohibitionists, the state was responsible for the people's well-being. Legislation to ban the liquor trade was thus justified. But the prohibitionists differed about whether or not they should work for legislation through the existing parties. Critics of the existing parties said that there were advocates who often preached temperance, but at election time supported the Whiskey Party to avoid having men go without bread if the Republicans were not elected. They denounced existing parties as run by corrupt self-seekers. Not only were major parties criticized, but also the Socialist Party was denounced by one writer for being deflected by liquor dealers from its true purpose of improving the lot of workers. Less hopefully, another writer felt that the slightness of the Prohibition Party vote proved the need to work through the victorious major parties.[37] But, if all temperance advocates did not expect much from the Prohibition Party, at least they did not dispute that prohibition laws would ensure a better life. They tried to demonstrate how such laws ended poverty, improved homes, filled churches, and emptied jails and poor houses. In this spirit one writer cited the example of the bachelor who formerly had spent his money each payday in saloons instead of buying needed clothing, but who now under a state prohibition law was well-clothed.[38] Surely then, the prohibitionists concluded, they were justified in their belief that the state could improve the life of its citizens through law.

Unlike the prohibitionists, socialists expected far-reaching reforms from their American Socialist Party. In keeping with their doctrines they maintained that political action was imperative. Before forming the Finnish Socialist Federation in 1906, immigrants interested in workingmen's organizations debated the desirability of losing their ethnic identity by joining the American Socialist Party.[39] Socialists compromised on the issue by forming the Federation, which retained its ethnic identity and, by collecting dues, acted for the Party, which did not have direct contact with Finnish members. The Federation aided the Party through financial contributions and election campaigning. But its political role was partly limited because not all its members were citizens. The organization was, moreover, plagued by doubts over the feasibility of political action. Such doubts were raised by the "impossibilists" and industrial unionists who questioned whether socialists could do much in a "bourgeois legislature." According to the critics, since economic power antedated the state, workers should start at the source of power by building up their economic organizations. In reply, party-minded socialists said that political action was essential to hasten economic betterment and that although capitalists controlled the state at the moment, there was no reason why workers should not gain control.[40] Subsequently, they retained control of the Federation, which reaffirmed loyalty to the American Socialists Party after the schism of 1913 and 1914.

In behalf of the American Socialist Party, its supporters argued that control of the state was essential for workers and their economic well-being. They stated that workers were in economic straits no matter which of the two major parties held office. Developing their organization during Republican administrations, they questioned if good times really existed. In 1910 a correspondent quipped that it was probably a sign of the "Republican good times" when workers lost jobs in Sandstone, Minnesota. Another said that no wonder the Republican era was golden, because it brought gold only to those who had plenty of it already. But then, socialists were not very surprised because they contended that both major parties served the same few capitalists who were free to run the economy as they wished. To remedy this situation socialists advocated changing the industrial economy by appropriate political reforms to ensure that workers would direct the new economic and social order. Above all, a writer said, workers needed laws guaranteeing their rights to a decent livelihood.[41] Logically, as long as private employers were free to hire and discharge men at will, socialists saw no hope of getting ahead through parties which did not challenge such prevailing practices. Instead, they preferred their own party.

By learning to seek political advance in such different ways, Finnish Americans helped complete the search for a place in their new homeland. It was not surprising, because they tried to advance in other fields of activity. Then, too, if for no other reason, they could not escape developing political ambitions because state power was evident all around them. As long as they had to live with the state, they decided to enter politics, hoping to share in the power of the state through the ballot. To do so they first sought citizenship. This took time and marked their formal break with any plan for returning immediately to their Old Country. Consequently, they found themselves fated to stay longer and longer in America.

CHAPTER VII

# FATE

*But then shall we regard America as a land strange to us, or ourselves as strangers in this land?*

JOH. BÄCK [1]

Gradually, Finnish immigrants no longer remained strangers in America. Even in the absence of any welcome, they organized to make themselves at home. As one of them wrote, America remained cold and forbidding unless familiarities were taken with her.[2] In general, Finns were so aware of staking claims on America that the question arose whether they would lose their ethnic identity and ties with the Old Country. But they could not undo their origin in Finland any more than they could avoid developing new roots in America. Finally, the immigrants decided that, in spite of their origin, their endeavors were not out of place in American life. And so they became Finnish Americans.

Moving about in search of work, immigrants also sought each other and congregated in the same areas. By 1900 they had found the thirteen states that were to attract most of them. According to the census of that year, of the 62,641 foreign-born persons from Finland 55,744 lived in Michigan, Minnesota, Massachusetts, New York, Washington, Ohio, Pennsylvania, Wisconsin, Illinois, California, Oregon, Montana, and New Jersey. In 1910 the thirteen states had 117,144 of the total 129,680 Finns, and ten years later they had 135,991 of the total 149,824. At census time each of the thirteen states almost always had 2,000 or more foreign-born Finns. Besides, there were nine other states which each had between 500 and 2,000. In short, the immigrants had settled mainly in a belt of northern states stretching from the Atlantic to the Pacific.[3]

Within each state, moreover, certain towns and cities became the focuses around which immigrants built their communities. Often such places were confined to one section of the state. Among them were Fitchburg, Massachusetts; Ashtabula, Ohio; Hancock, Michigan; Duluth, Minnesota; and Astoria, Oregon. The names of hundreds of other nearby places appeared in the press, which publicized many little-known hamlets and villages which had received immigrants. The press even revealed that settlers had christened places with Finnish names like Oulu in Wisconsin and Kaleva in Michigan. Indeed, by settling with their own kind, Finnish immigrants found the communities to which they could really belong in the midst of native-born Americans and other nationalities from Europe.

Finns developed their sense of belonging to some community especially through their organizations. Without such associations, they did not feel at home. According to a correspondent, there was really "no worthwhile news to report" from Wareham, Massachusetts, since the few immigrants had yet organized scarcely any common activities. Another correspondent despaired whether Delamar, Nevada, could ever become a Finnish center since people moved in and out so much that there were no organizations.[4] When employment was available in a place, immigrants did not move away, and they did not advise outsiders to remain away. Instead, immigrants looked forward to establishing ties with their new environment through organizations. To remain permanently required organizational pioneering, which was appropriately noted in reports about those who had arrived first on the scene. Within one year after the firstcomers had moved to Winlock, Washington, a correspondent reported progress not only in economic affairs but also in organizational matters, and he expected that a hall would be acquired shortly.[5] Certainly when such halls were acquired in the towns and cities of employment, the immigrant arrivals came to feel that they were really part of a Finnish-American community destined to survive.

In developing their associative life the immigrants maintained their national identity, which strengthened their sense of belonging to a special community. They shared a common cultural background in Finland. Homesickness and disappointment renewed tender feelings for, and sustained special interest in, their old homeland. Then, too, intellectual stimulus came through literature and visitors from Finland. Most important, language barriers kept the immigrants isolated as an ethnic group. In relatively few cases did they acquire sufficient command of English to feel at home in organizations outside their own Finnish community. Dissatisfied with existing leisure activities, they were also unwilling to depend upon others for corrective measures. As one said in 1914, they would lack coöperatives if they waited for action by Americans.[6] Finally, to conserve their energies Finns were often content only to organize themselves. Meeting in 1910, one temperance organization felt unable to organize other nationalities because all its efforts were needed to "elevate" the Finns.[7] Hence, immigrants formed their own language organizations based on common ideas and experiences gained in Finland or America.

Among the promoters of organizations were nationalists who emphasized ethnic consciousness. They declared that Finnish nationalism or culture could survive in America. By transmitting the language, customs, and patterns of thought which supposedly were Finnish, they expected that their children would acquire the parental culture. Through the language, said one writer, children had access to the "Finnish mind." If there were schools to teach the language, he added, the future of Finnish nationality was assured in America. Another writer expected that Finns could preserve their nationality even for a thousand years in America. This was possible, he said, because in America people could freely assert their national spirit and preserve their heritage.[8] In other words, the nationalists said that it was possible to organize and preserve their ethnic identity for a long time.

By affirming their ethnic origins nationalists believed that they drew strength. It was impossible to conceal one's origins, said one writer, since each nationality had its distinctive characteristics. In America, therefore, Finnish immigrants disclosed their origins, although nationalism required conscious cultivation. To impress this view in 1915 one pastor wrote a pamphlet explaining why he wanted to retain his ethnic ties and share the culture of an ancient race. He surveyed literature, music, art, language, and religion and concluded that from the viewpoint of the "laws of humanism, patriotism, and divinity" Finnish culture was self-sufficient and met the criteria for a great national civilization. No one else but the Finns, he said, had preserved so well their instincts of honesty and hospitality from their pastoral era. No one else, not even Job, the Jews, the Romans, or the Napoleonic French had had a more eventful history than the Finns. Not only Finland's culture but also its natural scenery inspired nationalist writers. Although many poverty-stricken people came to America each year, an editor asserted that the children of immigrants need not deride Finland as poor and insignificant. For the children did not know Finland's charms and its melancholic pines, rushing rapids, sunlit nights, song thrushes, nightingales, and numerous lakes. If only such assets were appreciated, concluded the nationalists, no one need be ashamed to proclaim his Finnish ancestry.[9]

Through their slogan, "One tongue, one mind," nationalists hoped to muster fellow immigrants behind various institutions. As immigrants lived in scattered places and differed in their institutional endeavors, nationalists appealed for unity. To support this appeal, a pastor argued that since history demonstrated that the Finns were a religious nationality, immigrants should unite and renew religious ties. One writer declared that in America Finns lived in danger of national extinction because they were indifferent to the disruption caused by unknown would-be leaders. Another writer warned that ethnic unity was lost through quarreling and accepting disruptive "unspiritual" ideas. To remedy this situation he called for the support of existing nationalist-minded organizations like churches and temperance societies. After 1898 the Knights of Kaleva and after 1904 the Ladies of Kaleva formed secret societies and chose as members those who they thought best represented their nationality and, as one said later, were active in churches, temperance organizations, and "other group endeavors which developed our compatriots to higher levels." Ethnic unity thus became another cause.

Then, when their ethnic consciousness was developed, different groups reduced their factional conflicts. In 1908 temperance societies met in efforts to settle quarrels. Newspapers were reported as ending some of their mutual bickering. The National and Synod Lutherans talked about merging. In 1920 Apostolic Lutherans in Hancock, Michigan, were reported as having friendlier relations with each other in contrast to earlier years. Rejecting class struggle, ex-socialists and utopian socialists like Matti Kurikka found refuge in nationalism and urged partisan organizations to embrace ethnic unity as a higher cause. In part, these various appeals for unity agreed with a pastor's view that temperance societies should strengthen themselves by organizing against the un-Finnish socialist admirers of international brotherhood.[10] Imbued with such a purpose, nationalist spokesmen then increasingly tried to offset socialist influences during the decade of World War I.

Under the impact of forces outside their own group also, immigrants found that the concept of ethnic unity was accentuated. Both at work and play they were classified according to national origin, and their behavior was ascribed to racial inheritance. At their places of employment the job hierarchy was based partly on nationality lines. Especially during World War I the campaign for Americanization suggested that an immigrant had a set of ethnic characteristics to be exchanged for an American set. Simultaneously, by defining American war aims, President Woodrow Wilson gave added prominence to the concept of ethnic differences with his plea for national self-determination in Europe. Consequently, immigrants could not escape awareness of their national origin in Finland.

Since dominant American elements typed immigrant behavior by race and nationality, Finns became concerned with how each of them was classified. In other words, they were self-conscious of their group reputation outside immigrant ranks. Until Finnish immigrants arrived, most Americans probably knew little, if anything, about the people of Finland and, after meeting the newcomers, developed stereotyped pictures of them. As Finland was ruled by Russia, the first immigrants were even regarded as Russians. This situation led one immigrant writer to declare that, as long as Finns were classed with Russians, they did not receive the same respect which they enjoyed in 1920 after Finland had become independent. More often, American observers declared that Finnish immigrants had "that inward and downward slant of the eye which proclaims the Mongol." Such statements were offensive to the nationalists, who attributed them to the inadequate information of Americans. Frequently, American writers generalized on what they regarded as characteristic Finnish traits even though their lists were contradictory at times. Their lists described Finns as taciturn, melancholic, sober, clannish, patient, racially sullen, even-tempered, "more phlegmatic than the Italian," ambitious to get on, and too self-contemplative. Most of all, their lists accentuated proneness to drink, fighting, and radicalism.[11]

Americans must first have learned about the Finns in the saloons in the opinion of the nationalists, who were greatly concerned about the reports on the intemperance and fighting among their compatriots. Since each immigrant was a "natural representative of his nationality," declared one pastor, fighting and drinking by the first-comers had lowered the reputations of all Finns who came later to America. Noting the Boston newspaper account which included data on Finns jailed for drunkenness, a writer was sure that Finnish reputations would be much better in the absence of the heavy drinkers. In Ironwood, Michigan, one correspondent complained that English-language newspapers were sure to misspell the surnames and to indicate the nationality whenever Finns were involved in crime. Their crimes, declared another writer, undid the efforts to raise Finnish reputations.[12] If drinking and fighting, which undoubtedly were represented as crimes in most instances, seemed bad enough, nationalists felt even more concerned about other matters.

When employers and others singled out Finnish socialists and strikers, the nationalists were aroused. They asserted that reports which described some Finns as "lawless young fellows who will not work" damaged the general reputation of Finns. They repudiated the claim of the New York *World* that, since every Finn was born a revolutionary, there were 300,000 Finnish-American Reds. They also were concerned when employers fired Finns for socialist and union activity. According to the United States Immigration Commission, in 1907 and 1908 on the Menominee Iron Range employers discharged more Finns in proportion to their number than any other race for their reputed "radical tendencies" and for being "much less tractable than any other race." It quoted a superintendent who said that his company refused to hire Finnish socialists, who were regarded as "good laborers" but "trouble breeders." After the copper strike in 1914, employers again singled out Finns and reportedly planned to get rid of them. Such policies led one writer to declare that labor agitation had lowered Finnish reputations and endangered their opportunities of finding employment. In 1914 a correspondent blamed labor reformers for creating disorder and rebellion against the government and, in turn, causing American newspapers to endorse boycotting Finnish workers and even sending them to Russia. In 1919 Herman Donner, a Swedish-speaking Finn, wrote that fifteen or twenty years earlier Americans had welcomed his countrymen as desirable immigrants with unlimited capacities for work, thrift, frugality, temperance, piety, and obedience. By 1911 on his tour of Michigan, he recalled, Americans were already showing antagonism and misunderstanding. Now, he wrote, Americans regarded them as socialistic and classed them, especially the newcomers, "as demagogues and agitators" who "contributed so greatly to labor unrest and disturbances more or less grave." In later years one pastor recalled that an American journal had interpreted Finnish life in a false light during the copper strike by alleging that every Finnish community had its center in the labor temple, but neglecting to mention the schools, churches, and other institutions. He also stated that another report about 150 Finns who were made to kneel and kiss an American flag had injured reputations and overlooked "hundreds of worthy deeds and sacrifices made by the better class of Finnish Americans."[13] No wonder then, in view of such reports and allegations, that nationalists urged ethnic unity to combat the socialists.

Although their ethnic self-consciousness was reinforced in America, the immigrants also lost ethnic identity in certain ways. It was debatable whether they had any innate national or racial attributes to lose, because someone in their midst was sure to match each supposed "Finnish characteristic" with its opposite. In truth, they retained, modified, or replaced traits, habits, and customs which were acquired in a particular historical past. If such traits, habits, and customs had been so unique and hereditary to them, there would have been no reason to worry about the loss of identity. As it was otherwise, Finns could not avoid sensing cultural changes in themselves.

Immigrants certainly were not all in sympathy with the nationalists. Socialists deplored nationalism as a barrier to class consciousness. No longer did they feel that it was useful and up-to-date. One group declared that the promoters of an excursion trip to Finland were impelled by a love of antiquity. To unite immigrants with the Old Country on the basis of nationality, a writer added, merely obscured the class struggle. Although the natural beauties of Finland were not to be scorned, still another wrote, workers had no time to make pleasure trips, and especially, they had no reason to sing the praises of the Finnish forests from which only the wealthy reaped the riches. If the Finnish race were preserved in America, still another writer declared, it would be a miraculous exception to all other nationalities who, although more numerous and powerful, had not been able to preserve their racial purity. History showed, moreover, that mankind was erasing all national barriers and instead was learning mutual help. Eventually, he predicted, people would find no need to be

Finns but would rather be individuals deserving justice. However, the socialists retained their ethnic identity when they joined the American Socialist Party through their own language federation. But unlike the nationalists, they did not promote language unity, because they believed that the Finnish language embodied unique aspirations. Eventually, socialists predicted, their federation would disappear after organizing the "foreigners" who thereby would cease to be foreign.[14]

In various ways the loss of cultural separateness was recognized by both the advocates and critics of Finnish nationalism. As part of his sociological studies at the University of Chicago, Clemens Niemi concluded that, by undergoing a process of adaptation, his fellow immigrants dissolved their "old ideals, standards and customs through contact with American life and finally, gradual adjustment to new conditions." Although everyone did not agree how far such adaptation went, they assumed that at least some changes had occurred in themselves. They felt conscious of adopting new methods, and even new ideas, in their institutions; one writer said that in the 1890's temperance work was relatively more widespread among the Finns of America than of the Old Country. Other changes were recognized in personal behavior. In 1910 a writer observed that businessmen had an art of "enslaving" immigrants to American styles by making women give up their woolen dresses for those made in America. When a suitor departed with the purse of a lady friend, one correspondent explained that the suitor had been long enough in America to lose his "Finnish honesty." Another writer noted that Finns changed their surnames, for example, from Korpi to Corbey and from Mattila to Madila.[15] Above all, linguistic changes were noted.

After they had learned some English words, immigrants combined Finnish case endings with English stems into "Finglish." They changed, for instance, "trammer" into *trammari,* "room" into *rooma,* and "cake" into *keeki*. Such words were given currency in part by editors who invented them when translating articles from English-language sources. So many new words were made that complaints appeared. A newspaper reader complained that his editors used too many "foreign words" like *mobiliseeraa* ("mobilize"), *analyseeraa* ("analyze"), and *absoluuttinen* ("absolute") without explaining their meaning to the uninitiated. Another reader lamented that Finns tried to adorn their language with all sorts of borrowed trimmings although linguists regarded their tongue as one of the most rich, melodious, and inflective languages. Such borrowings, he added, merely represented the view that everything which did not originate in Finland was desirable and clever. Reporting on a dramatic performance, one correspondent urged the actors to enunciate more clearly in Finnish and to avoid the use of "Finnish-English."[16] While immigrants coined new words in such ways, their children went further and entirely rejected the Finnish language.

The immigrant generation observed that its children increasingly preferred to speak English rather than Finnish. According to one pastor, the children of immigrants learned to regard themselves as Americans in the public schools and like "traitors" rejected Finnish culture in their homes. Another pastor felt that American-schooled children became ashamed of their Finnish connections and did not speak the language except perhaps for business reasons in immigrant communities. A temperance speaker complained that the American and foreign-born Finns drew apart and young people did not respect the experiences of their elders. As long as immigration continued, said an editor in 1913, immigrant communities received new strength, which was sapped, however, by the estrangement of their children schooled in America.[17] Unless children learned the language, it was evident that the cultural ways of their parents could not well survive beyond the immigrant generation.

Immigrants also drew away from their cultural roots when they sought inspiration from American history. Immigrant speakers and writers examined American history to discover what was common with their aspirations and, hence, they felt less isolated as an ethnic group. Defending secret societies like the Knights of Kaleva, one writer reminded his readers that Americans had had secret associations as early as 1733 when Bostonians formed a society of Free Masons.[18] To further their rise in economic and political matters aspiring politicians found encouragement in the history of the party of Abraham Lincoln. During World War I a loyalty league included the former president's name in its title to demonstrate that there were Finns who appreciated patriotic heroes from America's past. Lincoln's Birthday as well as the Fourth of July gave editors occasions to associate Finns with America's past. One newspaper writer concluded that immigrant successes in America demanded honoring great men, like Lincoln, found in both Finland and the United States. Another editor felt that Lincoln's exhortations to thrift and industry were still sound in 1920; undoubtedly the object lesson was meant for those with entrepreneurial aspirations.[19] Book publishers, likewise, in their publications gave lessons from the record of the Civil War president and the Republican Party.

In the 1890's immigrant publishers issued their first books surveying American history from the colonial period. Such works emphasized political matters and drew their material from English-language secondary accounts. Two of the three books which extended their surveys into the 1890's definitely favored the Republicans.[20] After covering the origins of the United States, one of them devoted most of its remaining space to the Civil War and its aftermath. In the earlier period it credited George Washington with freeing the colonies, and in the later era it credited Abraham Lincoln with saving the union. The post-war period was highlighted by a discussion of the rise of the Ku Klux Klan and of southern hostility towards Negroes. Carrying this discussion into the second administration of Grover Cleveland, on its last page the book concluded that the Republican Party was the only political agency continuing to support "the democratic and personal freedom upon which the United States was founded."[21] In the same way the other pro-Republican book stressed the Colonial, Revolutionary, and Civil War periods. Its survey ended with William McKinley's defeat of Grover Cleveland, who was described as having lost public favor during the economic crisis of the early 1890's. As a final observation, the book said that the new administration brought better times and improved business life.[22] But it was not surprising that Republicans were so treated, because many publishers agreed in the 1890's and the following decade that Republican victories improved economic conditions and assured better opportunities to individual businessmen.

To inspire their religious endeavors churchmen also drew on American history. At services dedicating a new church, an immigrant pastor spoke in English and referred to American history. He declared that Christianity had nurtured the rise of the American Republic, only Christians could have written the Constitution, and George Washington had asked for Divine help during the Revolution. This evidence, he concluded, demonstrated that religion had played and continued to play an important role in the progress of history. Another pastor, Salomon Ilmonen, prepared a historical survey on the religious inclinations of six American presidents ranging from George Washington to William McKinley. Later he wrote a book on the seventeenth-century colony of New Sweden and praised the Finnish and Swedish settlers for helping plant the seeds of religious endeavor in America.[23] Obviously, the two pastors tried to suggest that immigrant religious aspirations were in keeping with the work of men credited with setting the course of American history.

In their temperance crusade immigrants, likewise, searched the record of American history. Salomon Ilmonen declared in Pennsylvania that the elation of temperance crusaders rose to unlimited heights on learning that Abraham Lincoln had championed their cause. Presenting a section on the teachings of history in its handbook, the Finnish National Temperance Brotherhood declared that advocates of its cause could take their war cry from a book published in 1785 by the Philadelphia doctor, Benjamin Rush. It said that the doctor had wanted true freedom for Americans and had appreciated, moreover, the historical lesson that no nation could preserve its freedom if it was enslaved by debauchery. To make the lesson clearer in its temperance courses, the Brotherhood used a pamphlet on Benjamin Rush that was written by a temperance leader in Finland. Such courses also offered other historical lessons. In 1909, for instance, a lecturer surveyed the history of temperance and prohibition laws in the United States. He concluded that history showed promise of final victory for prohibition.[24] In such references to the past implication was clearly made that immigrants were destined to fulfill a mission in American history.

Like the temperance advocates, socialists found in American history promise of victory for their own cause. Their view was sustained in the translations of works by leaders of the American Socialist Party: for example, works by James Oneal, Morris Hillquit, and Algie Simons. Essentially historical, these books centered on the role of workingmen in America and their struggles to develop socialism and class consciousness.[25] In line with the views of such books, immigrant socialists declared that from the beginning American workers had sought to cast off their "chains." According to one speaker, the American forefathers had not actually tried to free workers. Instead, he argued, George Washington had really undertaken Revolutionary leadership to avoid arrest by the British for land-grabbing. Although Abraham Lincoln freed Negro slaves, an editorial writer asserted, the northern victory had enslaved white workers who now needed a new emancipator. Another writer said that Lincoln had brought power to northern industrialists who were opposed by the rising industrial working class, and, hence, Lincoln's importance came from his class consciousness in spite of the contrary claims of certain Finnish newspapers.[26] So immigrant socialists concluded that they were only continuing the historical struggle of American workers for real liberation.

Although searching for bonds with Americans of the past, immigrants also tried to establish common ground with contemporary Americans. Increasingly, they tried to win the respect of Americans whose esteem was deemed worthwhile, by pointing to common interests of the foreign and native-born. According to one temperance spokesman, if immigrants learned about American conditions and engaged properly in church and temperance activities, they would be closer to Americans and more respected by them. In particular, the nationalistic-minded assumed that Americans cherished culture and, hence, liked the best that was found in immigrant cultures. Unfortunately, in their view, there were Americans who felt that the native-born had a higher culture than the foreign-born, whose intellectual achievements and cultural activities through churches and newspapers were overlooked. One writer declared in 1920 that true Americans did not want immigrants to forsake their heritage from Finland since the high ideals of the foreign-born were used to make a better America. An editor asserted that, by maintaining their heritage, Finns would win respect since filial honor was the highest national virtue in the United States. By preserving their heritage, a pastor said, his Lutheran seminary did not obstruct Americanism but instead strengthened a sense of responsibility towards the United States in the "right American spirit." Socialists also agreed that it was desirable to win respect. During the copper strike socialist editors encouraged Finns to unite in behalf of the cause and thereby win more respect from "enlightened American workers." Others pointed out that Finnish workers who coöperated with different nationalities at a festival were inspired by the Red banner rather than by the slogans of patriotic nationalism.[27] When the immigrants assumed that such common grounds and mutual respect could be established with Americans, they had paved the way for direct contact with them.

After the early 1890's nationalists made efforts to impress Americans by participating in fairs and expositions. One of the first such efforts occurred in 1894 at an exposition in San Francisco, where Finnish immigrants had their special day with floats and paraders highlighting temperance activities. Again in 1915 they tried to organize a display for another exposition in San Francisco. According to the promoters, the display would help undo the harm of those who had broken "the reputation and good name of the Finnish people." Besides, it would correct American views about Finland and its people. The display, however, did not materialize except for paintings sent from Finland. After the close of World War I, Finns talked about displaying their national culture and arranged exhibits at various fairs and expositions. One writer encouraged them by saying that, since success depended upon reputation, immigrants should publicize their music, art, and literature. A woman wrote that they should display their folk culture to refute the view held by most Americans that immigrants were incapable of doing anything beyond "raw labor." Trying to carry out such ideas in 1920 at a Minnesota fair, another woman displayed rugs and knives, which she felt impressed visitors in regard to Finnish abilities.[28] Few such displays, however, were actually arranged.

Identifying themselves with American opponents of socialism and strikes, nationalist immigrants held public meetings and parades. To refute the view that Finns as a group were prone to joining strikes and socialist activities, they expressed their contrary view publicly. After the iron strikes of 1907 in Minnesota, they held public meetings to complain about lowered reputations and lost jobs, which were undeserved in their view. They argued that most Finns were Christian, law-abiding, hard workers who deserved the respect of true Americans. Again after the copper strike in 1914, Finnish businessmen, churchmen, temperance leaders, and even miners expressed similar views and formed antisocialist leagues. Said one of them, Finns had outlived their earlier reputation as drunkards; now they had to convince Americans that the immigrants as a group were not socialists. Another declared that they were united against "red socialism" and anxious to maintain their reputations. They resolved to drive out the agitators who created a false impression about Finnish attitudes toward socialism and anarchy and threatened the good name and reputation of Finns as American citizens. During World War I similar groups also denounced the socialists and industrial unionists as endangering Finnish reputations. Joining them was a writer who endorsed the Lincoln Loyalty League as a means to cleanse the tarnished reputations of Finnish workers. This attitude was carried over into the demonstrations, parades, and resolutions proclaiming loyalty to the government. For instance, the Knights and Ladies of Kaleva publicized the telegram sent from their convention to the American President, pledging "unswerving loyalty" to the war effort.[29] In other words, the nationalists tried to affirm common grounds with Americans who were not socialists.

Temperance groups also tried to reach people outside immigrant ranks in various ways. They even talked of working outside their own ranks in behalf of temperance; one temperance group decided to publicize its activities in the English-language press in the hope of encouraging English-speaking elements to organize. They passed resolutions and sent messages to public officials. They also invited such officials and local citizens to their temperance gatherings. At one of its annual meetings, for example, the Finnish National Temperance Brotherhood reported that its speakers included a congressman and that the local English-language press gave extensive coverage. The desire to impress Americans at such affairs was revealed by the reporter who felt that the failure on one occasion to provide proper after-dinner speeches in the "American manner" may have led the guests to decide that Finns did know how to conduct festivities. The annual meetings also provided opportunities to parade the streets of the host town or city. One such meeting held in Monessen, Pennsylvania, in 1908 had city officials precede the immigrant paraders, who walked two abreast in a line of almost half a mile.[30] Besides these efforts, temperance workers also got in touch with their counterparts in American organizations working for the same cause.

Like other immigrant groups, socialists did not evade contacts with their contemporaries. Instead they tried to cultivate such contacts by using methods similar to those of the temperance groups. Becoming the largest ethnic group within the American Socialist Party, Finnish socialists suggested that their organizational successes offered examples for others. In this spirit one socialist suggested that the Finnish Socialist Federation should seek to correct errors in the Party.[31] Socialists sent organizers among workers who did not speak Finnish and published an English-language weekly called the *Wage Slave*. At its national convention in 1912 the Federation resolved to help form English-language socialist clubs where none existed.[32] As important as any other means of contact, parades were featured at conventions and summer festivals. From Massachusetts to Oregon the socialists arranged parades somewhat in the manner of the temperance crusaders. However, socialists were not content with these methods, but like other groups looked constantly for new occasions to approach Americans.

When world-wide attention on Finland increased after 1899, immigrants made special efforts to acquaint Americans with their Old Country and its people. At the turn of the century famine and Russian actions in the Grand Duchy of Finland had aroused the outside world. Aided in part by political émigrés, immigrants formed action committees, made appeals in the English-language press, and petitioned American officials to capitalize on the world-wide interest in Finland. With the help of one of Michigan's senators in Congress in 1899 a petition reached President William McKinley from immigrants urging action by the Hague Conference.[33] On another occasion fifty immigrant organizations published statements in American newspapers to protest statements made by Russian officials about the Finns.[34] No doubt these various efforts made more Americans realize that there were Finns in America.

Identifying themselves with Finland between 1899 and 1905, immigrants suggested that the Finnish people merited respect by Americans who valued orderly democratic rule. As one writer said, at this time the immigrants reaching America were the flower of manhood from a doomed land, which was "a spectacle to make angels weep." He suggested that Finns had unusual innate abilities for self-government, which were stifled by Russian actions. Finns and Russians, he continued, had radical differences in their views on government; Finland had a government of, for, and by the people, who were led by educated and cultured officials; Russia had a government of, by, and for a privileged class, which despised the masses as ignorant. Emphasizing their desire to appear different from Russians, one group asked American census officials to list Finns henceforth separately from the Russians. Its request was based on the view that Finland was not a province like Poland but was "independent in domestic matters" and that Finns and Russians were entirely different races. According to one observer, when immigrant pastors and others spoke on the events of Finland, they "addressed themselves to the spirit of liberty inherent in the American character." Speaking to American readers, the representative of an immigrant committee said that Finland's real grievance was that it no longer had an inviolable constitution.[35] In the same way again after 1917 immigrants tried to explain events in Finland to Americans who were interested in self-government and national self-determination.

During World War I various American officials and private citizens joined the immigrants in showing special interest in Finland. Their interest was stirred after the Russian Revolution by the rival groups seeking control in Finland. In January, 1918, socialists formed a provisional government in Helsinki and civil war ensued; nonsocialist officials fled northward and returned after the defeat of their foes in April. In this situation, on the one hand, the United States government was concerned with the relationship of Russia and Finland; on the other hand, it was concerned when its German foe entered Finland to help defeat the socialists. As the United States refused to recognize any Finnish government until 1919, immigrants pressed for American action.[36]

When the rival governments sought American recognition, immigrants came to their aid. The provisional socialist government selected as its representative an immigrant editor who formed the Finnish Information Bureau supported in part by immigrant socialists. From Finland the opposing government sent representatives who coöperated with their immigrant friends in forming the Finland Constitutional League of America. The League also drew sponsors from American businessmen and professionals. Through the two new agencies as well as through public meetings, petitions, and newspapers immigrants appealed to Americans. They especially carried on a pen war in English-language papers published in immigrant communities: for example, in Waukegan, Illinois, at least five articles were published by each side in a local newspaper.[37] Finally, when America recognized a Finnish government, immigrants found new issues regarding Finland with which to gain American attention.

To secure American sympathies the immigrants stressed the democratic and anti-German themes. Helping Finland, argued a lawyer, proved the Americanism of the immigrants. As America had a mission "to democraticize the world," he said that Finns helped America to fulfill its "noble world mission" by pressing for recognition of Finland and its antisocialist government. Socialists declared that they were defamed by pro-German critics; in turn, the critics denied the charges. According to the Finland Constitutional League of America, Finns were not pro-German, and this point was proven by their presence in the American Army and shipbuilding industry. The League published a pamphlet which conceded that Germans had been welcomed in Finland, but only as a last resort against Russian Bolsheviks. Americans were assured by one of its officials that independence was being defended in Finland as it had been in America in 1776.[38] And it was the democratic theme which such immigrant groups continued to emphasize in the 1920's.

Although they approached Americans through different avenues, immigrants could not escape their cultural ties with Finland. Even if nothing else, language barriers kept them partly isolated in an environment which emphasized ethnic differences. Yet, when they broke that isolation in varying degrees, immigrants felt able to identify their endeavors with the aspirations of native Americans both past and present. In so doing they became Finnish Americans, destined to spend their days away from the Old Country and to become so attached to the United States that they tried writing their chapter of American history.

CHAPTER VIII

# LOOKING BACK

*I am driven by my longing,*
*And my understanding urges*
*That I should commence my singing*
*And begin my recitation.*
*I will sing the people's legends,*
*And the ballads of the nation.*

KALEVALA [1]

By 1920 Finnish Americans saw the end of an era in their associative life and they came to a milestone in their history as immigrants by continuing to stay in America. Although travel to Finland again became possible, they made no mass exodus from America because they were tied down by employment, families, and citizenship. Besides, they were very much attached to the associative activities which represented a generation of their effort. Having existed upwards of thirty years, their associations now faced the era when immigration virtually ceased to bring in new members from Europe. This meant that the survival of organizations depended upon recruiting the American-born children of the immigrants. Only the children, moreover, might repeat the original thrill of discovering the associations, because the immigrant generation already had experienced the thrill years ago. However, the immigrants tried to remind themselves of their original thrill by reviewing the history of their organized pursuit of paradise, of the happy, good life.

After World War I, immigration from Finland never again reached its prewar numbers. The war period had made travel uncertain, or even impossible, at times. Then legislative restrictions made it harder for immigrants to enter America. In the fiscal year ending June 30, 1914, 12,805 immigrants were admitted from Finland; the figure, never again half as large even before American quotas were imposed, dropped below 1,000 in 1919. Between 1920 and 1924 the highest number admitted in any one year barely exceeded 4,000. Under American law after June, 1924, 471 immigrants were permitted to enter annually from Finland; in July, 1929, the quota became 569.[2] Consequently, Finnish immigrants were diverted to Canada, but at the same time the pressure for departure lessened in Finland where industrial growth provided new jobs for the landless. Land reform in 1918 and later years also brought ownership to thousands of tenants and laborers. So the war period marked the virtual end of growth for immigrant communities in America.

But the resumption of travel between Finland and America after the war did not create any mass exodus from the New World. Although enthusiasm for the new Republic of Finland led both old and new arrivals to leave America, if immigrants left America, they did so mainly within their first five years away from the Old Country. Since the war period reduced immigration, there were fewer recent arrivals to leave America when travel became possible. In the four fiscal years before June 30, 1924, an average of about 1,100 Finns left annually from America compared to the average of nearly 3,600 who left in the four-year period ending June 30, 1914. As the war had kept the recent prewar arrivals in America, immigrants had increasingly acquired residency of more than five years, and so they had become less likely to leave.

When their stay lengthened in America, immigrants sank deeper roots. They became too involved with American life to think of leaving the country. As economic advancement did not come fast, they moved about seeking better jobs or becoming businessmen and farmers. They also sought economic advance through stock companies, trade unions, coöperative businesses, and educational endeavors. Becoming engrossed in such efforts, they extended their American stay and created more permanent roots by maintaining property, raising families, and exercising citizenship. Speaking about the immigrant farmers of Minnesota in 1910, a visiting teacher from the Old Country keynoted his report by saying that no one talked about returning to Finland. He observed that the farmers were too busy raising families and eking out a living on their rocky, stump-covered lands.[3]

Immigrant roots were also sunk through the sense of destiny

which imbued the numerous associations. By supporting associations, immigrants believed, a happy, good life was possible for them because knowledge becomes power when like-minded persons unite for action. Such a belief suggested that a kind of paradise was assured mainly to those active in some organization. Without such participation, of course, organizations could not survive. It followed that immigrants did not regard their communities as permanent until enduring associations were set up. In this spirit local correspondents evaluated immigrant life primarily in terms of the associations. According to them, there was nothing worthwhile to report until associative life developed. When organizations appeared, they saw a great future. Their elation increased as new recruits for the organizations arrived from Finland. On the other hand, their enthusiasm was dampened by those leaving the associations.

Even before the supply of new recruits from Finland was cut off, organizations had a foretaste of what would happen when their departing members were not replaced. Soon after forming their first associations, Finns found that the growth, decline, and revival of their institutional life were correlated to the number of Finns in the community. Growth came when new arrivals reached the community; decline resulted from their departure for work elsewhere; revival came when new ones arrived. Not far from New York Mills, Minnesota, a congregation was formed with a peak membership of about 100, but by 1906 it was non-existent because everyone except seven families had moved away. In Negaunee, Michigan, a temperance society had a peak membership of 192 in 1892. By October, 1893, its members totalled 23, and by 1898 there were 100, among whom was only one original member. The membership had fluctuated because iron mines opened and closed from time to time. During the panic of 1907 and 1908 the socialist local suspended in Carneyville, Wyoming, because its members moved away looking for work, and it was not revived until new arrivals came in 1916.[4] But as long as new immigrants arrived and employment was obtainable, there always existed opportunities to organize.

By 1920 the prospect for continued organizational growth was uncertain. Editors reported that immigrant firstcomers who had arrived in the 1860's, the 1870's, and later were starting to pass away.[5] Among such firstcomers were those who had pioneered in forming various associations. In 1919 death removed Juho Nikander, who had had thirty-four years of pastoral service. At this time, however, the virtual cessation of immigration was more important than death in limiting organizational growth. The ending of immigration meant that organizations were limited to working with those who had already reached America. In 1920 this fact was understood by a writer concerned with the survival of Finnish newspapers. He declared that publishers needed to find new methods to maintain newspapers for a clientele limited to the immigrant generation already in America. The ending of immigration, he explained, erased the possibility of obtaining new readers and, moreover, the American-reared children of immigrants preferred English-language newspapers more and more.[6] Although he saw little hope in the children, organizations generally saw a chance of survival with the growing second generation.

The ending of immigration spurred on efforts to secure future recruits for organizations from the second generation. This objective appeared more nearly possible than ever before because by 1920 almost one-half of all persons of Finnish stock had been born in America. Of course, almost as soon as the immigrants had formed their first organizations, efforts were made to attract the children, then few in number. But prior to the early 1900's, the organizations were concerned primarily with building up adult activities. Thereafter, when the number of children increased, the organizations expended more energy in developing suitable programs for them. Church, temperance, and socialist groups arranged Sunday schools and summer sessions and issued appropriate literature to train children in keeping with organizational purposes. They were also active in preparing Finnish grammars supplied with suitable texts teaching piety, sobriety, and class consciousness. As a result, by World War I the children's programs were more extensive than ever before.

In developing the children's programs it became common to assert that the future lay with youth. To emphasize this point, organizations even named their youth groups "Hope societies." No matter how they differed in purpose, every organization agreed that those who had the children, also had the future. Then, too, they concurred that it was easy for children to become alienated from parental values in America. To forestall this danger and to ensure survival, organizations accepted the task of training children. One pastor wrote that the future of churches lay in developing the Sunday schools. A temperance group agreed that Sunday schools were important, not only for preserving religious values, but also for retaining the Finnish language. Besides, another writer said, special temperance classes for children guaranteed greater victories in the future. Likewise, a socialist writer endorsed children's classes as means toward the future success of the socialist cause. Still another writer declared that such classes ensured that victory would be brought nearer for socialism when the immigrant generation was no longer alive to continue the struggle.[7] In short, they all had high expectations of a properly trained new generation.

By the 1920's most organizations were attracting children in greater numbers. In 1926 the three major Lutheran groups reported that their memberships were the largest ever and that about one-third of their members were under thirteen years. With few exceptions the young members undoubtedly were American-born. Besides, a number of the older members unquestionably had also been born in America. Such childhood participation led at least some of the American-born to retain organizational ambitions into adulthood. During the 1920's church groups had clergymen who were born and trained in America. One congregation in Fitchburg, Massachusetts, reported that its Sunday school teachers included fourteen American-born persons who had attended the school as children and now were able to teach in the Finnish language. At the time of World War I the loyalty committee in Ashtabula, Ohio, included among its leaders American-born Finns who had grown up in the local religious and temperance environment. At a training course for coöperative personnel in 1923, over one-third of the thirty-four students were American-born.[8] The increasing role of the American-born was also shown by the fact that organizations started to use the English language in some of their activities. The organizational role of the American-born was just starting, and only later decades could measure how well they carried on the work of their parents.

This recognition of the second generation coincided with the end of a generation of organizational effort by immigrants. As one churchman wrote in 1919, he was witnessing a period of transition. After promoting church activities for upwards of thirty years, he explained, immigrants were properly starting to give way to the second generation in the conduct of religious matters.[9] Although the second generation became stronger in the organizations, the immigrant generation remained dominant during the 1920's, because many who had arrived from Finland in the prewar decade still had years of vigorous activity ahead of them.

Indeed, Finns made special efforts to mark the end of the era. They were anxious to make sure that their work was not forgotten. In 1915 one group disinterred and reburied under a new tombstone the editor who had died in 1877 after publishing the first Finnish-language newspaper in America. Four years later another group erected tombstones to honor the work of two recently deceased temperance veterans. In 1921 history-minded persons gathered in Brooklyn, New York, to form the Finnish American Historical Society in the hope of encouraging the writing of history and the collecting of archival records.[10] During these years around World War I organizations were noticeably history-minded as they had occasion to mark anniversaries, often twenty-fifth anniversaries. To be sure, almost from the beginning, organizations marked their first anniversary. Thereafter they especially observed their fifth, tenth, fifteenth, twentieth, and twenty-fifth anniversaries. They arranged commemorative festivals and published souvenir books, pamphlets, and newspaper issues. In general, the associations were largely responsible for promoting interest in immigrant history.

During the period between 1910 and 1925 Finns surveyed their organizational past in special historical publications. In the order of their institutional appearance in America, churchmen first, temperance advocates next, and socialists last, celebrated and recounted their past. In 1911 came a history of the churches, most of which dated back less than thirty years. Four years later came the twenty-fifth anniversary publication of the Synod Lutherans, and in 1923 the National Lutherans issued a similar work. In 1912 came the book marking a quarter century of effort by the Finnish National Temperance Brotherhood. In 1925 came the survey of the labor movement, which started in the 1890's but really got underway about 1900 with socialist leadership. Local societies and newspapers also marked their anniversaries, ranging from the tenth to the twenty-fifth year, with special publications. All these various historical writings marked roughly a generation of effort.[11]

The historical publications were part of the literary flowering which also produced novels, memoirs, and short stories. Even though often disguised in fictional form, such writings usually dealt with the realities of immigrant life, drawing more often than not upon their authors' personal experiences.[12] They told about the struggles for a livelihood, the problems of settling in a strange land, and the role of the organizations. Openly drawing upon their past experiences of thirty years in America, Edward Hedman and Juho Jasberg related stories about fellow immigrants in America. They told about men searching for work, competing with other nationalities, and finding language difficulties.[13] Although he had spent almost twenty years in America by 1909, Martin Hendrickson based his autobiography mainly on a period of about ten years during which he had promoted socialist doctrines.[14] More common than these memoirs, however, were the novels which treated immigrant life in relation to matters like marriage, prostitution, recreation, employment, trade unions, and army service. Probably best remembered of the novelists was Kalle Potti whose novel, *The Happy Harbor,* at first serialized and later published in book form, concerned the early days of Ashtabula, Ohio, when temperance societies were first organized but suspended for the weekends, so he said, to permit members to imbibe in good conscience.[15] But such novels were rare compared to the scores of short stories which appeared in various publications and collected editions. As they were written often for organizational publications, the short stories were likely to emphasize the associative theme. With humor and satire, they dealt with the immigrant proclivity to organize. In this vein John Lauttamus depicted the organization of a chorus by leaders of rival church, temperance, and socialist groups and described their special vocal talents. Kalle Rissanen and Moses Hahl satirized the critics of socialism, the former once characterizing a town's culture before the coming of the socialists as revolving around saloon brawls and petty religious and political quarrels. As a theological student, Antti Lepistö wrote stories of contented immigrants building up churches.[16] Indeed, most writing was in part autobiographical and shaped by the associative interests of the authors.

No matter what literary medium they used, writers usually wrote on the basis of their active participation in organizations. The formal anniversary histories were largely written by members of the sponsoring organizations. Such histories often included writings by the original founders: Salomon Ilmonen and Frans Syrjälä wrote their histories partly on the basis of personal experiences in building up various organizations. After a career in temperance and religious endeavors, in 1920 Juuso Hirvonen wrote a general historical survey mainly on the associative life of his fellow immigrants in Michigan.[17] Likewise, the authors of works other than historical had organizational experience which ranged anywhere from about five to upwards of thirty years. Kalle Potti wrote his novel on Ashtabula after an American career of over twenty-five years in business, temperance, and religion. Moses Hahl was a socialist speaker and editor who started writing stories early in his American career of more than a quarter of a century. But of all the active promoters of organizations, Salomon Ilmonen was the most prolific in compiling the historical record.

In 1891, when temperance and church organizations were first appearing, Salomon Ilmonen arrived from Finland to help make their history which he later recorded. After working some years at various jobs, he went to Hancock, Michigan, and enrolled in the Lutheran seminary, becoming a member of its first group to be ordained as pastors. During his pastoral career he became more history-minded than ever before. In 1912 he prepared the history of the Finnish National Temperance Brotherhood. Four years later he retold the history of the Finns in the seventeenth-century colony of New Sweden. In 1919 he issued the first of a three-volume series on Finns in America since about 1850, with emphasis upon biographical data. In 1930 he issued the first of two books on immigrant institutions which he published before his death.[18] He also promoted historical endeavors by writing in newspapers and other publications, and he was the first secretary of the Finnish American Historical Society. But like other writers, he wrote history to point out milestones in organizational and individual achievements according to his moral predilections and associative commitments.

Searching for historical milestones, Finns looked partly to the record of their predecessors who came with the Swedes to found the colony of New Sweden on the banks of the Delaware River during the seventeenth century. Since William Penn had thought highly of the Finns in New Sweden, one writer concluded that contemporary immigrants should use them as models. Nationalist writers were especially interested in the colony and vied with Swedish writers to claim John Morton, who had signed the Declaration of Independence. According to a writer siding with Finnish claims, on one occasion except for George Washington's arrival, John Morton would have been hanged by the British in a matter of seconds and America thus would have had one less Finn for a "noble struggle." Churchmen like Salomon Ilmonen felt that the history of New Sweden showed Finns helping found a Christian civilization for later Americans. In 1925 Evert Louhi went even further and claimed that the Finnish settlers had laid the basis for "American civilization, and of all civilizations in the past, today and forever." Their descendants, moreover, he decided, were "the first real Americans" because they had lost all ties with Finland, while the English still were Englishmen and the Germans and Dutch still retained their languages at the start of the "noble campaign" for American independence. Writing his history of class-conscious immigrants, Frans Syrjälä referred to the spirit of rebellion which inspired one Finnish settler to stand up against the leaders of New Sweden.[19] Since New Sweden was so remote, however, to the immigrants of the twentieth century, writers were more concerned with evaluating their recent past since the American Civil War.

Surveying their recent history, Finns concluded that their organizational efforts had succeeded in lighting the way to happiness. Although the happy, good life had not yet been fully attained, religious, temperance, and socialist spokesmen agreed that their efforts had developed new ideals and aspirations in minds which once were solely content with drunken debauchery and intellectual and moral poverty. One churchman said that the general awakening which inspired congregations and temperance societies had drawn people to higher levels away from constant drinking and weekly knifings. In his history of temperance Salomon Ilmonen concluded that the crusade had brought a higher sense of Christian morality, which liberated people from drunken enslavement. Similarly, Frans Syrjälä believed that the socialist movement had served as a beacon to erase the darkness cast by saloons, and, he added, by churches and temperance societies.[20] All such writers, therefore, were certain that their fellow men had progressed to higher sources of "light." But they still saw shadows and offered lessons for a brighter morrow.

With its lessons the immigrant generation pledged itself to unite and work harder than before. As some participants were late-comers in the organizations, the historical lessons were partly meant to instruct and inspire them. Even more important, the lessons re-affirmed and renewed devotion to original purposes after years of internal factionalism. The twenty-fifth anniversary book of the National Lutherans wished to correct misrepresentations about their original doctrines and early founders. On its tenth anniversary in 1915 the socialist local of Waukegan, Illinois, issued a booklet affirming the belief that its past endeavors had been worthwhile and were still instructive to everyone in spite of the divisive elements then existing in the labor movement. To promote a union of the divided temperance societies, in 1908 one writer concluded that their past history showed the struggles were not in vain. Upon surveying the institutions beset with conflict in Michigan, Juuso Hirvonen hoped that his book would inspire greater mutual love and unity to sustain all the best idealistic organizations, mainly religious and temperance in character. Celebrating the twentieth anniversary of a socialist society, one speaker called for renewed efforts to enlist even more people in the battle.[21] Surely then, intimated these various spokesmen, future history would record their final triumph.

To ensure continued success, the second generation was given its own lessons from history. Young people were advised to seek inspiration and guidance from the devoted and farsighted work of their elders. Juuso Hirvonen hoped that from his book youth would learn to heed the example of an early immigrant arrival who had worked hard to further religious endeavor. At a twentieth-year anniversary celebration a youthful speaker assured his audience that young people were learning to collect strike aid and to distribute socialist literature in the spirit of those who came before them. The Lutheran Synod approved the collection of historical church literature to help show the right direction for the future. In honoring deceased temperance workers, speakers urged young people to join the cause and remember those who preceded them.[22] In other words, from the textbook of history youth was to learn to emulate its elders' aspirations.

Scanning their past for lessons, immigrants sensed that the freshness and innocence of discovering the associations was now lost to them. By the 1920's only their inexperienced children could make the discovery for the first time. Their early years consequently acquired a glory and a charm which had been lost, perhaps because of the constant bickering, quarreling, and breaking-up within the organizations. In 1920 Juuso Hirvonen saw a bygone golden age of intense activity in organizing congregations, temperance societies, and other groups in the Copper Country of Michigan. Now when people were leaving the area and organizations were splintered, or even virtually non-existent, he urged the youth to check these trends by promoting the associations' work of spreading enlightenment.[23] About the same time Frans Syrjälä saw the socialist organization torn asunder, but was hopeful that it again would have "beautiful days" as it had had in its youth.[24] To be sure, during the decade of World War I there were signs of unity and coöperation between various groups. Churches, however, still went in different directions. Temperance societies failed to unite around a single program. Labor organizations went in three ways. And other societies headed towards still different destinations. But from their sense of unity immigrants yet hoped to find the momentum which they had lost when they no longer felt the spell of their first enthusiasm for starting organizations.

Inevitably then, the history-minded immigrants concluded, their organizations would some day develop more fully the paradise or the happy, good life. They had left Finland with dreams of a better life and even with ideas of how to make real their dreams. In America new circumstances roused their proclivity to set up organizations, and so they reshaped or rebuilt their dreams and ideas brought from the Old Country. As their dreams had not yet been fully realized after a generation of organizational endeavor, they sought renewed inspiration from their past record. At the same time they began to feel that now perhaps only their children might have success with the organizations. The future alone could tell whether or not the rising generation really had found America in the spirit of its immigrant parents. Indeed, the Finnish Americans were at the end of one era and the start of a new one in their organized search for paradise.

NOTES

SOURCES

INDEX

# NOTES

*Chapter I*

1 O. K. Kilpi, "Statistics of Population," *Finland: The Country, Its People and Institutions* (Helsinki, 1926), p. 96.

2 Mrs. Alec Tweedie, *Through Finland in Carts* (New York and London, 1898), p. 124. Other English-language books of travel and description on Finland generally note the transformation of Finnish life during the second half of the nineteenth century. They particularly emphasize nationalism, economic changes, and literary developments.

3 Quoted in Niilo Liakka, "Adult Education—Libraries," *Finland: The Country, Its People and Institutions,* p. 445.

4 Viljo Hytönen, *Yleinen Raittiusliikkeen Historia* (Helsinki, 1911), p. 210.

5 The agricultural changes are surveyed in *Suomen maatalous,* ed. J. E. Sunila *et al.,* 2 vols. (Porvoo, 1922), and Eino Jutikkala, *Suomen talonpojan historia: Sekä katsaus talonpoikien asemaan Euroopan muissa maissa* (Porvoo and Helsinki, 1942), pp. 497–641.

6 *Suomen Tilastollinen Vuosikirja: Uusi sarja, kahdeskymmenesneljäs vuosikerta, 1926* (Helsinki, 1926), pp. 130–31.

7 Johannes Linnankoski, *Kootut teokset, IV nidos: Sanomalehti- ja yhteiskunnallisia kirjoituksia, puheita, kaunokirjallisia ja esteettisiä kirjoituksia* (Porvoo, 1914), 16–28, 218–23.

8 O. K. Kilpi, *Suomen siirtolaisuus ja 19. vuosisadan kansantalous,* Taloustieteellisiä Tutkimuksia, XXII (Helsinki, 1917), 81, 84; *Yhteiskuntatilastollinen kartasto Suomen maalaiskunnista v. 1901,* ed. Hannes Gebhard, text ed. (Helsinki, 1908), p. 18; Heikki Waris, *Työläisyhteiskunnan syntyminen Helsingin pitkänsillan pohjoispuolelle, I* (Helsinki, 1932), 87; Väinö Voionmaa, "Maanomistus Suomessa," *Työväen kalenteri, XIII, 1920* (Helsinki, 1919), 160. See also Heikki Waris, *Suomalaisen yhteiskunnan rakenne* (Helsinki, 1948), *passim.*

9 K. T. Jutila, "Maatalouden merkitys Suomen talous- ja yhteiskuntaelämässä," *Suomen maatalous,* I, 247.

10 Waris, *Työläisyhteiskunnan syntyminen, passim.*

11 Population data based on *Suomen tilastollinen vuosikirja: Uusi sarja—XLVIII—vuonna 1951* (Helsinki, 1952), 5.

12 Based on data in *Suomen Tilastollinen Vuosikirja, 1926,* p. 72. During the years, 1893–1920, Vaasa sent 49 percent, Oulu sent 14 percent, and Turu-Pori provided 13 percent of all emigrants leaving Finland. As the years passed, the relative share of Vaasa and Oulu decreased. In the 1890's Vaasa alone sent as many as over 60 percent in one year.

13 Waris, *Työläisyhteiskunnan syntyminen,* p. 78.

14 *Ibid.,* pp. 78–79, 110–12.

15 O. K. Kilpi, "Suomen siirtolaisuudesta," *Oma maa: Tietokirja Suomen kodeille,* ed. E. G. Palmén *et al.,* V (Porvoo, 1910), 696.

16 Following data taken from "Immigration into the United States, Showing Number, Nationality, Sex, Age, Occupation, Destination, etc., from 1820 to 1903," *Monthly Summary of Commerce and Finance of the United States,* U.S. Dept. of Treasury, Bureau of Statistics (June, 1903), p. 4349; U.S. Dept. of Treasury, Commissioner-General of Immigration, *Annual Report . . . ,* 1896–1903 (Washington, 1896–1903); U.S. Dept. of Commerce and Labor, Commissioner-General of Immigration, *Annual Report . . . ,* 1904–13 (Washington, 1904–14); U.S. Dept. of Labor, Commissioner-General of Immigration, *Annual Report . . . ,* 1914–20 (Washington, 1915–20). Until 1899 the immigrants were classified by country of citizenship or last residence and thereafter by "race."

TOTAL FINNISH IMMIGRANT ARRIVALS AT AMERCAN PORTS FOR THE FISCAL YEARS ENDING JUNE 30

| | |
|---|---|
| 1872–1883 | 1,942 |
| 1884–1893 | 27,443 |
| 1894–1900 | 35,527 |
| 1901–1910 | 133,065 |
| 1911–1920 | 61,347 |

17 Following data taken from *Suomen Tilastollinen Vuosikirja, 1926,* p. 72, and *Suomen virallinen tilasto. XXVIII. Siirtolaisuustilasto. 1. Siirtolaisuus vuosina 1900–1902* (Helsinki, 1905), 10.

TOTAL FINNISH PASSPORTS ISSUED TO EMIGRANTS FROM

| | | |
|---|---|---|
| Vaasa | 1,616 | 1883 |
| Vaasa and Oulu | 34,785 | 1884–1892 |
| All provinces | 47,557 | 1893–1900 |
| All provinces | 158,832 | 1901–1910 |
| All provinces | 67,346 | 1911–1920 |

18 *Suomen Tilastollinen Vuosikirja, 1926,* pp. 72–73; U.S. Dept. of Commerce and Labor, Commissioner-General of Immigration, *An-*

*nual Report,* 1911–13; U.S. Dept. of Labor, Commissioner-General of Immigration, *Annual Report,* 1914–20. The figures cited from the reports of the Commissioner-General do not include Finns who left American ports and planned to return nor those who came temporarily to visit in America.

19 Rafael Engelberg, *Suomi ja Amerikan suomalaiset: Keskinäinen yhteys ja sen rakentaminen* (Helsinki, 1944), pp. 34–35.

20 Ernest Young, *Finland: The Land of a Thousand Lakes* (New York and London, 1912), pp. 87–88.

21 Notebook of Karl Siren of Virginia, Minnesota, and other places [*ca.* 1913–20] (MS in present writer's possession).

22 *Letter from the Secretary of the Treasury, Transmitting a Report of the Commissioners of Immigration upon the Causes which Incite Immigration to the United States,* H. Exec. Doc. No. 235, Pt. 2, Serial 2957, 52d Cong., 1st Sess. (Washington, 1892), 36, 100.

23 Victor Ek, "Finland," *Emigration to the United States,* Special Consular Reports, U.S. Dept. of Commerce and Labor, Bureau of Statistics, XXX (Washington, 1904), 108.

24 John I. Kolehmainen, *Suomalaisten siirtolaisuus Norjasta Amerikkaan* (Fitchburg, Massachusetts, [1946]), pp. 20, 50–52; S. Ilmonen, *Amerikan suomalaisten historia, II: Ja elämäkertoja* (Jyväskylä, 1923), 25–28, 65.

25 James B. Hedges, "The Colonization Work of the Northern Pacific Railroad," *The Mississippi Valley Historical Review,* XIII (December, 1926), 319, 322; Ilmonen, *Amerikan suomalaisten historia, II,* 32–35; New York State Department of Agriculture, *Fifteenth Annual Report of the Commissioner of Agriculture for the Year 1907* (Albany, 1908), p. 185. References to the solicitation of Finnish immigrants by American railroads are also made in the research notes and drafts of the incompleted study, marked Works Projects Administration, "Finns in Minnesota," Writers' Project, Section II (MSS in the Minnesota Historical Society, MSS Division, St. Paul).

26 Letter from Andrew Kangas, Franklin, Minnesota, to Johan Kimari, Finland, March 30, [1892?] (MS in present writer's possession).

27 U.S. Dept. of Commerce and Labor, Commissioner-General of Immigration, *Annual Report,* 1908–13; U.S. Dept. of Labor, Commissioner-General of Immigration, *Annual Report,* 1914–20.

28 *Työmies* (Hancock, Michigan), December 23, 1909, p. 12.

29 Kilpi, "Suomen siirtolaisuudesta," p. 705.

30 Engelberg, *Suomi ja Amerikan suomalaiset,* pp. 66–67. This work emphasizes the reaction to emigration in Finland.

31 Konni Zilliacus, *Siirtolaisia: Kertomuksia Ameriikan suomalaisten*

*elämästä,* trans. into Finnish by Juhanni Aho (Porvoo, 1897), pp. 3–4.

32 *Suomen pappissäädyn pöytäkirjat valtiopäiviltä v. 1891,* I (Helsinki, 1892), 78–80, 335–36; *Suomen talonpoikaissäädyn keskustelupöytäkirjat 1894 vuoden valtiopäiviltä,* I (Jyväskylä, 1894), 401; Akseli Järnefelt [-Rauanheimo], *"Amerikkaan"* (Helsinki, 1899), p. 39; "Vanha ukko puhuu," Juhani Aho, *Katajainen kansani,* 4th ed. (Porvoo, 1909), pp. 165–69.

33 Järnefelt [-Rauanheimo], *"Amerikkaan";* Matti Tarkkanen, *Siirtolaisuudesta, sen syistä ja seurauksista,* Kansantaloudellisen Yhdistyksen Esitelmiä, Sarja III, No. 16 (Helsinki, 1903).

34 Engelberg, *Suomi ja Amerikan suomalaiset,* pp. 62–63, 65.

35 *Liite. Olojen kehitys viime vuosina* (Helsinki, 1904), p. 27 (This pamphlet is bound in some copies of *Suomalaiset Amerikassa* by Akseli Järnefelt [-Rauanheimo] that were originally printed in Helsinki in 1899); Akseli [Järnefelt-] Rauanheimo, "Amerikan suomalaiset," *Oma maa,* III (Porvoo, 1908), 435–36; Juho Saari, "Mitä Amerikan suomalaisista kotimaassa, Suomessa, ajatellaan," *20:nen vuoden Muisto-Julkaisu, 1906–1926,* Monessen ja Mononga-helan Jokilaakson Suomalaisten Loukkaus-, Sairaus-, ja Hautaus-apurengas (Monessen, Pennsylvania, n.d.), pp. 29–30; Rafael Engelberg, *Pöytäkirja Ulkosuomalaisneuvotteluista Hämeenlinnassa heinäk. 23 p. 1927* (Helsinki, 1927), pp. 12–15.

36 "Työväenasiain valiokunnan mietintö N:o 6 anomusehdotuksen johdosta, joka tarkoittaa tutkimuksen toimittamista siirtolaisuudesta," 1914.—Anomusmietintö No. 31 [Suomen eduskunta], *Valtiopäivät 1914 asiakirjat,* V, Pt. 2 (Helsinki, 1914), 21.

37 Yrjö Koskinen, *Kansallisia ja yhteiskunnallisia kirjoituksia,* Suomalaisen Kirjallisuuden Seuran Toimituksia, CVIII, Pt. 4 (Tampere, 1930), 586–88.

38 [Suomen eduskunta], *Valtiopäivät 1910 pöytäkirjat, I: Istunnot 1–26 valtiopäivien alusta toukokuun 10 päivään* (Helsinki, 1910), 407; *Alexandra Gripenberg's A Half Year in the New World: Miscellaneous Sketches of Travel in the United States (1888),* ed. and trans. by Ernest J. Moyne, (Newark, Delaware, 1954), p. 165; Kilpi, *Suomen siirtolaisuus,* pp. viii–ix, 50–54; Edvard Gylling, "Siirtolaisuutemme ja tilaton väestö," *Sosialistinen aikakauslehti,* No. 3 (January, 1906), 34–39; "Siirtolaisuus," *Työmiehen illanvietto,* II (August 28, 1903), 280.

39 *Suomen Tilastollinen Vuosikirja, 1926,* p. 72. The total figure for passports cited is slightly different from the total cited earlier in this chapter because the present total excludes 369 emigrants whose place of origin was not known.

40 Based on figures in *Suomen tilastollinen vuosikirja: Uusi sarja—XLIII—vuosina 1946–47* (Helsinki, 1948), 81.

41 *Uusi Kotimaa* (New York Mills, Minnesota), April 9, 1896, p. 4; *Siirtolainen* (Brooklyn, New York), 1895: October 30, p. 4; November 27, p. 4.

42 U.S. Dept. of Treasury, Commissioner-General of Immigration, *Anual Report,* 1901–3; U.S. Dept. of Commerce and Labor, Commissioner-General of Immigration, *Annual Report,* 1904–13; U.S. Dept. of Labor, Commissioner-General of Immigration, *Annual Report,* 1914–20; F. L. Dingley, *European Emigration: Studies in Europe of Emigration Moving out of Europe, Especially That Flowing to the United States,* Special Consular Reports, U.S. Dept. of State, Bureau of Statistics, II (Washington, 1890), 258; Stanley Levine's untitled report on his interview with Nestor Willows, Kettle River, Minnesota, October 30, 1938, in Works Projects Administration, "Finns in Minnesota"; Ralph H. Smith, "A Sociological Survey of the Finnish Settlement of New York Mills, Minnesota and Its Adjacent Territory" (Master's Thesis, University of Southern California, 1933), pp. 15–16. Smith reported that according to a survey of 341 immigrants of New York Mills, Minnesota, 209 gave economic reasons for coming to the United States.

43 Letters from Herman Donner to T. F. Bayard, July 7, 1886, and to Jas. D. Parker, April 12, 1887 (American Consular Correspondence and Reports from Helsinki, January 1, 1851—August 14, 1906, U.S. Dept. of State, National Archives); *Amerikan Uutiset* (Calumet, Michigan), April 4, 1900, p. 2; John I. Kolehmainen, "Why We Came to America: The Finns," *Common Ground,* V (Autumn, 1944), 77.

44 Yrjö Alanen, *Siirtolaisemme ja kotimaa: Siirtolaisuuden vaikutuksesta kansamme oloihin ja luonteeseen* (Helsinki, 1910), p. 42.

45 It should be remembered that Finns found reasons to leave their country in peak numbers just when other European emigrants also left in great numbers. Finnish emigration was not thus exceptional in its origins. European emigrants in general were the landless, "driven" or "uprooted" from the countryside to seek urban employment.

*Chapter II*

1 Emil Elo, *Seppä* (Marquette, Michigan, n.d.), p. 5.

2 Albert Edelfelt, "Sketches in Finland," *Harper's New Monthly Magazine,* LXXXII (February, 1891), 348–51.

3 Arthur W. Wright, "Professor John A. Porter's Translation of the 'Kalevala,' " *The New Englander,* XXVII (April, 1868), 372.

4 Domenico Comparetti, *The Traditional Poetry of the Finns,* trans. by Isabella M. Anderton (London, 1898), pp. 17–18.

5 All the proverbs are adapted from Aino Tuomiokoski, "Finnish [Proverbs]," *Racial Proverbs: A Selection of the World's Proverbs Arranged Linguistically,* comp. by Selwyn Gurney Champion (New York, 1938), pp. 134–40; Marjorie Edgar, "Finnish Proverbs in Minnesota," *Minnesota History,* XXIV (September, 1943), 226–28; *Suomen kansan sananparsikirja,* ed. R. E. Nirvi and Lauri Hakulinen (Porvoo and Helsinki, 1948), pp. 87, 177.

6 John H. Wuorinen, *Nationalism in Modern Finland* (New York, 1931), pp. 67–68, 74.

7 Alexis Kivi, *Seven Brothers,* trans. by Alex Matson (New York, 1929).

8 *Suomen Tilastollinen Vuosikirja: Uusi sarja, kahdeskymmenesneljäs vuosikerta, 1926* (Helsinki, 1926), pp. 42–43.

9 U.S. Immigration Commission, *Reports of the Immigration Commission: Review of Immigration, 1820–1910; Distribution of Immigrants, 1850–1900,* S. Doc. No. 756, Serial 5878, 61st Cong., 3d Sess. (Washington, 1911), 84–85.

10 Quoted in Charles B. Cheney, "A Labor Crisis and a Governor," *The Outlook,* LXXXIX (May 2, 1908), 26.

11 *Työmies* (Hancock, Michigan), May 28, 1913, p. 7. Of the 136 students 51 had had no school experience, 32 had attended and 44 had finished their studies in grammar schools, and 9 had attended other schools. Actually the report listed 18 as attending other schools besides grammar schools. As 51 had not attended, 9 of the 76 attending grammar school must have also attended a second school. Reports for other academic years also revealed the lack of schooling. See *Industrialisti* (Duluth), June 9, 1919, p. 3; May 27, 1920, p. 2.

12 Kalle Kajander, *Nälkämailta: Kuvia ja havaintoja koillis-Suomesta nälkävuodelta 1902* (Helsinki, 1903), p. 186.

13 K. Kerkkonen, "Silmäys kansakoululaitoksemme puoliwuosisataiseen kehitykseen," *Kansanvalistusseuran Kalenteri, 1916* (Helsinki, 1915), pp. 7–8.

14 Statements based partly on data in "Edistysseuroista," *Kansanwalistus-Seuran Kalenteri, 1906,* Pt. II (Helsinki, 1905), 80–81; "Kirjastoliike," *Kansanvalistusseuran tietokalenteri, 1917* (Helsinki, 1916), p. 119; "Raittiusliike," *ibid.,* p. 121; John I. Kolehmainen, "Finnish Temperance Societies in Minnesota," *Minnesota History,* XXII (December, 1941), 392.

15 Such examples of provincial behavior are still revealed in the anecdotes told by immigrants to the present writer.

16 Oskari Tokoi, *Sisu, "Even Through a Stone Wall": The Autobiography of Oskari Tokoi* (New York, 1957), p. 93.

17 "Pohjanmaa," *Oma maa: Tietokirja Suomen kodeille* ed. E. G. Palmén *et al.*, IV (Porvoo, 1909), 157–72. See also Yrjö Koskinen, *Kansallisia ja yhteiskunnallisia kirjoituksia,* Suomalaisen Kirjallisuuden Seuran Toimituksia, CVIII, Pt. 1 (Helsinki, 1904–5), 14–24, 125–37.

18 "Suomenmaan Säätyjen alamainen anomus, joka koskee toimiin ryhtymistä maasta siirtymisen tuottamien epäkohtain johdosta," Säät. Anom.—Anomusmiet. No. 8 [Suomen eduskunta], *Asiakirjat valtiopäiviltä Helsingissä vuonna 1891,* V (Helsinki, 1892), 3; W. R. [William Rautanen], "Miksi lähdimme Amerikaan?" *Kirkollinen Kalenteri wuodelle 1922* (Hancock, 1921), pp. 168–71.

19 *Työmies,* 1909: December 16, p. 4; December 28, p. 8; January 29, 1910, p. 6; *Raivaaja* (Fitchburg, Massachusetts), December 20, 1910, p. 6; August 30, 1913, p. 2.

20 Henry Samuel Heimonen, "Finnish Rural Culture in South Ostrobothnia (Finland) and the Lake Superior Region (U.S.)—A Comparative Study" (Doctoral Thesis, University of Wisconsin, 1941), pp. 224–25, 260–63, 273–74.

21 Juuso Hirvonen, "Suomalaisten Joulun Vietosta," *Kansan Henki,* II (December, 1917), 22.

22 This paragraph draws on sources like Nyrkkilehti of Tyyni Raittius Seura, Erie, Pennsylvania, No. 5, 1911; July 11, 1915 (MSS in present writer's possession); Sirkka, " 'Kukkaset,' " *ibid.,* July 9, 1914; Richard Pesola, "Rikkaiden ja köyhien kevät," *Sorretun Kevät* (Astoria, Oregon, 1908), pp. 5–8; Mikael Rutanen, "Toukokuu," *Pelto ja Koti & Osuustoimintalehti,* VII (May 1, 1918), 183; John Parkkila, *Siirtolaisen kannel: Kokoelma runoja* (Hancock, 1907), pp. 60–61, 135–36; M. Johansson, "Juhlaruno, lausuttu raittiuskansan vuosijuhlassa Elyssä, Minn., heinäk. 26 p. 1913," *Raittius-kalenteri, 1914* (Fitchburg, 1913), pp. 179–85; S. I——nen [Ilmonen], "Kevät luonnossa,—kevät elämässä," *Kansan ääni: Raittiusmielisten kevätalbumi, I, 1899* (Brooklyn, 1899), 9–11; Anni M. Pennanen, *Kevät-Esikoita* (Ironwood, 1914), pp. 98–99; J. H. Erkko, "Kewätruno," *Kokoelma Raittiusrunoja,* S.K.-R.-V: seuran Kirjasia No. 4 (Brooklyn, 1896), 27–30; J. H. Heimonen, "Ajan vaihteluista," *Syyslehti,* Kansalliskirkon Juhlajulkaisut, II (Ironwood, 1911), 22–23.

23 Richard M. Dorson, *Bloodstoppers & Bearwalkers: Folk Traditions of the Upper Peninsula* (Cambridge, Massachusetts, 1952), pp. 130–31. The present writer was told a slightly different version

of the fish story as well as other stories suggesting the inferior board received by hired hands in Finland.

24 J. Elenius-Rantamäki, *"Sven-Duuva" nuorempi* (Hancock, 1921).

25 *Humoreski: Kokoelma humoorisia runoja ja kupletteja* (Worcester, Massachusetts, 1911), pp. 79–81.

26 Proverbs cited are taken mainly from Evi Aronen, "Lapset ja raittiusseura," *Raittius-kalenteri, 1915* (Duluth, 1914), p. 119; *Työmies,* May 12, 1910, p. 7; *Raivaaja,* February 4, 1911, p. 4; August 29, 1912, p. 5; *Toveritar* (Astoria), 1916: January 11, p. 5; October 31, p. 6; *New Yorkin Uutiset* (Brooklyn, New York), March 6, 1915, p. 6; November 2, 1920, p. 4; *Amerikan Sanomat* (Ashtabula, Ohio), March 24, 1898, p. 4; *Lännen Uutiset* (Rock Springs, Wyoming), October 28, 1896, p. 2; *Sankarin maine* (Hancock), June 25, 1880, p. 3.

27 A. H., "Kotilähetystoimemme," *Juhla-albumi Suomi-synoodin 25-vuotisjuhlan muistoksi, 1890–1915* (Hancock, 1915), pp. 124–25; Martin Hendrickson, *Muistelmia Kymmenvuotisesta Raivaustyöstäni* (Fitchburg, 1909), pp. 106–7; [H. Tanner], "Kertomus allekirjoittaneen lähetysmatkasta Wyoming'in y. m. waltiossa asuttuneiden suomalaisten seassa," *Paimen-Sanomia,* III (January 21, 1891), 3; K. O. [Kalle Ojajärvi], "Raittiuspuhujana," *Raittiuslehti,* No. 5 (May, 1901), 4.

28 *Raivaaja,* July 8, 1911, p. 5; K. O., "Raittiuspuhujana," p. 4; Hendrickson, *Muistelmia,* pp. 81–82; T. H., "Työmiehen kymmenvuotisen elämän vaiheet," *Työmies kymmenvuotias, 1903–1913: Juhlajulkaisu* (Hancock, 1913), p. 11; Uuras Saarnivaara, *Amerikan laestadiolaisuuden eli Apostolis-luterilaisuuden historia* (Ironwood, Michigan, 1947), p. 215.

29 *Käsikirja: Perustuslaki, siwulait, paikallis-yhdistysten säännöt, järjestys- ja työ-ohjeet, lasten raittiusosaston säännöt, sairastus-apuyhdistyksen säännöt,* Amerikan Suomalaisen Kansallis-Raittius-Weljeysseura, 7th ed. (Hancock, 1906); *Käsikirja Suomalaiseen Raittius-Ystäwien Yhdistykseen Kuuluwille Raittiusseuroille Amerikassa* (Red Jacket, Michigan, 1890).

30 Minute Book of Discussion Meetings of Tyyni Raittius Seura, Erie, Pennsylvania, for 1914–15 (MS in present writer's possession).

31 John I. Kolehmainen, "The Finnish Immigrant *Nyrkkilehti,*" *Common Ground,* IV (Autumn, 1943), 105–6; Nyrkkilehti of Tyyni Raittius Seura, 1911–19; Nyrkkilehti "Pölkky Pää" of Suomalainen Sosialisti Osasto, Munising, Michigan, October 24, [1910?], and Nyrkkilehti "Oras" of Pohjan Tähti Raittius Seura, Hancock, Michigan, 1907–12 (MSS were in archives of Finnish Historical Society of Hiawatha Land, Crystal Falls, Michigan, but

were lost or misplaced in the transfer of the archives to the Finnish American Historical Library, Hancock).

32 A. O. Hokkanen, "Kertomus Los Angeles'in s. s. osaston kymmenvuotisesta toiminnasta," *Toveri kymmenvuotias, 1907–1917: Muistojulkaisu* (Astoria, 1917), p. 86; Kertoja, "Astorian s. s. osaston toiminnasta," *ibid.*, pp. 92–93. See also T. Tainio, "Hullu yritys," *Raivaaja Kymmenen Vuotta* (Fitchburg, 1915), p. 10.

33 *Kalevala: The Land of the Heroes,* trans. by W. F. Kirby, II (London and New York, 1951), 274.

34 There are 38 poetry titles and 60 prose titles in a list of works published before 1921. See titles in John I. Kolehmainen, *The Finns in America: A Bibliographical Guide to Their History* (Hancock, 1947), pp. 113–21.

35 *Ibid.*, pp. 110–11; *Amerikan Sanomat,* March 9, 1899, p. 3; Matti Johansson, *Manifestin mainninkeja* (Hancock, 1904), p. 3.

36 In interviews the present writer was twice reminded of this poem but he has failed to locate a copy of it.

37 Discussion on the poet is mainly based on [Eelu Kiwiranta], *Eelu Kiwirannan tekemiä Kansan Runoja,* Nos. 1–5 (n.p., n.d.), *Eelu Kiwirannan sepittämiä Kansan Runoja,* Nos. 3–4 (n.p., n.d.), and *Eelu Kiwirannan sepittämiä Weitikkamaisia Runoja. Luikasta lukemista Hauskuutta haluawille,* Nos. 1, 5–6 (n.p., n.d.). The present writer also interviewed the son and three friends of the poet.

38 *Muisto-Julkaisu: "Suomen Sävel" Lauluseuran 25 vuotisesta toiminnasta* (Calumet, Michigan, [1918]).

39 The role of one such army musician is recalled in "George H. Wahlström," *Siirtokansan kalenteri, 1953* (Duluth, [1952]), pp. 62–66.

40 S. Ilmonen, "Amerikan suomalaisen raittiusliikkeen historia," *Juhlajulkaisu suomalaisen kansallis-raittius-veljeysseuran 25-vuotisen toiminnan muistoksi* (Ishpeming, Michigan, 1912), p. 106. See also A. V. H. [Havela], "Kansanjuhlista sananen," *Kansan ääni,* 1899, pp. 69–70.

41 Juli O——, "Vieraalla maalla," *Viesti,* I (June, 1915), 420; Song No. 131, *Kansan laulukirja,* comp. by Vilho Reima *et al.* (Ishpeming, 1907), p. 101; Linda Mahlberg, *Tunnelmia* (Fitchburg, 1909), p. 50; Notebook of Oscar Keturi, Eveleth, Minnesota [*ca.* 1902] (MS in present writer's possession); *Amerikan Sanomat,* February 24, 1898, p. 6.

42 Swante Luoma, "Eksynyt ja löydetty," *Kirkollinen Kalenteri wuodelle 1921* (Hancock, 1920), p. 74; Song No. 77, *Hartauslauluja (Vanhoja ja uusia)*, ed. N. Saastamoinen (Hancock, 1915),

pp. 58–59; *Siirtolainen* (Superior, Wisconsin), February 16, 1894, p. 1; M. Seura, "Kodista lähtö," *Raittiuslehti,* No. 11 (November, 1902), 9; K. I——n, "Kulkurit," *Raivaajan työvainiolta, VI. Raivaajan vuosijulkaisu* ([Fitchburg], 1910), 140; M. Hahl, "Kulkurin lempijälle," *Raivaajan Työvainiolta, I: Amerikan suomalaisten sosialistien kirjailija-alpumi* (Fitchburg, 1905), 46. Other poems on the wanderer include Kalle Koski, *Runoja* (Calumet, 1896), pp. 9–10; N. Kangas, "Kulkuri," *Säkeniä,* I (August, 1907), 251–52; W. Hywönen, "Weljelleni wierahalle," *Raittiuslehti,* No. 9 (September, 1904), 9.

43 Song No. 11, *Evankeliumi lauluja* (n.p., n.d.), p. 10; Song No. 177, *Pyhäkoulun laulukirja: Kokoelma lauluja ja virsiä pyhäkoululle ja kodille,* ed. Axel Keihänen (Hancock, 1918), pp. 84–85; Richard Pesola, "Kulkurin laulu," *Uusi työväen laulukirja* (Hancock, 1910), pp. 105–6; "Kulkuripoikain laulu," *Proletaari lauluja* (Duluth, [1918?]), pp. 55–56; Aili Kolehmainen Johnson, "Finnish Labor Songs from Northern Michigan," *Michigan History,* XXXI (September, 1947), 338–39; Matti Kurikka, "Voi Malkosaari," *Kalevan Kansan Sointuja. I. V. 1903. Sointula, B.C.* (Vancouver, n.d.), 8–14; Song No. 44, *Kansan laulukirja,* pp. 38–39; L. K., "Juopporaukka," *Raittius-Kalenteri, 1897* (Brooklyn, 1896), pp. 42–44. See also Hugo Hillilä, *Tuokiokuvia* (Hancock, 1917), pp. 65–66, and *Auttaja* (Ironwood), August 19, 1909, p. 5.

44 This paragraph draws on sources like Parkkila, *Siirtolaisen kannel,* pp. 30–31; V. Kuusisto, "'Olen tahtonut koota,'" *Juhla-albumi Suomi-synoodin 25-vuotisjuhlan muistoksi,* pp. 9–10; Song No. 73, *Hartauslauluja,* p. 56; Auno Ala-Wirta, "Nouse sorron alta!" *Raittius-Kalenteri wuodelle 1905* (Hancock, 1904), p. 23; Annaliisa, "Kansalleni," Nyrkkilehti of Tyyni Raittius Seura, March 14, 1911; Edw. Mäki, "Juhlaruno (Raittiusseura Murtajan 21:een vuosijuhlaan elok. 3 p. 1914, San Franciscossa, Cal.)," *Raittius-Kalenteri, 1915,* pp. 65–66; M. K——a [Matti Kurikka], "Vuosisadan raunioilla," *Työväen Laulukirja* (Hancock, 1905), pp. 21–22; Aku Päiviö, "Kohti Edeniä: Pohjois-Minnesotan suom. sos. kesäjuhlaan 24/6 1911," *Säkeniä,* V (September, 1911), 364–65; M. Kiikka, "Uusi yhteiskunta luokka," *Vihan vasamia* (Duluth, [1919?]), pp. 47–49.

*Chapter III*

1 Heikki Anias, "Raittiustyön merkitys kansallisena kehitystyönä," *Raittius-Kalenteri wuodelle 1905* (Hancock, Michigan, 1904), pp. 63–64.

2 E. Merijärvi, "Kuparialueen raittiusliitto," *Rauhankokous ja pääpiirteitä Amerikan suomalaisten raittiustyön historiasta* (Hancock, 1908), p. 212; H. H., "Katsahduksia raittiuteen," *Kansan Ääni: Raittiusmielisten Kewätalbumi, III, 1901* (Hancock, 1901), 16; "Historian opetuksia. Taistelu tarpeellista," *Aseita raittiustaistelussa* (Fitchburg, Massachusetts, 1908), p. 5; H. S——mi, "Uuden ajan aatoksia," *Uusi aika* (February—March, 1914), p. 66; *Työmies* (Hancock), September 13, 1913, p. 4; Aku Päiviö, "Elämän tie," *Raivaajan Työvainiolta, IV. Raivaajan vuosijulkaisu* (Fitchburg, 1908), 11; "Pastori K. L. Tolosen juhlapuhe Suomi-Opiston nurkkakivijuhlassa opistopaikalla tuokok. 30 p. 1899," *Suomi-opiston albumi, 1896–1906* (Hancock, 1906), pp. 133–38; John Parkkila, *Siirtolaisen kannel: Kokoelma runoja* (Hancock, 1907), pp. 33–35, 88–94; J. Wargelin, "Awajaispuhe, pidetty Suomi-Opiston syysluku. awajaisissa w. 1919," *Kirkollinen Kalenteri wuodelle 1920* (Hancock, 1919), p. 188; John Haaro, "Ajatus on onnen mahti!" *Nuori Suomi: Amerikan suomalaisten joulualbumi, 5, 1907* (Duluth, 1907), 82–95.

3 A. W. H., "Toimittaja J. W. Lähde," *Kansan Henki*, I (December, 1916), 1–2; A. F. Tanner, "Silmäys taaksepäin," *Työväen Kalenteri, I, 1905* (Hancock, 1904), 99.

4 Some biographical data is given in [Lauri Lemberg?], "John A. ja Martha L. Harpet," *Siirtokansan kalenteri, 1957* (Duluth, [1956]), pp. 131–33.

5 Hijoppi Rotilainen [*pseud.* of Moses Hahl], *Agitaattori Räyhäsuu: Juttuja 2* (Port Arthur, Canada, 1913), p. 14.

6 Mikko Raunio, *Hypnotismi* (Seattle, n.d.), pp. 3–4; *Teosofian valo*, III (Cleveland, February, 1915), 31–32; Advertisement of *New Yorkin Uutiset* in *Kalenteri Amerikassa asuville suomalaisille vuodelle 1910*, Finland Steamship Company Agency (New York, n.d.); *New Yorkin Uutiset* (Brooklyn, New York), August 8, 1914, p. 4; M. K——a [Kurikka], "Onniko vai tieto?" *Kalevainen, III: Kalevan naisten ja kalevan ritarien kalevalapäivän juhlajulkaisu, 1915* (Hancock, n.d.), 5–7.

7 *Amerikan Suomalainen Työmies* (Worcester, Massachusetts), November 25, 1903, p. 4.

8 *Amerikan Uutiset* (Calumet, Michigan), October 27, 1898, p. 4.

9 The tenor of the debates is revealed for example in *Amerikan Uutiset*, 1898: May 26, p. 4; June 23, p. 3; August 25, p. 4; October 27, p. 6; *Paimen-Sanomia*, X (February 2, 1898), 36; *ibid.* (July 6, 1898), 212; *Sankarin maine* (Hancock), 1880: February 27, p. 2; April 23, pp. 2–4; H. Tanner, *Suomi-Synodista* (Hancock, 1893);

J. K. Nikander, "Lyhyt silmäys kirkkokuntamme 25-vuotiseen toimintaan," *Juhla-albumi Suomi-synoodin 25-vuotisjuhlan muistoksi, 1890–1915* (Hancock, 1915), pp. 19–32.

10 J. Wargelin, "Yleinen mielipide ja totuus," *Kirkollinen Kalenteri wuodelle 1915* (Hancock, 1914), pp. 57–63; John F. Saarinen, "Yksi on tarpeellinen," *Kirkollinen Kalenteri wuodelle 1916* (Hancock, 1915), p. 27; J. E. Saari, "Waloa——warjoa," *Raittius-kalenteri, 1898* (Hancock, 1897), pp. 77–79; M. A. Tiura, "Toimeenpaneva," *Kansan Henki*, II (September, 1917), 5; "Nykyaika," *Juhlajulkaisu Kuparialueen Raittiusliiton Vuosijuhlaan Elokuun 25 päivänä 1907, Hancockissa, Michiganissa* (n.p., n.d.), p. 13; M. Johansson, "Yhdistysten aikakausi," *Raittiuslehti*, No. 12 (December, 1903), 4.

11 Akseli Järnefelt [-Rauanheimo], *Suomalaiset Amerikassa* (Helsinki, 1899), pp. 257–58.

12 Sources on religious developments include Uuras Saarnivaara, *Amerikan laestadiolaisuuden eli Apostolis-luterilaisuuden historia* (Ironwood, Michigan, 1947), and *The History of the Laestadian or Apostolic-Lutheran Movement in America* (Ironwood, 1947); Juuso Hirvonen, *Michiganin kuparialue ja suomalaiset siirtolaiset* (Duluth, 1920); *Evankelis-Luterilainen kansalliskirkko: Ensimmäiset 50 vuotta* (Ironwood, [1949]); S. Ilmonen, *Amerikan suomalaisten sivistyshistoria: Johtavia aatteita, harrastuksia, yhteispyrintöjä ja tapahtumia siirtokansan keskuudessa*, 2 vols. (Hancock, 1930–31); V. Rautanen, *Amerikan suomalainen kirkko* (Hancock, 1911); *Amerikan Suom. Ev. Luth. Kansalliskirkkon 25-vuotisjulkaisu, 1898–1923* (Ironwood, 1923).

13 Ilmonen, *Amerikan suomalaisten sivistyshistoria*, I, 136–37; U.S. Dept. of Commerce, Bureau of the Census, *Religious Bodies: 1926*, II: *Separate Denominations, Statistics, History, Doctrine, Organization, and Work* (Washington, 1929), 804, 821, 826; E. Määttälä, *English-Finnish Vest Pocket Encyclopedia and Dictionary* (Hancock, 1911), p. 62; John I. Kolehmainen and George W. Hill, *Haven in the Woods: The Story of the Finns in Wisconsin* (Madison, 1951), p. 107.

14 John I. Kolehmainen, "A History of the Finns in Western Reserve" (Doctoral Thesis, Western Reserve University, 1937), pp. 73–75.

15 Rafael Engelberg, *Suomi ja Amerikan suomalaiset: Keskinäinen yhteys ja sen rakentaminen* (Helsinki, 1944), pp. 194–96.

16 Works on the temperance movement include *Rauhankokous;* S. Ilmonen, "Amerikan suomalaisen raittiusliikkeen historia," *Juhlajulkaisu suomalaisen kansallis-raittius-veljeysseuran 25-vuotisen toiminnan muistoksi* (Ishpeming, Michigan, 1912), pp. 3–317.

17 Henry Askeli, "Suomalainen sosialisti-järjestö," *Kalenteri Amerikan suomalaiselle työväelle, 1918* (Fitchburg, n.d.), pp. 31–32.

18 Writings on the labor movement include F. J. Syrjälä, *Historia-aiheita Ameriikan Suomalaisesta Työväenliikkeestä* (Fitchburg, [1925]); Elis Sulkanen, *Amerikan Suomalaisen Työväenliikkeen Historia* (Fitchburg, 1951); William Lahtinen, *50. vuoden varrelta* (Superior, Wisconsin, 1953); John I. Kolehmainen, "The Inimitable Marxists: The Finnish Immigrant Socialists," *Michigan History,* XXXVI (December, 1952), 395–405.

19 Emil Rinne, "San Franciscon Suomalainen Veljeysseura," *Y. s. k. v. ja s.-liiton 50-vuotishistoria: Muistojulkaisu* (Duluth, 1937), p. 165.

20 C. H. S., "Katsaus Kalevaisten järjestöön," *Kalevainen,* III (February, 1917), 58; Määttälä, *English-Finnish Vest Pocket Encyclopedia,* p. 133.

21 John Syrjamaki, "Mesabi Communities: A Study of Their Development" (Doctoral Thesis, Yale University, 1940), pp. 468–69, 477–78.

22 "Raittiuskurssi-kirjat," *Raittius-Kalenteri wuodelle 1910* (Hancock, 1909), pp. 43–44.

23 *Viisitoista vuotta New Yorkin suomalaisten sosialistien historiaa, 1903–1918* (Fitchburg, [1919]), pp. 30–31.

24 Robert E. Park, *The Immigrant Press and Its Control* (New York and London, 1922), pp. 7–10.

25 Järnefelt [-Rauanheimo], *Suomalaiset Amerikassa,* pp. 302–3.

26 *Amerikan Uutiset,* December 8, 1898, p. 6.

27 Quoted in John I. Kolehmainen, *The Finns in America: A Bibliographical Guide to Their History* (Hancock, 1947), p. 74. See *ibid.,* pp. 73–97, for short survey and list of immigrant publications and see also the same author's "Finnish Newspapers and Periodicals in Michigan," *Michigan History Magazine,* XXIV (Winter, 1940), 119–27.

28 F. Tolonen, "Muutamia historiatietoja Amerikan suomalaisista sanomalehdistä," *Amerikan Suometar, 1899–1919: Muistojulkaisu* (Hancock, 1919), p. 92.

29 N. J. Ahlman, "Amerikan suomalaisen kirjallisuuden seura," *Tiedon henki,* I (September, 1910), 20–23. See also *Lännetar* (Astoria, Oregon), January 7, 1897, p. 2, and Chas. H. S——nen, "Vieläkin Amerikan suomalaisen kirjallisuuden seuran puolesta," *Viesti,* I (June, 1915), 467–72.

30 *New Yorkin Uutiset,* November 5, 1913, p. 4; F. V. Kava, "Amerikan Suomettaren historia v. 1899–1919," *Amerikan Suometar, 1899–1919,* p. 25; *Raivaaja* (Fitchburg), January 13, 1916, p. 2; J. Lauttamus, "Valioköörin kolmas osasto," *Kansan Henki,* I (De-

cember, 1916), 49.

31 J. W. Lilius, "Johdanto," *Rauhankokous,* pp. 5–6.

32 Kalle Tähtelä, "Amerikan suomalainen kirjallisuus," *Säkeniä,* VI (February, 1912), 77–79; Aa—— ja ——oo, "Sana kirjallisuuden puolesta," *Kalevainen, II: Kalevan naisten ja kalevan ritarien kalevalapäivän juhlajulkaisu, 1914* (n.p., n.d.), 8; *New Yorkin Uutiset,* June 16, 1917, p. 6; J. Wargelin, "Uskonto ja tietopuolinen siwistys," *Kirkollinen Kalenteri wuodelle 1911* (Hancock, 1910), p. 95; Tikka, "Siirtolaiskirjallisuudesta," *Kaukomieli jouluna 1913* (Hancock, 1913), p. 2.

33 See prose titles in Kolehmainen, *The Finns in America, passim.* Immigrant literature is surveyed by George Sjöblom, "Finnish-American Literature," *The History of the Scandinavian Literatures: A Survey of the Literatures of Norway, Sweden, Denmark, Iceland and Finland, from Their Origins to the Present Day, Including Scandinavian-American Authors, and Selected Bibliographies,* ed. Frederika Blankner (New York, 1938), pp. 311–18. See also Ernest John Moyne, "Studies in Cultural Relations Between Finland and America, 1638–1938" (Doctoral Thesis, Harvard University, 1947), pp. 428–32.

34 S. Ilmonen, "Suomen kirkon lahja Amerikan suomalaisille," *Kirkollinen Kalenteri wuodelle 1922* (Hancock, 1921), pp. 81–98.

35 Engelberg, *Suomi ja Amerikan suomalaiset, passim;* Tanner, "Silmäys taaksepäin," p. 96; "Neiti Alma Hinkkanen, S. K.-R.-Weljeysseuran nykyinen raittiuspuhuja," *Raittius-Kalenteri wuodelle 1909* (Hancock, 1908), p. 163.

36 *Suomi-opiston vuosikertomus lukuvuonna 1909–1910* (Hancock, n.d.), p. 21; *Evankelis-Luterilainen kansalliskirkko,* pp. 97–98; Ilmonen, "Amerikan suomalaisen raittiusliikkeen historia," p. 154; Alex Halonen, *Sosialismin Perusteet* ([Fitchburg], 1907), pp. 14–15; Julmisen Sakka, "Muistelmia 'ens' kutsunnan' ajoilta," *Vallankumous, II, Työväen Opiston Toverikunnan Julkaisu v. 1909* (Hancock, 1909), p. 108; *Pöytäkirja Co-operative Central Exchangen Vuosikokouksesta, Pidetty Keskusosuuskunnan Talolla Maaliskuun 22 ja 23 päivinä 1919* (Superior, n.d.), p. 19; *Kuparisaaren Sanomat* (Hancock), May 15, 1896, p. 2; Annual Report Book No. 2 of President of Suomalaisen Kansallis-Raittius-Weljeysseura for 1907–34, report of July 23, 1907 (MS in possession of Finnish American Historical Library, Hancock).

37 *Evankelis-Luterilainen kansalliskirkko,* pp. 53–54; *Siirtolainen* (Brooklyn), May 20, 1895, p. 1; *New Yorkin Uutiset,* July 29, 1914, p. 8.

38 J. K. N. [Juho K. Nikander], "Wertailua wuosien 1896 ja 1911 wälillä," *Tartu kiinni,* Suomi-Opiston Juhla-Julkaisu ([Hancock? 1911?]), p. 10. Early years of the school are covered in *Suomi-opiston albumi, 1896–1906.*

39 Olga Fast, "Oppilaan havaintoja," *Vallankumous, VII. Työväen-opiston toverikunnan kevätjulkaisu, 1914* (Hancock, 1914), 13. Early fortunes of the school are noted by one of its officials, K. L. Haataja, "Piirteitä Kansan-Opiston toiminnasta," *Vallankumous: Kansan-opiston toverikunnan albumi* No. 1, 1908 (Hancock, 1908), pp. 5–13.

40 Hirvonen, *Michiganin Kuparialue,* p. 84; H. A. [Heikki Anias], "Raittiuskurssit talwella 1904–1905. A. S. K.-R.-W.-Seuran ensimmäiset," *Raiwaustyössä. Raittiuskurssien, A. S. K.-R.-W.-Seuran ensimmäisten, johdosta* (Hancock, 1905), pp. 86–95; Halonen, *Sosialismin Perusteet,* pp. 14–15.

41 Ilmonen, "Suomen kirkon lahja," pp. 81–98; *New Yorkin Uutiset,* February 5, 1957, p. 5; John Wargelin, *The Americanization of the Finns* (Hancock, 1924), pp. 129–30; *Report of the Proceedings of the Fourth Congress of the Co-operative League, New York, N.Y., November 6, 7, 8, 9 and 10, 1924* (New York, 1924), p. 182; "Education at Superior," *Co-operation,* VI (November, 1920), 168.

42 S. Ilmonen, "Seurakunnan wirkailijat," *Kirkollinen Kalenteri wuodelle 1907* (Hancock, 1906), p. 62; *Saarnaaja Johan Mursun Elämäkerta* (New York Mills, Minnesota, 1912); K. O., "Kirkollinen politiikka ja uskonnolliset asiat Amerikan suomalaisten kesken," *Kirkollinen Kalenteri wuodelle 1915,* pp. 159–60; J. K. N. [Juho K. Nikander], "Suomalaisten kirkollinen tila Amerikassa ennen Suomi-Synoodin perustamista," *Kirkollinen Kalenteri Wuodelle 1903* (Hancock, 1902), p. 40.

43 *Käsikirja: Perustuslaki, siwulait, paikallis-yhdistysten säännöt, järjestys- ja työ-ohjeet, lasten raittiusosaston säännöt, sairastus-apuyhdistyksen säännöt,* Amerikan Suomalaisen Kansallis-Raittius-Weljeysseura, 7th ed. (Hancock, 1906), pp. 6–7; Viljo Hytönen, *Yleinen Raittiusliikkeen Historia* (Helsinki, 1911), p. 253; M. P.-Mäki, "Juho Heikki Jasberg," *Kirkollinen kalenteri vuodeksi 1930* (Hancock, 1929), p. 178; Richard Pesola, "Hajamuistelmia," *Työmies 20 vuotta* (Superior, 1923), pp. 97–98; *Vallankumous, V: Työväen-opiston toverikunnan kevätjulkaisu, 1912* (Hancock, 1912), 128; *Raivaaja,* January 1, 1914, p. 5.

44 Akseli [Järnefelt-] Rauanheimo, "Amerikan suomalaiset," *Oma maa: Tietokirja Suomen kodeille,* ed. E. J. Palmén *et al.,* III (Porvoo, 1908), 433; Heikki Anias, "Raittiustyön merkitys kan-

sallisena kehitystyönä," *Raittius-Kalenteri wuodelle 1905,* p. 64; *Amerikan Kaiku* (Brooklyn), July 29, 1905, p. 4.

45 Joh. Bäck, "Kirkollinen asemamme Amerikassa," *Kirkollinen Kalenteri wuodelle 1907,* pp. 48–52; Alvar Rautalahti, *Juho Kustaa Nikander* (Hancock, 1920), p. 23; Yrjö Joki, "Muutamia piirteitä seurakuntatyöstä Monessenissa," *Kirkollinen Kalenteri wuodelle 1916,* pp. 138–40; Kalle Mäkinen, "The Land Where a Man Is Free to Work," *The World's Work,* XLI (January, 1921), 274–75; A. R——hti [Alvar Rautalahti], "Sanomalehti ja kirkko," *Amerikan Suometar, 1899–1919,* pp. 56–57; Hannes Leiviskä, *Piirteitä Amerikan suomalaisten seurakunnallisista oloista* (Helsinki, 1908), p. 11; V. Rautanen, "Amerikan suomalaisesta kirkosta ja kirkkosillasta," *Tervehdys Suomelle* (Brooklyn, 1920), pp. 31–33; J. S——nen, "Papit ja sanankuulijat," *Paimen-Sanomia,* IX (February 3, 1897), 34.

46 J. K. N. [Juho K. Nikander], "Suomi-Synoodin perustaminen ja sen kolme ensimmäistä wuotta," *Kirkollinen Kalenteri Wuodelle 1904* (Hancock, 1903), pp. 49–50; V. F., "Sanomalehti," *Amerikan Suomalaisille: Selostuksia tärkeistä asioista* (Hancock, n.d.), pp. 6–8; Saarnivaara, *Amerikan laestadiolaisuuden eli Apostolisluterilaisuuden historia,* pp. 43–45. See also the two charts comparing factional developments in the Laestadian movements of America and Finland, *ibid.,* pp. 363–64.

47 Kalle H. Mannerkorpi, "Conneautin suomal. ew.-luth. seurakunnan historia 20-wuotisajalta 1895–1915," *Paimen Sanomia,* XXVII (July 12, 1915), 539; ——r——, "Muistelmia," *Raittius-Kalenteri wuodelle 1902* (Hancock, 1901), p. 104; Järnefelt [-Rauanheimo], *Suomalaiset Amerikassa,* p. 283; [Järnefelt-] Rauanheimo, "Amerikan suomalaiset," p. 433; A. M., "Yhteispyrintömme," *Kansan ääni: Raittiusmielisten kevätalbumi, I, 1899* (Brooklyn, 1899), 42; Wesa, "Miltä kannalta ajamme raittiusasiaa," *Raittius-kalenteri, 1898,* p. 104; Hytönen, *Yleinen Raittiusliikkeen Historia,* pp. 252–53.

48 Tanner, "Silmäys taaksepäin," p. 97; *Raivaaja,* November 8, 1910, p. 8; December 20, 1915, p. 2. See also Leonard C. Kercher *et al., Consumers' Cooperatives in the North Central States,* ed. Roland S. Vaile (Minneapolis, 1941), p. 31.

49 Santeri Mäkelä, "Vertailun vuoksi," *Köyhälistön nuija, VI, 1912* (Hancock, 1911), pp. 20–31. See also reports cited in *Raivaaja,* July 7, 1910, p. 4; *Työmies* (Hancock), July 12, 1910, p. 4; Kolehmainen, "The Inimitable Marxists," pp. 397–99.

50 Y. K. Laine, *Suomen poliittisen työväenliikkeen historia, III: Luokkataisteluun!* (Helsinki, 1946), 193–218; *Työmies kymmen-*

*vuotias, 1903–1913: Juhlajulkaisu* (Hancock, 1913), pp. 14–15; G. H., "Kuinka I.W.W. Tuli Suomalaisille Tunnetuksi," *Industrialistin Joulu, 1927* (Duluth, n.d.), p. 19; F. J. S——ä [Syrjälä], "Poimintoja ja muistelmia," *Raivaaja Kymmenen Vuotta* (Fitchburg, 1915), p. 34; Wilho Boman, "Piirteitä suomalaisesta sosialistisesta liikkeestä Amerikassa," *Säkeniä,* VII (July, 1913), 209–16.

*Chapter IV*

1 Quoted in U.S. Industrial Commission, *Reports of the Industrial Commission on Immigration, Including Testimony, with Review and Digest, and Special Reports, and on Education, Including Testimony, with Review and Digest,* H. Doc. No. 184, Serial 4345, 57th Cong., 1st Sess. (Washington, 1901), 510.

2 U.S. Immigration Commission, *Reports of the Immigration Commission: Immigrants in Industries,* Pt. 18: *Iron Ore Mining,* S. Doc. No. 633, Serial 5677, 61st Cong., 2d Sess. (Washington, 1911), 395, 404.

3 Advertisements in *New Yorkin Uutiset* (Brooklyn, New York), July 29, 1914, p. 8, and *Almanakka karkausvuodelle 1904,* Suomen Höyrylaiva Osakeyhtiö (Helsinki and New York, n.d.).

4 Based on data in U.S. Dept. of Treasury, Commissioner-General of Immigration, *Annual Report . . . ,* 1901–3 (Washington, 1901–3); U.S. Dept. of Commerce and Labor, Commissioner-General of Immigration, *Annual Report . . . ,* 1904–13 (Washington, 1904–14); U.S. Dept. of Labor, Commissioner-General of Immigration, *Annual Report . . . ,* 1914–20 (Washington, 1915–20). During the fiscal years 1901–20 officials recorded 194,412 arrivals of whom 78,211 were destined for Michigan and Minnesota and 59,450 were headed for Massachusetts and New York.

5 U.S. Immigration Commission, *Reports of the Immigration Commission: Immigrants in Industries,* Pt. 18: *Iron Ore Mining, passim,* and *Reports of the Immigration Commission: Immigrants in Industries,* Pt. 17: *Copper Mining and Smelting,* S. Doc. No. 633, Serial 5677, 61st Cong., 2d Sess. (Washington, 1911), *passim.*

6 *Amerikan albumi: Kuvia Amerikan suomalaisten asuinpaikoilta* (Brooklyn, [1905?]), p. x; "Tilasto Ishpemingin Suomalaisista Huhtikuulla 1907," *Raittius-Kalenteri wuodelle 1908* (Hancock, Michigan, 1907), p. 31; *Amerikan Sanomat* (Ashtabula, Ohio), October 20, 1898, supplement, p. 3. Immigrant compilers generally did not distinguish between foreign-born and native-born persons of Finnish stock.

7 William B. Gates, Jr., *Michigan Copper and Boston Dollars: An*

*Economic History of the Michigan Copper Mining Industry* (Cambridge, 1951), p. 111.

8 U.S. Immigration Commission, *Reports of the Immigration Commission: Review of Immigration, 1820–1910; Distribution of Immigrants, 1850–1900,* S. Doc. No. 756, Serial 5878, 61st Cong., 3d Sess. (Washington, 1911), 96, *Reports of the Immigration Commission: Immigrants in Industries,* Pt. 17: *Copper Mining and Smelting,* 88, and *Reports of the Immigration Commission: Immigrants in Industries,* Pt. 18: *Iron Ore Mining,* 311, 343.

9 *Ibid.,* p. 343.

10 Kurkistelia, "'Jänkkistailiin,'" *Jätkäin Virsiä, I* (Fitchburg, Massachusetts, n.d.), 71–73; H. Haines Turner, *Case Studies of Consumers' Cooperatives: Successful Cooperatives Started by Finnish Groups in the United States Studied in Relation to Their Social and Economic Environment* (New York, 1941), p. 38; U.S. Immigration Commission, *Reports of the Immigration Commission: Immigrants in Industries,* Pt. 18: *Iron Ore Mining,* 305, 336; Gates, *Michigan Copper and Boston Dollars,* p. 107; U.S. Industrial Relations Commission, "The Situation in Butte, Montana," processed report prepared by Daniel O'Regan (n.p., 1914), pp. 2–3 (copy in State Historical Society of Wisconsin, Madison).

11 *Strike in the Copper Mining District of Michigan: Letter from the Secretary of Labor Transmitting in Response to a Senate Resolution of January 29, 1914, a Report in regard to the Strike of Mine Workers in the Michigan Copper District which Began on July 23, 1913,* S. Doc. No. 381, Serial 6575, 63d Cong., 2d Sess. (Washington, 1914), 26.

12 *Amerikan Sanomat,* February 17, 1898, p. 3; Hans R. Wasastjerna, *Minnesotan suomalaisten historia* (Duluth, 1957), p. 137; clipping from *Uusi Kotimaa* (New York Mills, Minnesota), January 24, [1907], in Scrapbook of Newspaper Clippings (volume in possession of Finnish American Historical Library, Hancock); letter from Wäinö J. Lehto, Kearsarge, Michigan, to Julius Sarin Wirta, July 27, 1903 (MS in present writer's possession).

13 U.S. Dept. of Commerce and Labor, Commissioner-General of Immigration, *Annual Report,* 1911–13; U.S. Dept. of Labor, Commissioner-General of Immigration, *Annual Report,* 1915–20. According to the reports, between July, 1910, and June, 1920, 20,545 Finns left permanently from the United States and reported continuous residence in America as follows: less than 5 years, 8,422; 5–10 years, 4,108; 10–15 years, 786; 15–20 years, 141; over 20 years, 127; unknown, 6,961.

14 Letter from Antti Kangas, Franklin, Minnesota, to Wilhelm

Kangas, Finland, July 1, 1883 (MS in present writer's possession). Other "America letters" are found in Artturi Leinonen, *Atlanttia ja Amerikkaa katselemassa* (Porvoo and Helsinki, 1938), pp. 126–31.

15 *Amerikan Sanomat,* November 3, 1898, p. 4; April 27, 1899, p. 4; March 4, 1903, p. 4; *Siirtolainen* (West Superior, Wisconsin), February 16, 1894, p. 6; *Lännetar* (Astoria, Oregon), October 21, 1897, p. 1; March 5, 1898, p. 1.

16 John I. Kolehmainen, "A History of the Finns in Western Reserve" (Doctoral Thesis, Western Reserve University, 1937), pp. 66–69; A. Mäläskä, "Jatkuwa rikoskirja," *Kansan Ääni: Raittiusmielisten Kewätalbumi, III, 1901* (Hancock, Michigan, 1901), 126; *Raivaaja* (Fitchburg), August 10, 1911, p. 2.

17 Matti Herneshuhta, *Trämppejä: Romaani* (Worcester, Massachusetts, 1911); *New Yorkin Uutiset,* April 23, 1918, p. 5; *Raivaaja,* March 16, 1911, p. 6; S. I——nen [Ilmonen], "Amerikan suomalaisten väkilukutilastoa, tuhatluvuissa ja valtioittain," *Raittiuskalenteri, 1913* (Hancock, 1912), pp. 21–22.

18 Kalle Sippola, "Ilmiö-raittiusseura, Biwabikissa, Minn.," *Raittius-Kalenteri wuodelle 1906* (n.p., [1905]), p. 158; *Työmies* (Hancock), January 6, 1910, p. 8; *Raivaaja,* January 7, 1911, p. 7; *Amerikan Sanomat,* April 20, 1899, p. 5.

19 J. H., "Suomalaisia Pankkimiehiä," *Kansan Henki,* II (December, 1917), 38; *Ohjaaja onnellisuuteen eli jokainen on oman onnensa seppä* (Ashtabula, n.d.), pp. 20–22; *Sankarin maine* (Hancock), December 17, 1880, p. 2; *Amerikan Sanomat,* November 13, 1912, p. 6.

20 Siiri Kantonen, " 'Jokainen on oman onnensa seppä,' " *Juhannuslehti,* Suomi-Opiston Juhla-Julkaisut, XII (Hancock, June 10, 1919), 23; A. N., "Opin arwo ja merkitys. Muutamia mietteitä wanhoille ja nuorille," *Raittius-Kalenteri wuodelle 1911* (Ishpeming, 1910), p. 117; *Raivaaja,* August 22, 1912, p. 5; Hijoppi Rotilainen [*pseud.* of Moses Hahl], *Jumalan karitsat* (Port Arthur, Canada, 1914), pp. 5–7.

21 *Opas* (June [1911?]), p. 2.

22 Jacob Laurila, *Massachusettsin suomalaisia liikemiehiä vuosina 1890–1945* (Fitchburg, [1946]); Juuso Hirvonen, *Michiganin kuparialue ja suomalaiset siirtolaiset* (Duluth, 1920), pp. 43, 49, 149–51; F. Tolonen, "Amerikan suomalaisten liike-elämästä," *Suomimatka 1921,* Liikemiesten ja Laulajain Suomimatkatoimikunta (Hancock, 1921), pp. 99–106; *Amerikan Suometar* (Hancock), March 23, 1910, p. 4; C. H. S., "Pankkiiri Albert Budas, Red Lodge, Montana," *Kansan Henki,* II (June, 1917), 22–23.

23 M. P., "Our Present Need," *Tiedon henki,* I (September, 1910), 39–41; A. N., "Opin arwo," p. 117; Mina Walli, *Suomalais-amerikalainen keittokirja* (New York, 1914), p. 3; "Pastori J. Bäckin puhe Suomi-Opiston nurkkakivijuhlan iltana Germania haalissa toukok. 30 p. 1899," *Suomi-opiston albumi, 1896–1906* (Hancock, 1906), p. 149.

24 *Suomi-opiston vuosikertomus lukuvuonna 1909–1910* (Hancock, n.d.), p. 25.

25 Based on figures listed in S. Ilmonen, *Amerikan suomalaisten sivistyshistoria: Johtavia aatteita, harrastuksia, yhteispyrintöjä ja tapahtumia siirtokansan keskuudessa,* II (Hancock, 1931), 224.

26 Yrjö Sirola, "Työväen-opisto ja suomalaisen sosialistijärjestön suhde siihen," *Suomalaisten sosialistiosastojen ja työväenyhdistysten viidennen eli suomalaisen sosialistijärjestön kolmannen edustajakokouksen pöytäkirja 1–5, 7–10 p. kesäkuuta, 1912* (Fitchburg, n.d.), p. 16.

27 *New Yorkin Uutiset,* March 30, 1918, p. 5.

28 *Työmies,* November 29, 1910, p. 4.

29 See chapter on stock companies, mainly mining, in S. Ilmonen, *Amerikan suomalaisten sivistyshistoria: Johtavia aatteita, harrastuksia, yhteispyrintöjä ja tapahtumia siirtokansan keskuudessa,* I (Hancock, 1930), 196–206.

30 See advertisements in *Työmies,* 1910: February 5, p. 2; March 15, p. 5; September 8, p. 6; November 19, p. 3; *New Yorkin Uutiset,* March 21, 1912, p. 7. See also *Finnish-American Mining Co. raportti Joulukuun 31 p:ään 1909* ([Duluth? 1910?]) and *Mustan karhun kaivanto-yhtiö kaivokset Coloradon valtiossa, San Miguel ja Ouray kauntissa* (Hancock, 1907).

31 *New Yorkin Uutiset,* July 29, 1914, p. 6; *Raivaaja,* March 19, 1914, p. 2; *Siirtolainen* (Duluth), February 12, 1918, p. 3; Annikki, "Surun tarina New Yorkista," *Kaukomieli jouluna 1913* (Hancock, 1913), pp. 18–20.

32 U.S. Immigration Commission, *Reports of the Immigration Commission: Immigrants in Industries,* Pt. 18: *Iron Ore Mining,* 332; "Kauhea kaiwantoonnettomuus Scofield, Carbon Co., Utahissa. 63 suomalaistakin saanut kaiwannon kaasu-räjäyksessa [*sic*] surmansa," *Raittiuslehti,* No. 5 (May 15, 1900), 1; *Amerikan Sanomat,* July 15, 1903, p. 4.

33 *Ohjelma sekä perus- että ohje-Säännöt,* Suomalainen Apuyhdistys Imatra (n.p., n.d.).

34 " 'Tuon toisen' työnteko," *Työwäen Ystäwä,* No. 5 (March 15, 1897), 5.

35 Matti Halminen, *Sointula: Kalevan Kansan ja Kanadan suomalais-*

*ten historiaa* (Mikkeli, 1936); A. B. Mäkelä, "Miksi Malkosaaren yhtiöhomma ei menestynyt," *Työväen kalenteri, III, 1910* (Helsinki, 1909), 66–98; Kaapro Jääskeläinen [*pseud.* of A. B. Mäkelä], *Muistoja "Malkosaarelta": Kuvia ja kuvauksia "kalevan kansan" kommunistisesta siirtola-yrityksestä Sointulassa, Malcolm saarella, Brittiläis-Columbian rannikolla Kanadassa v. 1901–1905* (Helsinki, 1907); John. I. Kolehmainen, "Harmony Island. A Finnish Utopian Venture in British Columbia," *The British Columbia Historical Quarterly,* V (April, 1941), 111–23; Matti Kurikka, "Tervehdys Malkosaarelta," *Työmiehen illanvietto,* I (November 28, 1902), 107–8, and "Kirje Sointulasta. II. Luonne ja työkyky," *ibid.* (December 12, 1902), 119.

36 *Amerikan Suomalainen Työmies* (Worcester), 1903: August 26, p. 2; September 16, p. 1; October 28, p. 2; November 4, pp. 1–3, 11; December 23, pp. 1–2. See also T. H., "Työmiehen kymmenvuotisen elämän vaiheeet," *Työmies kymmenvuotias, 1903–1913: Juhlajulkaisu* (Hancock, 1913), pp. 7–13; F. J. Syrjälä, "Alkuvaikeuksien ajoilta," *ibid.*, pp. 63–66.

37 J——i R——o, "Demokratinen sosialismi, teosofia ja kristillinen sosialismi," *Soihtu,* II (July—August, 1906), 239–44; M. Hahl, *Uudempi kansantalous* (Fitchburg, 1906), pp. 3, 34–36; Richard Pesola, *Sorretun poluilta: Kertomuskokoelma* (Astoria, 1909), p. 9; Adolph Salmi, *Amerikalaisessa kaivoskylässä: Murhenäytelmä 6:ssa näytöksessä* (Hancock, 1910); Eemeli Parras, *Villit vuoret: Nelinäytöksinen näytelmä* (Hancock, 1911).

38 *New Yorkin Uutiset,* July 24, 1912, p. 4; March 12, 1913, p. 4; January 6, 1915, p. 4; *Amerikan Suometar,* April 1, 1908, p. 4; *Eveleth News* (Minnesota), February 12, 1908, p. 1; J. Katajamaa, "Muutamia Huomioonotettawia Seikkoja," *Siirtolaisen Opas,* Suomen Merimieslähetysseura and Suomi Synoodi (Helsinki, 1910), pp. 29–30; unidentified clipping [*ca.* 1908] in Scrapbook of Newspaper Clippings, Finnish American Historical Library, Hancock.

39 *Conneaut News-Herald,* 1908: July 1, p. 1; July 9, p. 1; *Ashtabula Beacon Record,* July 8, 1908, p. 1.

40 Elis Sulkanen, *Amerikan Suomalaisen Työväenliikkeen Historia* (Fitchburg, 1951), pp. 125–26. Through a probable misprint, this source misstates the year of the strike as 1905.

41 Vernon H. Jensen, *Heritage of Conflict: Labor Relations in the Nonferrous Metals Industry up to 1930* (Ithaca, 1950), p. 248.

42 The course of the strike can be traced not only in American newspapers but also in Finnish ones like the *Työmies* and *Amerikan Suometar.* The last named paper also published *Lakko tutkimus,* Michiganin Kuparialueen Liikemies-Yhdistyksen Komitea (Han-

cock, 1913), which was a translation of the report, *Strike Investigation* (Chicago, 1913), by the Committee of the Copper Country Commercial Club of Michigan. Official reports include *Strike in the Copper Mining District of Michigan* and *Conditions in the Copper Mines of Michigan: Hearings before a Subcommittee of the Committee on Mines and Mining; House of Representatives, Sixty-Third Congress, Second Session, Pursuant to H. Res. 387, a Resolution Authorizing and Directing the Committee on Mines and Mining to Make an Investigation of Conditions in the Copper Mines of Michigan*, 7 Pts. (Washington, 1914). See also Jensen, *Heritage of Conflict*, pp. 272–88.

43 Sulkanen, *Amerikan Suomalaisen Työväenliikkeen Historia*, pp. 149–50; *Työmies* (Hancock), 1911: May 28, p. 2; June 29, p. 2; November 17, p. 2; *Raivaaja*, December 10, 1910, p. 4; 1911: June 24, p. 4; August 16, p. 2; December 21, p. 8; September 29, 1913, p. 6; February 9, 1914, p. 2; Selig Perlman and Philip Taft, *History of Labor in the United States, 1896–1932*, IV: *Labor Movements* (New York, 1935), 388–90; Fred Thompson, *The I.W.W., Its First Fifty Years (1905–1955): The History of an Effort to Organize the Working Class* (Chicago, 1955), pp. 101–4.

44 *Pöytäkirja Amerikan s. s. järjestön itäpiirin edustajakokouksesta joka pidettiin Fitchburgissa, Mass., s. s. kustannusyhtiön (raivaajan) talolla helmikuun 24, 25 ja 26 p:nä 1917* (Fitchburg, n.d.), pp. 29–30.

45 F. J. Syrjälä, *Historia-aiheita Ameriikan Suomalaisesta Työväenliikkestä* (Fitchburg, [1925]), pp. 210–11; Wasastjerna, *Minnesotan suomalaisten historia*, p. 453; *History of the Finnish Settlement in Brown and Dickey Counties of South and North Dakota, 1881–1955* (New York Mills, 1956), p. 16.

46 *Report of the Proceedings of the First American Co-operative Convention Held at Springfield, Illinois, September 25th, 26th, and 27th, 1918, under the Auspices of the Co-operative League of America* (New York, 1919), pp. 252–53.

47 "Pöytäkirja pidetty Co-operative Central Exchangen vuosikokouksessa helmikuun 9 ja 10 päivä 1918, Superiorissa, Wis., s. s. osaston talolla," *Pelto ja Koti & Osuustoimintalehti*, VII (April 1, 1918), 130.

48 *New Yorkin Uutiset*, July 20, 1920, p. 6; "Muutamia piirteitä Ashtabula Harborin Suomalailaisen [*sic*] ruoka-osuuskaupan toiminnasta," *Pelto ja koti*, III (November 1, 1914), 423; Harlan J. Randall and Clay J. Daggett, *Consumers' Cooperative Adventures: Case Studies* (Whitewater, Wisconsin, 1936), p. 112; *Raivaaja*,

February 5, 1916, p. 5; Turner, *Case Studies of Consumers' Co-operatives,* pp. 55, 166–67.

49 *Raivaaja,* October 4, 1915, pp. 2–3; *Report of the Proceedings of the First American Co-operative Convention,* pp. 71–72; *Meidän Jokapäiväinen Leipämme,* Co-operative Central Exchange'in Lentokirjanen No. 2 (Superior, Wisconsin, [1918?]), 6; Wuorensyrjän Topias, " 'Jukola,' " *Pelto ja koti,* III (April 1, 1914), 163.

50 Paul H. Landis, *Three Iron Mining Towns: A Study in Cultural Change* (Ann Arbor, 1938), pp. 50, 110; *New Yorkin Uutiset,* March 26, 1918, p. 5; *Raivaaja,* July 16, 1910, p. 6; April 11, 1914, p. 4; *Työmies,* May 28, 1910, p. 8.

51 "Suomalaisella farmiseudulla Amerikassa," *Amerikan Joulukaikuja 1904* (Brooklyn, n.d.), p. 16; John I. Kolehmainen, "Amerikan suomalaisten historiaa Osuustoimintalehdelle, II: Takaisin Maalle! —'Maaemo se meidät kaikki elättää,' " *Työväen Osuustoimintalehti,* XVII (February 2, 1946), 5; *New Yorkin Uutiset,* 1920: January 3, p. 6; July 15, p. 6; *Tiedon henki,* I (September, 1910), 59; John I. Kolehmainen and George W. Hill, *Haven in the Woods: The Story of the Finns in Wisconsin* (Madison, 1951), p. 41; *Amerikan Suometar,* June 25, 1902, p. 4; October 13, 1909, p. 2; *Päivälehti* (Calumet, Michigan), March 18, 1902, p. 2; "Aikanaan maalle," *Pellervo* (June 15, 1913), p. 2; *Uusi Kotimaa,* February 15, 1900, p. 2; May 2, 1901, p. 5.

52 C. H. S., "Kansallista kevytmielisyyttä," *Kalevainen,* VI (February, 1919), 19; *New Yorkin Uutiset,* May 14, 1918, p. 4; September 22, 1921, p. 6; *Työmies,* October 1, 1910, p. 5; *Kolmannen Amerikan Suomalaisen Sosialistijärjestön edustajakokouksen pöytäkirja, Kokous pidetty Hancockissa, Mich., 23–30 p. elok., 1909* (Fitchburg, n.d.), pp. 134–63; *Raivaaja,* June 21, 1916, p. 2.

53 U.S. Dept. of Commerce, Bureau of the Census, *Fourteenth Census of the United States Taken in the Year 1920,* V: *Agriculture, General Report and Analytical Tables* (Washington, 1922), 319, 323, and *Fourteenth Census of the United States Taken in the Year 1920,* II: *Population, 1920, General Report and Analytical Tables* (Washington, 1922), 768, 958.

## *Chapter V*

1 T., "Lännen mailta," *Tiedon henki,* I (September, 1910), 27.

2 Following data taken from *Suomen virallinen tilasto. XXVIII. Siirtolaisuustilasto. 17. Siirtolaisuus vuosina 1921 ja 1922* (Helsinki, 1923), 7.

MARITAL STATUS OF EMIGRANTS APPLYING FOR PASSPORTS

| | *1901–10* | | *1911–20* | |
|---|---|---|---|---|
| | *Male* | *Female* | *Male* | *Female* |
| Unwed | 76,307 | 40,800 | 29,540 | 22,337 |
| Married | 26,161 | 13,426 | 7,541 | 6,729 |
| Widows, divorced, and widowers | 527 | 970 | 211 | 738 |
| Unknown | 582 | 59 | 226 | 24 |
| Total | 103,577 | 55,255 | 37,518 | 29,828 |

3 In the 1880's the Finnish government started to record the age of passport applicants. But not until 1900 did its reports use the following age categories as given in *International Migrations,* I: *Statistics,* ed. Walter F. Willcox (New York, 1929), 776.

AGE GROUPS OF EMIGRANTS APPLYING FOR PASSPORTS

| | *1901–10* | | *1911–20* | |
|---|---|---|---|---|
| | *Male* | *Female* | *Male* | *Female* |
| Under 16 years | 8,239 | 8,406 | 4,499 | 4,564 |
| 16–20 years | 25,846 | 14,724 | 7,905 | 7,741 |
| 21–30 years | 48,391 | 22,931 | 17,160 | 11,636 |
| 31–40 years | 15,002 | 5,734 | 5,621 | 3,962 |
| 41–50 years | 4,338 | 1,640 | 1,671 | 1,012 |
| Over 50 years | 1,192 | 1,017 | 522 | 689 |
| Age unknown | 569 | 803 | 140 | 224 |
| Total | 103,577 | 55,255 | 37,518 | 29,828 |

4 Following data based on *Suomen Tilastollinen Vuosikirja: Uusi sarja, kahdeskymmenesneljäs vuosikerta, 1926* (Helsinki, 1926), pp. 70–71, and *Suomen virallinen tilasto. XXVIII. Siirtolaisuustilasto. 1. Siirtolaisuus vuosina 1900–1902* (Helsinki, 1905), 10.

DISTRIBUTION OF EMIGRANT PASSPORT APPLICANTS BY SEX
(Only data from 1893 on covered entire country)

| *Years* | *Male* | *%* | *Female* | *%* |
|---|---|---|---|---|
| 1883–85 | 2,315 | 78.6 | 629 | 21.4 |
| 1886–90 | 16,772 | 76.3 | 5,196 | 23.7 |
| 1891–92 | 7,910 | 68.9 | 3,579 | 31.1 |
| 1893–95 | 8,977 | 61.8 | 5,540 | 38.2 |
| 1896–1900 | 19,809 | 59.9 | 13,231 | 40.1 |
| 1901–5 | 52,920 | 65.2 | 28,136 | 34.8 |
| 1906–10 | 50,657 | 65.1 | 27,119 | 34.9 |
| 1911–15 | 29,626 | 58.4 | 21,042 | 41.6 |
| 1916–20 | 7,892 | 47.3 | 8,786 | 52.7 |

5 Based on U.S. Dept. of Treasury, Commissioner-General of Immigration, *Annual Report . . . ,* 1901–3 (Washington, 1901–3); U.S. Dept. of Commerce and Labor, Commissioner-General of Immigration, *Annual Report . . . ,* 1904–13 (Washington, 1904–14); U.S. Dept. of Labor, Commissioner-General of Immigration, *Annual Report . . . ,* 1914–20 (Washington, 1915–20). During the fiscal years 1901–20 the Finnish immigrant arrivals totalled 194,412 and included 68,982 women and 125,430 men.

6 Based on data in U.S. Dept. of Commerce, Bureau of the Census, *Thirteenth Census of the United States Taken in the Year 1910, I: Population, 1910, General Report and Analysis* (Washington, 1913), 830, 866, and *Fourteenth Census of the United States Taken in the Year 1920,* II: *Population, 1920, General Report and Analytical Tables* (Washington, 1922), 693.

7 Following data taken from *ibid.,* p. 898.

WHITE STOCK OF FINNISH ORIGIN IN AMERICA

| *Nativity* | *1910* | *1920* |
|---|---|---|
| Foreign-born | 129,669 | 150,770 |
| Native-born of | | |
| both parents foreign-born | 76,261 | 130,083 |
| only one parent foreign-born | 5,096 | 15,423 |
| Total | 211,026 | 296,276 |

8 *Amerikan Sanomat* (Ashtabula, Ohio), December 22, 1898, p. 4; *Amerikan Suomalainen* (Hancock, Michigan), March 16, 1897, p. 3; "Tilasto Ishpemingin Suomalaisista Huhtikuulla 1907," *Raittius-Kalenteri wuodelle 1908* (Hancock, 1907), p. 31.

9 Nyrkkilehti of Tyyni Raittius Seura, Erie, Pennsylvania, February 11, 1915; May 11, 1916 (MS in present writer's possession).

10 J. J. Hoikka, "Siirtolaisuudesta awioliittoon nähden Amerikan suomalaisten kesken," *Kirkollinen Kalenteri Wuodelle 1905* (Hancock, 1904), pp. 140–42.

11 G. G. Rosenqvist, *Ehtoollispakko: Historiallisesti ja kriitillisesti valaistu* (Helsinki, 1903), pp. 4–6; *Kuparisaaren Sanomat* (Hancock), July 17, 1896, p. 3; *New Yorkin Uutiset* (Brooklyn, New York) , August 23, 1913, p. 4; "Avio-kysymys Malkosaarella," *Työmiehen illanvietto,* I (October 3, 1902), 42; Wäinö Paananen, *Uusia aatteita. Näytelmä yhdessä näytöksessä* (Fitchburg, Massachusetts, 1903); D. A. S., "Welwollisuuksistamme perhettämme, itseämme, kansaamme, maatamme ja Kristusta kohtaan," *Kirkollinen Kalenteri wuodelle 1915* (Hancock, 1914), pp. 40–45.

12 John Syrjamaki, "Mesabi Communities: A Study of Their Develop-

ment" (Doctoral Thesis, Yale University, 1940), pp. 175, 178.

13 Minute Book of Discussion Club of Toivola Raittius Seura, Crystal Falls, Michigan, for 1911–12, minutes of February 21 and March 13, 1912 (MS in possession of Finnish American Historical Library, Hancock). See also, P. Wuori, "Naiset auttamaan Kansan Opistoa!" *Ylöspäin: Kansalliskirkkokunnan kirkollinen Kalenteri vuodelle 1904* (Ironwood, Michigan, 1903), p. 17–19.

14 V. Rautanen, *Amerikan suomalainen kirkko* (Hancock, 1911), p. 189; *Evankelis-Luterilainen kansalliskirkko: Ensimmäiset 50 vuotta* (Ironwood, [1949]), p. 100.

15 ——a, "Sananen nais-asiasta," *Yhteistyössä: Kuparialueen raittiusliiton julkaisu* (Hancock, 1908), pp. 49–55; Augusta Riihimäki, "Sananen kansamme naisille," *Raittius-Kalenteri wuodelle 1906* (n.p., [1905]), pp. 154–57.

16 *Työwäen Ystäwä,* No. 5 (March 15, 1897), 4–5.

17 Nyrkkilehti of Tyyni Raittius Seura, May 1, 1913.

18 *New Yorkin Uutiset,* 1918: March 21, 1912, p. 12; January 12, p. 3; *Työmies* (Hancock), 1910: June 21, p. 3, July 23, p. 3; *Industrialisti* (Duluth), March 20, 1919, p. 3; *Raivaaja* (Fitchburg), January 1, 1917, p. 7; January 20, 1919, p. 3; *Siirtolainen* (Kaleva, Michigan), May 11, 1906, p. 7; *Amerikan Sanomat,* 1903: January 7, p. 8; January 21, p. 8; *Amerikan Kaiku* (Brooklyn), January 17, 1906, p. 7.

19 Elis Sulkanen, *Amerikan Suomalaisen Työväenliikkeen Historia* (Fitchburg, 1951), p. 309.

20 *New Yorkin Uutiset,* 1914: July 29, p. 5; August 8, p. 5; August 12, p. 5.

21 Sara Röyhy, *Murtunut nuoruus eli rikkaus voitti rakkauden* (Brooklyn, 1914).

22 N. N., *Rakkauden woima. Nowelli* (Brooklyn, 1896). This example of such works was translated and revised from the original.

23 Titles listed in *Raittius kertomuksia* (Ashtabula, n.d.).

24 A. F. Tanner, *Lapsikysymyksiä ja Ehkäisyoppi,* 5th ed. (New York, 1912). See also A. F. Tanner, *Elämän pitentämisestä,* 2d ed. (Brooklyn, 1915), for list of at least ten works by the same author on sex and marriage.

25 *Avioliitto ja Siitinelo: Tärkeitä lääketieteellisiä neuvoja naineille ja naimattomille* (Brooklyn, 1900), pp. 8, 28.

26 John Parkkila, *Siirtolaisen kannel: Kokoelma runoja* (Hancock, 1907), pp. 165–69; Notebook of Karl Siren, Virginia, Minnesota, and other places [*ca.* 1913–20] (MS in present writer's possession).

27 Bernarr MacFadden and Marion Malcolm, *Terveys, kauneus,*

*sukupuolielämä tytöstä naiseksi: Tytöille yksinkertaisia ohjeita, jotka tulevat olemaan arvokkaita heidän kehittyessään tytöstä naiseksi* (Worcester, Massachusetts, 1910), pp. 7–8, 16–18; Selma Jokela, *Nainen kodissa ja työmarkkinoilla* (Hancock, 1911), pp. 9–10, 19; Eva M. Vitkala, *Suomalainen Orjatyttö: Ainoa alkuperäinen suomalainen novelli valkosesta orjakaupasta* (Duluth, 1917). See also Eva Vitkala's denunciation of "male tyranny" over women in *New Yorkin Uutiset,* March 8, 1913, p. 2.

28 *Amerikan Suometar* (Hancock), July 16, 1902, p. 6; April 3, 1912, p. 5; H. Halonen, "Onko tarpeellista, että naiset käyvät koulua," *Kevätesikko: Suomi-opiston konventin kevätjulkaisu, I* (Hancock, 1907), 117–19; Rpp., "Naisillemme," *Kansan ääni: Raittiusmielisten kevätalbumi, I, 1899* (Brooklyn, 1899), pp. 65–66; *Suomalainen* (Rockport, Massachusetts), December 24, 1896, p. 4; M. Laitala, "Nykyisen [yh]teiskuntajärjestelmän vaikutus perheonneen," *Raivaajan Työvainiolta, I: Amerikan suomalaisten sosialistien kirjailija-alpumi* (Fitchburg, 1905), p. 63; Miina Autio, "Naisasiasta," Nyrkkilehti "Oras" of Pohjan Tähti Raittius Seura, Hancock, Michigan, November 3, 1907 (MS was in archives of Finnish Historical Society of Hiawatha Land, Crystal Falls, Michigan, but was lost or misplaced in the transfer of the archives to the Finnish American Historical Library).

29 Of course, views about marriage and family life began to change in Finland, particularly as a part of the general awakening in the cities. See Armas Nieminen, *Taistelu sukupuolimoraalista: Avioliitto; ja seksuaalikysymyksiä suomalaisen hengenelämän ja yhteiskunnan murroksessa sääty-yhteiskunnan ajoilta 1910-luvulle,* I (Helsinki, 1951).

30 During the years 1901–10, emigrants left behind in Finland 89,328 dependents who included 27,429 wives, 377 husbands, and 61,522 underage children. During this period 103,577 men and 55,255 women received passports to emigrate. Although no records were kept, probably a majority of the dependents later came to America. Statistics on dependents are taken from *Suomen virallinen tilasto. XXVIII. Siirtolaisuustilasto. 1,* 38, and *Suomen virallinen tilasto. XXVIII. Siirtolaisuustilasto. 17,* 18.

31 H. T., "Kertomus allekirjoittaneen lähetysmatkasta Wyoming'in, Oregon'in, Washington'in, Montana'n ja Etelä-Dakotan waltioissa asuttuneiden suomalaisten seassa," *Paimen-Sanomia,* II (December 3, 1890), 195–96; J. K. N., [Juho K. Nikander], "Siirtolaiskansamme juomarina ja raittiina," *Raittius-Kalenteri, 1897* (Brooklyn, 1896), pp. 38–40; Aini Kaukonen, "Juoppouden tiellä,"

*Wuonna 1898 Palkitut Kilpakirjoitukset,* S. K.-R.-W:seuran Kirjasia No. 7 (Hancock, 1898), 3–20; Selma Jokela, "Kuka hävittää kodin?" *Säkeniä,* V (September, 1911), 348–49; R. Pesola, "Koti," *Köyhälistön Nuija, V, 1911* (Hancock, 1910), 75–84; *Amerikan Suometar,* April 17, 1912, p. 5.

32 "Työväenasiain valiokunnan mietintö N:o 6 anomusehdotuksen johdosta, joka tarkoittaa tutkimuksen toimittamista siirtolaisuudesta," 1914.—Anomusmietintö No. 31, [Suomen eduskunta], *Valtiopäivät 1914 asiakirjat,* V, Pt. 2 (Helsinki, 1914), 31.

33 N. Toppari, "Mikä on ollut tarkoituksena?" *Raittius-Kalenteri wuodelle 1906,* p. 134.

34 A. W. Hawela, "Joulu-aattona," *Amerikan Suomalaisten kansankirjailiain kertomuksia. Amerikan Sanomain kilpailu kirjoituksia* (Ashtabula, 1899–1900), pp. 34–40.

35 Paul H. Landis, *Three Iron Mining Towns: A Study in Cultural Change* (Ann Arbor, 1938), pp. 32, 62; Syrjamaki, "Mesabi Communities," pp. 270–72, 317–19.

36 U.S. Immigration Commission, *Reports of the Immigration Commission: Immigrants in Industries,* Pt. 18: *Iron Ore Mining,* S. Doc. No. 633, Serial 5677, 61st Cong., 2d Sess. (Washington, 1911), 341; S. Ilmonen, "Lastunen länsi-Pennsylwanian Suomalaisten historiasta," *Voiton Kaiku: "Voiton Lippu" Raittiusseuran Juhlajulkaisu* (Fitchburg, 1908), pp. 12–13; Akseli Järnefelt [-Rauanheimo], *Suomalaiset Amerikassa* (Helsinki, 1899), p. 74.

37 K. O., "Ohion ja Pennsylvanian suomalainen raittiusliitto," *Raittius-kalenteri, 1914* (Fitchburg, 1913), pp. 174–75; J. H. J., "Suomalaisten kehitys Amerikassa," *Juhla-albumi Suomi-synoodin 25-vuotisjuhlan muistoksi, 1890–1915* (Hancock, 1915), p. 159; Hugo Hillilä, *Valinkauhassa* (Hancock, 1950), p. 15.

38 Artturi Leinonen, *Atlanttia ja Amerikkaa katselemassa* (Porvoo and Helsinki, 1938), p. 127; *Työmies,* October 3, 1913, p. 8; *Raivaaja,* July 28, 1913, p. 5; *Ashtabula Star and Beacon,* January 30, 1918, p. 1; *Siirtolainen* (Brooklyn), May 15, 1895, p. 6; S. Ilmonen, *Amerikan suomalaisten sivistyshistoria: Johtavia aatteita, harrastuksia, yhteispyrintöjä ja tapahtumia siirtokansan keskuudessa,* I (Hancock, 1930), 31.

39 Anders Nygren, *Agape and Eros: A Study of the Christian Idea of Love,* trans. by A. G. Hebert, Pt. 1 (London and New York, 1941), xi, xiii.

40 Rakso, "Sananen kodista," Nyrkkilehti "Oras" of Pohjan Tähti Raittius Seura, April 30, 1910.

41 Hilda Heikkilä, "Kertomus uljas koitto r.-seuran synnystä, kehityk-

sestä ja toiminnasta 25:n vuoden aikana," *Uljas koitto raittiusseuran joulujulkaisu 25:n vuotisen toiminnan muistoksi, 1915* (Fitchburg, n.d.), pp. 19–21.

42 Sulkanen, *Amerikan Suomalaisen Työväenliikkeen Historia,* p. 108.

43 *Toveritar* (Astoria), January 9, 1917, p. 7.

44 Uuras Saarnivaara, *Amerikan laestadiolaisuuden eli Apostolis-luterilaisuuden historia* (Ironwood, 1947), and *The History of the Laestadian or Apostolic-Lutheran Movement in America* (Ironwood, 1947); *Pöytäkirja Tehty Ap. Luth. Kristittyjen yleisistä kokouksista Republicissa, Michigan, Kesäk. 19, 20, 21, 22, ja 23 p. 1916* (Ironwood, 1916), p. 46.

45 Saarnivaara, *Amerikan laestadiolaisuuden eli Apostolis-luterilaisuuden historia,* pp. 344–45; J. Wargelin, "Jesaijan näky," *Raittius-Kalenteri wuodelle 1908* (Hancock, 1907), pp. 91–95; A. H., "Muutamia hawainnoita aikamme reformiluonteesta," *Uskonpuhdistuksen Muisto,* Suomi-Opiston Juhla-Julkaisut, I (October 1, 1908), pp. 12–13; E. P. Saaranen, "Parantajat, parantakaa itsenne!" *Kirkollinen Kalenteri wuodelle 1907* (Hancock, 1906), pp. 90–95; A. H., "Uutta taiwalta alottaessa," *Kirkollinen Kalenteri wuodelle 1921* (Hancock, 1920), pp. 31–32; *Suomen Ewankelis-Lutherisen Kirkon Katekismus* (Hancock, 1918), pp. 17–18; Joh. Bäck, "Kristityn suhde raittiusseuroihin," *Raittius-Kalenteri wuodelle 1902* (Hancock, 1901), pp. 35–73; S. Ilmonen, "Idän suom. ew.-lut. seurakuntain hengelliset juhlat," *Kirkollinen Kalenteri wuodelle 1906* (Hancock, 1905), pp. 148–59; J. J. Hoikka, "Kirkollisesta ja seurakunnallisesta järjestyksestä muutama sana yleensä," *Kirkollinen Kalenteri Wuodelle 1903* (Hancock, 1902), pp. 55–68; *Amerikan Suometar,* August 29, 1906, p. 4; June 14, 1911, p. 4; V. R., "Kirkko ja sosiaaliset kysymykset," *Kirkollinen Kalenteri wuodelle 1914* (Hancock, 1913), pp. 59–64; M. Kkk., "Mikä on Suomen kansan tulevaisuus Amerikassa?" *Raittius-kalenteri vuodelle 1899* (Brooklyn, 1898), pp. 95–96; *Lännetar* (Astoria), April 16, 1898, p. 2.

46 *Evankelis-Luterilainen kansalliskirkko, passim;* M. K., "Amerikan Suom. Ew. Luth. Kansalliskirkkokunnan synty ja kehitys," *Ev. Luth. Kansalliskirkkokunnan kalenteri karkausvuodelle 1908* (Fitchburg, 1907), pp. 64–74; *Amerikan Suom. Ev. Luth. Kansalliskirkon 25-Vuotisjulkaisu, 1898–1923* (Ironwood, 1923), *passim; Auttaja* (Ironwood), February 1, 1912, p. 4.

47 K. F. Henrikson, *Sosialismi ja Matti Kurikan teoria* (Fitchburg, 1902), p. 3.

48 F. V. K., "Raittiusväen ja kirkolisten [*sic*] suhteesta," *Raittius-kalenteri, 1912* (Fitchburg, 1911), pp. 159–66; M. Kiwisto, "Kristityn suhde raittiusseuroihin," *Kewät-Albumi, 1902* (Hancock, 1902), pp. 13–18; J. Katajamaa, "Sananen sosialismista ja sen suhteesta uskontoon," *Raittius-Kalenteri wuodelle 1907* (n.p., [1906]), pp. 129–48; H. T., "Mistä on ihmiskunnan parantaminen aijettawa?" *Raittius-kalenteri, 1898* (Hancock, 1897), pp. 38–42; Nyrkkilehti of Tyyni Raittius Seura, January 28, 1912; *New Yorkin Uutiset,* February 16, 1918, pp. 6–7.

49 W. A. Groenlund, "Alkoholi lääkärin kannalta," *Raittius-kalenteri, 1914,* pp. 73–74; *New Yorkin Uutiset,* February 9, 1918, p. 5; "Onko alkohooli myrkkyä?" *Raittiuslehti,* No. 7 (July, 1904), 1–3; K. A. Jurwa, *Kappale Kapakka elämää* (Ashtabula, n.d.); J. Kaminen, "Muutama sana raittiusopetuswälineistä," *Raiwaustyössä. Raittiuskursien, A. S. K.-R.-W.-Seuran ensimmäisten, johdosta* (Hancock, 1905), pp. 41–51; Olawi Laulaja, "Raittiustyön yhteiskunnallisesta merkityksestä," *ibid.,* pp. 79–84.

50 Based on chart attached to p. 384 in *Juhlajulkaisu suomalaisen kansallis-raittius-veljeysseuran 25-vuotisen toiminnan muistoksi* (Ishpeming, 1912).

51 Minute Book of Annual Meetings and Directors' Meetings of Suomalaisen Kansallis-Raittius-Weljeysseura for 1888–97, minutes of July 18, 1890 (MS in possession of Finnish American Historical Library).

52 H. T., "Teaatterista," *Raittius-kalenteri vuodelle 1899,* pp. 103–11; W. A——la, "Seuranäytelmät raittiusaatteen palveluksessa," *Juhlajulkaisu Ohion ja Pennsylvanian raittiusliiton vuosijuhlaan vuonna 1913* (Hancock, n.d.), p. 17; S. Ilmonen, "Muutamia raittiustyön menestymisehtoja," *Raittiuskalenteri, 1913* (Hancock, 1912), pp. 93–94; K. V. M., "Katsauksia," *Raittius-kalenteri, 1914,* p. 51; "Raittius Seura 'Onnen Alku:n' Säännöt," Minute Book of Onnen Alku Raittius Seura, Neihart, Montana, for 1899–1907 (MS in possession of Finnish American Historical Library).

53 T. Tainio, *Juoppouden Syitä* (Fitchburg, 1905); *Pöytäkirja Amerikan Suomalaisten Sosialistiosastojen Edustajakokouksesta, Hibbingissä, Minn., Elokuun 1–7 päivinä 1906* (Hancock, 1907), pp. 68–79; *Kolmannen Amerikan Suomalaisen Sosialistijärjestön edustajakokouksen pöytäkirja, Kokous pidetty Hancockissa, Mich. 23–30 p. elok, 1909* (Fitchburg, n.d.), pp. 163–79.

54 M. Hahl, *Lihan evankeliumi: Moraalin arvostelua* (Fitchburg, 1914); Alex Halonen, *Sosialismin Perusteet* ([Fitchburg], 1907); Antti Kilkkinen, "Sosialistit vai kapitalistiko hävyttömiä?" *Taisto:*

*Ashtabulan Suom. Sosialisti Osaston Juhannusjulkaisu* (Fitchburg, [1908?]), pp. 42–46; *Työmies,* February 10, 1910, p. 2.

55 *Kolmannen Amerikan Suomalaisen Sosialistijärjestön edustajakokouksen pöytäkirja,* pp. 41–44, 59–62; *Pöytäkirja Amerikan s. s. järjestön itäpiirin edustajakokouksesta joka pidettiin Fitchburgissa, Mass., s. s. kustannusyhtiön (raivaajan) talolla helmikuun 24, 25 ja 26 p:nä 1917* (Fitchburg, n.d.), pp. 19–20, 55, 67; *Amerikan S. S. järjestön Länsipiirin toisen piirikokouksen pöytäkirja Pidetty Astoriassa, Ore. huhtik. 16–18 p:nä 1912* (Astoria, n.d.), p. 33; *Toveritar,* 1916: January 11, p. 7; January 18, p. 7; *Työmies,* August 18, 1910, p. 7; December 4, 1913, p. 3.

56 *Raivaaja,* December 15, 1910, p. 4; *Sosialisti* (Duluth), January 13, 1915, p. 1.

57 E. M. V——ja, "Voimistelemaan," *Kesäjulkaisu, 1917,* O., Pa. & W.Va. suomalaisen raittiusliitto (Hancock, n.d.), pp. 14–15; "Urheilun alalta," *Säkeniä,* V (September, 1911), 376–77; Victor Sunell, "Yleispiirteitä urheilun merkityksestä työväenluokan keskuudessa," *Urheilu-viesti, II, Julkaisu urheilu- ja voimisteluharrastuksen elvyttämiseksi Amerikan suomalaisten keskuudessa* (Hancock, 1910), pp. 57–58; *Raivaaja,* December 16, 1909, p. 5; Victor Sunell, "Lääketieteen ja voimistelun vertailua," *Raivaajan työvainiolta, V. Raivaajan vuosijulkaisu* (Fitchburg, 1909), pp. 87–92; [Hilda Hannu], "Urheilua on harrastettava," Nyrkkilehti of Tyyni Raittius Seura, February, 1914.

58 "Painiurheilun alalta," *Urheilu-viesti, II,* pp. 40–48.

59 *Työmies,* November 29, 1910, p. 2.

60 J. K., "Patenttilääkkeet," *Kirkollinen Kalenteri wuodelle 1911* (Hancock, 1910), p. 202.

61 *Kansan Henki,* IV (June, 1919), 39; Louis Kuhne, *Uusi Lääketiede eli Oppi tautien yhtenäisyydestä ja niiden siihen perustuwasta parantamisesta ilman lääkkeitä ja leikkauksia,* trans. into Finnish by Anna Kurimo, 6th ed. (Hämeenlinna, 1911).

62 *Amerikan Suometar,* June 3, 1903, p. 5; Martin Hendrickson, *Muistelmia Kymmenvuotisesta Raivaustyöstäni* (Fitchburg, 1909), p. 10; *New Yorkin Uutiset,* April 15, 1914, p. 4; *Työmies,* 1913: July 25, p. 1; November 11, p. 8; November 28, p. 5; December 4, p. 8; *Pohjan Tähti* (Fitchburg), April 19, 1906, p. 6; *Amerikan Uutiset* (Calumet, Michigan), July 7, 1898, p. 4.

63 J. H. J., "Suomalaisten kehitys Amerikassa," p. 162; Halonen, *Sosialismin Perusteet,* pp. 7–8; *Päiwän Uutiset* (Calumet), July 28, 1898, p. 2; *Amerikan Uutiset,* October 22, 1896, p. 4; July 7, 1898, p. 8; March 14, 1900, p. 3; *Lännen Uutiset* (Astoria), March 29,

1906, p. 7; January 30, 1908, p. 6; *Paimen-Sanomia,* IX (December 15, 1897), 396; X (June 22, 1898), 196; *Työmies,* January 17, 1905, p. 5.

64 *Amerikan Uutiset,* July 7, 1898, p. 4; *New Yorkin Uutiset,* September 14, 1920, p. 2; *Raivaaja,* January 22, 1916, p. 6; *Työmies,* October 26, 1913, p. 2.

65 P. Vuori, "Paha siemen," *Evankelinen lehti: Kesäkukkia* ([Fitchburg], 1906), pp. 22–23; *Raivaaja,* July 7, 1913, p. 5; May 31, 1916, p. 2; *Amerikan Suometar,* October 2, 1912, p. 1; *New Yorkin Uutiset,* September 30, 1920, p. 3.

66 *Raivaaja,* April 8, 1912, p. 5; *Työmies,* March 15, 1910, p. 5; *New Yorkin Uutiset,* January 16, 1915, p. 6; *Amerikan Suometar,* September 18, 1907, p. 4; *Amerikan Uutiset,* October 22, 1896, p. 6; *Paimen-Sanomia,* VII (August 7, 1895), 251.

*Chapter VI*

1 ——a, "Tosioloihin perustuwa kuwaus elämästä," *Raittius-Kalenteri wuodelle 1910* (Hancock, Michigan, 1909), p. 92.

2 Väinö Voionmaa, "Suomen työväenliike," *Oma maa: Tietokirja Suomen kodeille,* ed. E. G. Palmén *et al.,* VI (Porvoo, 1911), 886; Antti Mikkola, "Äänioikeusasia," *Kansanwalistus-Seuran Kalenteri, 1906,* Pt. II (Helsinki, 1905), 48–60; *Äänioikeusasia perustuslakivaliokunnassa valtiopäivillä 1904–05* (Helsinki, 1905), *passim;* Arthur Reade, *Finland and the Finns* (New York, 1915), pp. 196–97; Y. K. Laine, *Suomen poliittisen työväenliikkeen historia, I: Kansan valtaisuuden läpimurto* (Helsinki, 1946), 39–40; *Suomen historian käsikirja,* ed. Arvi Korhonen, II (Porvoo and Helsinki, 1949), 385–86; *Finland and Its Geography: An American Geographical Society Handbook,* ed. Raye R. Platt (New York, 1955), pp. 54–56.

3 *Alexandra Gripenberg's A Half Year in the New World: Miscellaneous Sketches of Travel in the United States (1888),* trans. and ed. by Ernest J. Moyne (Newark, Delaware, 1954), p. 167.

4 H. Tanner, "Kertomus allekirjoittaneen lähetysmatkasta Wyoming'in y. m. waltiossa asuttuneiden suomalaisten seassa," *Paimen-Sanomia,* III (January 28, 1891), 2–3; K. H., "Väärän wapauden ylistyksestä," *ibid.,* IV (November 16, 1892), 2; [H. T.], "Arwostelua sanomalehdistöstä," *ibid.,* V (September 13, 1893), 2–4; Joh. Bäck, *Raittiusesitelmiä* (New York Mills, Minnesota, 1897), pp. 40–51; K. W. Ojajärwi, *Wiisi Raittiusesitelmää. Ihanteellisuutta työssä ja aatteessa* (Hancock, 1898), p. 5.

5 *New Yorkin Uutiset* (Brooklyn, New York), January 17, 1918, p. 6.

6 *Ibid.*, April 10, 1912, p. 5; *Amerikan Sanomat* (Ashtabula, Ohio), November 9, 1899, p. 4.

7 *Päivälehti* (Calumet, Michigan), March 5, 1902, p. 2.

8 *Sankarin maine* (Hancock), August 27, 1880, p. 2.

9 *Nuori Suomi: Kaunokirjallinen Joulualbumi, I, 1903* (Brooklyn, n.d.), 5–6.

10 A. Könönen, "Piirteitä Fitchburgin ew. luth. seurakunnan waiheista," *Ev. Luth. Kansalliskirkkokunnan kalenteri karkausvuodelle 1908* (Fitchburg, Massachusetts, 1907), pp. 34–36; Minute Book of Annual Meetings and Directors' Meetings of Suomalaisen Kansallis-Raittius-Weljeysseura for 1908–10, minutes of July 28, 1909, and Minute Book of Annual Meetings and Directors' Meetings of Suomalaisen Raittius-Ystäwäin Yhdistys for 1890–1902, minutes of June 22–23, 1897 (MSS in possession of Finnish American Historical Library, Hancock).

11 J. L. Ollila, "Kuparialueen kauppaloista ja suomalaisesta asutuksesta," *Amerikan Suometar, 1899–1919: Muistojulkaisu* (Hancock, 1919), p. 124; Paul H. Landis, *Three Iron Mining Towns: A Study in Cultural Change* (Ann Arbor, 1938), pp. 33–35, 63; *Eveleth News* (Minnesota), April 2, 1914, p. 1; *History of the Finnish Settlement in Brown and Dickey Counties of South and North Dakota, 1881–1955* (New York Mills, 1956), p. 11; Hans R. Wasastjerna, *Minnesotan suomalaisten historia* (Duluth, 1957), pp. 470, 524–26, 550, 553, 658, 686.

12 Landis, *Three Iron Mining Towns,* pp. 36–40, 88–89.

13 *Strike in the Copper Mining District of Michigan: Letter from the Secretary of Labor Transmitting in Response to a Senate Resolution of January 29, 1914, a Report in regard to the Strike of Mine Workers in the Michigan Copper District which Began on July 23, 1913,* S. Doc. No. 381, 63d Cong., 2d Sess., Serial 6575 (Washington, 1914), pp. 135–36.

14 *Amerikan Suomalainen* (Hancock), April 2, 1897, p. 2.

15 A. L., "Häwäistyksen päiwät," *Raittius-Kalenteri wuodelle 1907* (n.p., [1906]), pp. 158–70; *Wage Slave* (Hancock), March 26, 1909, p. 1; T. Hiltunen, "Eräs kymmenvuotis-muistelma," *Toveri kymmenvuotias, 1907–1917: Muistojulkaisu* (Astoria, Oregon, 1917), pp. 114–15; *Copper Country Evening News* (Calumet), 1907: July 29, pp. 1, 4; August 3, pp. 1, 5; *Ely Miner* (Minnesota), August 23, 1907, p. 4; *Duluth News Tribune,* July 22, 1907, p. 1; *Mesaba Ore* (Hibbing, Minnesota), August 24, 1907, p. 5.

16 Based on figures in William B. Gates, Jr., *Michigan Copper and Boston Dollars: An Economic History of the Michigan Copper Mining Industry* (Cambridge, 1951), pp. 132–33.

17 *Conditions in the Copper Mines of Michigan: Hearings before a Subcommittee of the Committee on Mines and Mining; House of Representatives, Sixty-Third Congress, Second Session, Pursuant to H. Res. 387, a Resolution Authorizing and Directing the Committee on Mines and Mining to Make an Investigation of Conditions in the Copper Mines of Michigan,* Pt. I (Washington, 1914), 401–9, 453–58.

18 *Complete Report of the Chairman of the Committee on Public Information, 1917: 1918: 1919* (Washington, 1920), pp. 85–86.

19 S. Ilmonen, *Amerikan suomalaisten sivistyshistoria: Johtavia aatteita, harrastuksia, yhteispyrintöjä ja tapahtumia siirtokansan keskuudessa,* II (Hancock, 1931), 8; *New Yorkin Uutiset,* June 27, 1918, p. 6.

20 *Raivaaja* (Fitchburg), April 2, 1914, p. 4; F. J. Syrjälä, *Historia-aiheita Ameriikan Suomalaisesta Työväenliikkeestä* (Fitchburg, [1925]), pp. 138–39; Elis Sulkanen, *Amerikan Suomalaisen Työvaenliikkeen Historia* (Fitchburg, 1951), pp. 221–22.

21 *Industrialisti* (Duluth), May 8, 1918, p. 3; *Ashtabula Star and Beacon* (Ohio), June 6, 1918, p. 1; Sulkanen, *Amerikan Suomalaisen Työväenliikkeen Historia,* pp. 205–6, 222–23; *New Yorkin Uutiset,* February 21, 1918, p. 5; Harrison George, *The I.W.W. Trial: Story of the Greatest Trial in Labor's History by One of the Defendants* (Chicago, [1918]), pp. 41, 147–48, 190; *Duluth News Tribune,* September 20, 1918, p. 8; Väinö Wesman, "Suomalaisten joukkovangitsemisesta ja heidän puolustuksestaan," *Ahjo,* II (September, 1917), 65–68.

22 *New Yorkin Uutiset,* April 11, 1917, p. 4; May 11, 1918, p. 4; V. H. Gran, "Liikemiestemme Lojaalisuus," *Kansan Henki,* II (December, 1917), 34; O. J. Larson, "The Loyalty of Finnish-Americans," *The Finland Sentinel,* I (July 4, 1918), 37–39; *Duluth Herald,* November 12, 1917, p. 2.

23 Impi Liisa Miettinen, "Naisten äänioikeustaistelu ja voitto Amerikan Yhdysvalloissa," *Siirtokansan kalenteri, 1921* (Duluth, 1920), p. 183.

24 Appropriate publications for naturalization and learning English are listed in John I. Kolehmainen, *The Finns in America: A Bibliographical Guide to Their History* (Hancock, 1947), pp. 100–104.

25 U.S. Dept. of Commerce, Bureau of the Census, *Thirteenth Census of the United States Taken in the Year 1910,* I: *Population, 1910, General Report and Analysis* (Washington, 1913), 1072, and *Fourteenth Census of the United States Taken in the Year 1920,* II: *Population, 1920, General Report and Analytical Tables* (Washington, 1922), 805–6. In 1910 of the Finnish males who were

twenty-one years and older 30.6 percent were naturalized, 15.9 percent had first papers, 45.9 percent were aliens, and 7.5 percent were unreported.

26 U.S. Immigration Commission, *Reports of the Immigration Commission: Abstracts of Reports of the Immigration Commission with Conclusions and Recommendations and Views of the Minority,* S. Doc. 747, Serial 5865, 61st Cong., 3d Sess., I (Washington, 1911), 484–85, 488–89; U.S. Industrial Relations Commission, Report of Investigation of the Michigan Copper District Strike, untitled processed report prepared by Luke Grant (Hancock, February 11, 1914), p. 4 (copy in possession of State Historical Society of Wisconsin, Madison); *Wage Slave* (Hancock), February 7, 1908, p. 1; *Raivaaja,* February 28, 1912, p. 2; G. O. Virtue, *The Minnesota Iron Ranges,* Bulletin of the Bureau of Labor, U.S. Dept. of Commerce and Labor, XIX, No. 84 (Washington, 1909), 354; John I. Kolehmainen, "Suomalainen rotu punnittavana yhdysvaltalaisessa oikeudessa," *Siirtokansan kalenteri, 1949* (Duluth, [1948]), pp. 39–45; U.S. Dept. of Commerce, Bureau of the Census, *Thirteenth Census of the United States Taken in the Year 1910,* I, 1068–69.

27 The local nature of Finnish office-holding is shown by the biographical sketches in *Amerikan suomalaisia: Muotokuvia ja lyhyitä elämäkerrallisia tietoja,* comp. by Werner Nikander (Hancock, 1927). See also Ilmonen, *Amerikan suomalaisten sivistyshistoria,* II, 143–53.

28 *Työmies* (Hancock), April 16, 1910, p. 3; William J. Schereck, "Collecting Wisconsin Ethnic Material," *Wisconsin Magazine of History,* XXXIX (Summer, 1956), 265. The present writer has been unable to find further information on the official records reportedly kept in Finnish.

29 C. H. S., "Lakimies O. J. Larson," *Kansan Henki,* II (June, 1917), 4–6.

30 Kolehmainen, *The Finns in America,* p. 127; *Kuparisaaren Sanomat* (Hancock), November 6, 1896, p. 2; *Amerikan Uutiset* (Calumet), August 16, 1904, p. 2; *Raivaaja,* January 22, 1914, p. 3; *New Yorkin Uutiset,* July 5, 1913, p. 2; 1914: November 14, p. 6; November 28, p. 6; *Päivälehti,* October 29, 1904, p. 4; *Siirtolainen* (Duluth), March 2, 1917, p. 6; *Amerikan Suometar* (Hancock), 1911: March 22, p. 5; March 29, p. 3; *Suomalaisille äänestäjille,* handbill (n.p., [1900]).

31 M. P.-Mäki, "Juho Heikki Jasberg," *Kirkollinen kalenteri vuodeksi 1930* (Hancock, 1929), p. 186; "Oscar J. Larson," *Kansan Kuwalehti,* No. 2 (February, 1901), 19; *Lännetar* (Astoria), November 1, 1900, p. 4; *Amerikan Uutiset,* February 3, 1898, p. 4.

32 Such successful officeholders are cited in Juuso Hirvonen, *Michiganin kuparialue ja suomalaiset siirtolaiset* (Duluth, 1920), pp. 124–74.

33 *Työwäen Ystäwä,* No. 5 (March 15, 1897), 1.

34 *Kuparisaaren Sanomat,* 1896: October 30, pp. 1–2, November 6, p. 2; *Amerikan Uutiset,* October 31, 1900, p. 8; *Päivälehti,* October 15, 1904, p. 2.

35 *New Yorkin Uutiset,* 1912: August 14, p. 4; September 11, p. 4; *Amerikan Suometar,* 1912: July 31, p. 1; October 16, p. 4; October 23, p. 4; *Raivaaja,* May 21, 1912, p. 2..

36 S. Ilmonen, "Amerikan suomalaisen raittiusliikkeen historia," *Juhlajulkaisu suomalaisen kansallis-raittius-veljeysseuran 25-vuotisen toiminnan muistoksi* (Ishpeming, Michigan, 1912), pp. 120, 122, 130–31, 142, 148, 225–26, 265; *Auttaja* (Ironwood, Michigan), November 24, 1910, p. 1; Minute Books of Annual Meetings and Directors' Meetings of Suomalaisen Kansallis-Raittius-Weljeysseura for 1910–12 and for 1916–19, minutes of July 29, 1910; August 8–9, 1912; and July 11, 1918 (MSS in possession of Finnish American Historical Library).

37 Matti Lehtonen, "Sananen yleisestä mielipiteestä ja elämän tavoista," *Rauhan kilpi kalenteri* (Chisholm, Minnesota, [1910?], p. 65; A. J., "Raittiuspuolueen waalitulokset," *Raittiuslehti,* No. 11 (November 20, 1896), 1–2; J. W. Lilius, "Raittiustyö ja politiikka," *ibid.,* No. 4 (April 25, 1908), 1–3; Raittiusseuralainen, "Taisteluun," Nyrkkilehti of Tyyni Raittius Seura, Erie, Pennsylvania, May 11, 1916 (MS in present writer's possession).

38 M. S., "Kuiva Michigan," *Raittius-Kalenteri Vuodelle 1919* (Ishpeming, 1918), pp. 86–89; Salomon Ilmonen, "Mikä tulee raittiuswäen suhde olla kieltolakiin?" *Raittius-Kalenteri wuodelle 1903* (Hancock, 1902), pp. 31–60; *Kieltolaki voittoon! Kaikki muut väkijuomalait jo sitä ennen käytäntöön!* (Hancock, 1908), *passim;* J. Kaminen, "Vakijuomakysymys yhteiskunnallisena kysymyksenä," *Yhteistyössä: Kuparialueen raittiusliiton julkaisu* (Hancock, 1908), pp. 26–41.

39 *Pohjan Tähti* (Fitchburg), August 17, 1904, p. 2; February 1, 1905, p. 1.

40 *Työmies,* March 26, 1910, p. 6; *Raivaaja,* 1910: May 5, pp. 4–5; June 7, p. 4; *Sosialisti* (Duluth), July 2, 1914, pp. 2–3; January 13, 1915, p. 1, 3; Leo Laukki, *Teolliseen yhteiskuntaan* (Duluth, 1917).

41 F. J. S——ä [Syrjälä], "Vaalitaistelu v. 1912," *Tietokäsikirja, 1913: Amerikan suomalaisille* (Fitchburg, n.d.), pp. 66–87; *Työmies,* 1904: August 16, p. 3; September 13, p. 2; July 18, 1905, p. 6;

October 11, 1910, p. 7; *Raivaaja,* December 1, 1910, p. 4; November 2, 1912, p. 2.

*Chapter VII*

1 Joh. Bäck, "Kirkollinen asemamme Amerikassa," *Kirkollinen Kalenteri wuodelle 1907* (Hancock, Michigan, 1906), p. 48.
2 Toimitus, "Lukijalle," *Tiedon henki,* I (May, 1911), 10.
3 Following data taken from U.S. Dept. of Commerce, Bureau of the Census, *Thirteenth Census of the United States Taken in the Year 1910,* I: *Population, 1910, General Report and Analysis* (Washington, 1913), 834–39, and *Fourteenth Census of the United States Taken in the Year 1920,* II: *Population, 1920, General Report and Analytical Tables* (Washington, 1922), 698.

DISTRIBUTION IN AMERICA OF FOREIGN-BORN FINNS

| *State* | *1900* | *1910* | *1920* |
|---|---|---|---|
| Michigan | 18,910 | 31,144 | 30,096 |
| Minnesota | 10,727 | 26,637 | 29,108 |
| Massachusetts | 5,104 | 10,744 | 14,570 |
| New York | 4,048 | 8,760 | 12,504 |
| Ohio | 2,814 | 3,988 | 6,406 |
| California | 2,763 | 6,159 | 7,053 |
| Washington | 2,732 | 8,719 | 11,863 |
| Wisconsin | 2,198 | 5,705 | 6,757 |
| Oregon | 2,131 | 4,734 | 6,050 |
| Montana | 2,103 | 4,111 | 3,577 |
| Pennsylvania | 988 | 2,413 | 2,818 |
| Illinois | 859 | 2,390 | 3,080 |
| New Jersey | 367 | 1,640 | 2,109 |

4 *Amerikan Sanomat* (Ashtabula, Ohio), May 17, 1898, p. 2; March 30, 1899, p. 5.
5 *Lännen Uutiset* (Astoria, Oregon), December 7, 1905, p. 2.
6 "Amerikalainen osuustoiminta ja suomalaisten suhtautuminen siihen," *Pelto ja koti,* III (December 1, 1914), 451.
7 Minute Book of Marquetti Kauntin Raittius Liito for 1907–12, minutes of January 6, 1908, and September 25, 1910 (MS in possession of Finnish American Historical Library, Hancock).
8 M. Kkk, "Mikä on Suomen kansan tulevaisuus Amerikassa?" *Raittius-kalenteri vuodelle 1899* (Brooklyn, New York, 1898), pp. 98–99; P. K——nen, "Työmme ja aseet," *Tartu Kiinni,* Suomi-Opiston Juhla-Julkaisu ([Hancock, 1911?]), p. 32; *H——a* [Historia] *K. R. Y. M. Kokouksessa Ishpemingissä, Mich. Elok. 22, 23, 24, 25 ja 26 p:nä 1910* (Ishpeming, Michigan, 1910), pp. 26–32.
9 K——nen, "Työmme ja aseet," p. 31; Evert Määttälä, *Miksi tahdon*

*olla suomalainen?* (Hancock, 1915), pp. 159–60; J. W. Lähde, "Säilyttäkäämme nuorisomme suomalaisena, siveellisenä ja raittiina," *Raittuskalenteri, 1913* (Hancock, 1912), p. 139.

10 K——nen, "Työmme ja aseet," p. 31; "Pastori K. L. Tolosen juhlapuhe Suomi-Opiston nurkkakivijuhlassa opistopaikalla toukok. 30 p. 1899," *Suomi-opiston albumi, 1896–1906* (Hancock, 1906), p. 136; A. M., "Säilyttäwätkö Amerikan suomalaiset kansallisuutensa?" *Kansan Ääni: Raittiusmielisten Kewätalbumi, III, 1901* (Hancock, 1901), pp. 56–59; "Amerikan suomalaisten Kaleva-Seurat," *Jouluviesti, 1946* (Brooklyn, [1946]), p. 34; S. Ilmonen, "Muutamia raittiustyön menestymisehtoja," *Raittiuskalenteri, 1913*, p. 98; Juuso Hirvonen, *Michiganin kuparialue ja suomalaiset siirtolaiset* (Duluth, 1920), p. 67; "Uusi käänne ja rauhankokous," *Rauhankokous ja pääpiirteitä Amerikan suomalaisten raittiustyön historiasta* (Hancock, 1908), pp. 71–72; *New Yorkin Uutiset* (Brooklyn), January 21, 1914, p. 4; *Siirtolainen* (Duluth), July 9, 1919, p. 2.

11 *New Yorkin Uutiset,* November 9, 1920, p. 4; Antti Lepistö, "Paljon työtä suomalaisuuden hyväksi," *Siirtokansan kalenteri, 1920* (Duluth, 1919), pp. 122–24; *Sunday Herald* (Boston), December 18, 1904, magazine section, p. 4; Eldridge Mix, "The Pilgrims of Today—The Finns," *The Worcester Magazine,* VII (January, 1904), 17; Edward Alsworth Ross, "The Lesser Immigrant Groups in America," *The Century Magazine,* LXXXVIII (October, 1914), 934; Minnesota House of Representatives, "Hearings Before Committee on Labor and Labor Legislation: Labor Troubles in Northern Minnesota," carbon copy of transcript, II (St. Paul, 1917), 751–52 (MS in John Lind Papers, Minnesota Historical Society, St. Paul), *Times* (Chicago), June 12, 1886, p. 13; P. B. McDonald, "The Michigan Copper-Miners," *The Outlook,* CVI (February 7, 1914), 298.

12 *New Yorkin Uutiset,* August 8, 1914, p. 6; S. Koskela, "Kansamme maineen kohottajia," *Airut, I: Sibelius seuran julkaisu* (Duluth, 1917), 32; J. Laurila, "Eräs huomioni," *Juhlajulkaisu suomalaisen kansallis-raittius-veljeysseuran 25-vuotisen toiminnan muistoksi* (Ishpeming, 1912), pp. 368–69; S. Ilmonen, *Historiallisia Kuvauksia Juoppoudesta ja Raittiudesta* (Calumet, n.d.), pp. 1–3.

13 U.S. Immigration Commission, *Reports of the Immigration Commission: Immigrants in Industries,* Pt. 18: *Iron Ore Mining,* S. Doc. No. 633, Serial 5677, 61st Cong., 2d Sess. (Washington, 1911), 340, 398; "Impending Labor Changes in Lake Superior Region," *The Engineering and Mining Journal,* XCVII (April 18, 1914), 793–94; "The Proposed Elimination of the Finns," *ibid.* (May 2,

1914), 920; Ilmari Varjo, "Nuorisomme siveellinen tilanne," *Raittius-kalenteri, 1916* (Duluth, [1915]), p. 99; *New Yorkin Uutiset*, May 13, 1914, p. 6; Herman Montagu Donner, "Problem of the Finns in America," *The National Civic Federation Review*, IV (May 15, 1919), 14; John Wargelin, *The Americanization of the Finns* (Hancock, 1924), pp. 13, 168–69; *Mesaba Ore* (Hibbing, Minnesota), July 27, 1907, p. 2; *Siirtolainen*, October 12, 1917, p. 4; November 5, 1919, p. 2.

14 *Raivaaja* (Fitchburg, Massachusetts), 1911: September 8, p. 5; September 12, p. 5; December 18, p. 5; July 16, 1912, pp. 2–3; April 15, 1914, p. 4; J. W. Kannasto, "Voiko suomalainen kansallisuus säilyä Amerikassa?" *Taisto: Ashtabulan Suom. Sosialisti Osaston Juhannusjulkaisu* (Fitchburg, [1908?]), p. 48–52; *National Convention of the Socialist Party Held at Indianapolis, Ind., May 12 to 18, 1912* (Chicago, n.d.), p. 239.

15 "Pääpiirteitä Amerikan suomalaisten raittiusliikkeestä," *Rauhankokous*, p. 56; *New Yorkin Uutiset*, August 8, 1914, p. 8; Elina, "Siirtolaisten puolesta," *Tiedon henki*, I (September, 1910), 15; Aho-Kunnas, "Mistä se johtuu?" *ibid.*, 15–19, and (October, 1910), 17–21; Clemens Niemi, *Americanization of the Finnish People in Houghton County, Michigan* (Duluth, 1921), p. 43. Niemi's work was originally prepared as a Master's Thesis at the University of Chicago in 1919.

16 *New Yorkin Uutiset*, August 8, 1914, p. 5; *Raivaaja*, January 20, 1910, p. 7; January 12, 1915, p. 3.

17 Määttälä, *Miksi tahdon olla suomalainen?* p. 4; Lähde, "Säilyttäkäämme nuorisomme," pp. 138, 140; W. Rautanen, "Miksi Suomi-Opistoa muutamat wastustawat," *Kirkollinen Kalenteri wuodelle 1911* (Hancock, 1910), p. 103; Minute Book of Annual Meetings and Directors' Meetings of Suomalaisen Kansallis-Raittius-Weljeysseura for 1910–12, minutes of July 25–28, 1911 (MS in possession of Finnish American Historical Library).

18 A. R., "Salaseuroista," *Kalevainen*, VI (February, 1919), 10.

19 *New Yorkin Uutiset*, February 12, 1920, p. 6; *Amerikan Suometar* (Hancock), February 7, 1912, p. 4.

20 The third book was a translation which ended its coverage in 1891. Its last paragraph, which mentioned the Populists for the first time, merely said that the future would determine their success. See *Lyhykäinen Yhdyswaltain Historia. Pohjois-Amerikan ensimäisestä löytämisestä nykyaikaan asti* (New York Mills, Minnesota, 1891). A fourth book also appeared but it only covered the period through 1787. See T. Vallenius, *Amerikan Yhdysvaltojen synty* (Hancock, 1904).

21 *Yhdyswaltain Historia* (Ashtabula, 1908).

22 *Yhdysvaltain Historia* ([Brooklyn], 1897; 2d ed., Kaleva, Michigan, 1906).

23 J. Wargelin, "Puhe," *Kirkollinen Kalenteri wuodelle 1910* (Hancock, 1910), p. 79; S. Ilmonen, *Piirteitä Yhdysvaltain Presidenttien uskonnollisestä elämästä* (Hämeenlinna, 1909); S. Ilmonen, *Amerikan ensimäiset suomalaiset eli Delawaren siirtokunnan historia* (Hancock, 1916).

24 S. Ilmonen, *Abraham Lincoln raittiusmiehenä ja lyhyitä piirteitä hänen elämänkerrastaan* (Pori, 1909), p. 5; "Historian opetuksia. Taistelu tarpeellista," *Aseita raittiustaistelussa* (Fitchburg, 1908), pp. 7–9; "Raittiuskurssi-kirjat," *Raittius-Kalenteri wuodelle 1910* (Hancock, 1909), p. 43; Jacob P. Niemi, "Piirteitä raittiustyön historiasta ja kunnallisista kieltolakioloista Amerikan Yhdyswalloissa," *ibid.*, p. 73–91; A. A. Granfelt, *Benjamin Rush ja raittiusliikkeen aikaisimmat waiheet,* Raittiuden Ystäwien Kirjasia No. 13 (Helsinki, 1891).

25 Morris Hillquit, *Yhdysvaltain sosialismin historia* (Fitchburg, 1912); James O'Neil [Oneal], *Työn orjat: Lehtia Amerikan työväen historiasta* (Astoria, 1913); A. M. Simons, *Luokkataistelut Amerikassa* (Hancock, 1908; 2d ed., 1913).

26 *Raivaaja,* July 8, 1911, p. 2; November 14, 1912, p. 2; *Työmies* (Hancock), November 8, 1913, p. 4.

27 *Raivaaja,* July 11, 1913, p. 5; June 11, 1914, p. 6; *Työmies,* November 14, 1913, p. 6; *Amerikan Sanomat,* November 10, 1898, p. 4; August 24, 1899, p. 6; Hilja Kruka-Gran, "Tervehdys Aallottaren Tuvalta, Duluth, Minn.," *Kalevainen,* VII (February, 1920), 21–22; A. Riippa, "Heimomme tulevaisuus Amerikassa," *ibid.*, III (February, 1917), 3; J. Wargelin, "Suomi-opiston oppilasluwun kohottamisesta," *Juhannuslehti,* Suomi-Opiston Juhla-Julkaisut, XII (June 10, 1919), 11; Minute Book of Annual Meetings and Directors' Meetings of Suomalaisen Kansallis-Raittius-Weljeysseura for 1912–16, minutes of July 27–30, 1915 (MS in possession of Finnish American Historical Library).

28 Lizzie Ahlberg-Luoto, "Muistelmia raittiusseura murtajan toiminnasta San Franciscossa, Calif.," *Y. s. k. v. ja s.-liiton 50-vuotishistoria: Muistojulkaisu* (Duluth, 1937), pp. 168–69; *New Yorkin Uutiset,* October 29, 1913, p. 4; August 8, 1914, p. 6; February 20, 1915, p. 7; Milma S. Lappala, "Suomalainen osasto St. Louis kauntin näyttelyssä Hibbingissä, Minn. syyskuulla 1920," *Siirtokansan kalenteri, 1921* (Duluth, [1920]), pp. 187–89; J. A. Karkkainen, "Suomalaisen siirtokansan kansallisesta tehtävästä

Amerikassa," *Kansan Henki,* I (December, 1916), 4–5; Impi Liisa Miettinen, "Suomalaisen sivistyksen tunnetuksi tekeminen Amerikassa," *Kalevainen,* VII (February, 1920), 11–12.

29 *Amerikan Suometar,* February 19, 1908, p. 5; *Calumet News* (Michigan) March 1, 1913, pp. 3, 4; *Duluth Herald,* November 13, 1917, p. 8; *Sosialismi—Antisosialismi* ([Hancock? 1914?]); *Antisosialistiliiton Perus- ja Sivusäännöt* (Hancock, 1915); "Big Copper Barons of Northern Michigan," *The Miners' Magazine,* XV (April 1, 1915), 1; A. E., "Uusi toimiala raittiusseuroissa," *Kesäjulkaisu, 1919,* Ohion, Pennsylvanian ja West Virginian Suomalaisen Raittiusliitto ja Sibelius Seura (Duluth, 1919), p. 19; *Historia K. R. Y. Majan Kokouksessa Waukegan'issa, Ill. elok. 5–10 p. 1918* (Duluth, 1918), pp. 34, 40; Minute Book of Antisosialistinen Liitto, Hancock, Michigan, for 1914–15 (MS in possession of Finnish American Historical Library).

30 Alex Pantti, "S. K.-R.-Weljeysseuran wuosikokous," *Raittius-Kalenteri wuodelle 1903* (Hancock, 1902), p. 66; J. K., "Weljeysseuran 19:sta yleinen wuosikokous ja juhla," *Raittius-Kalenteri wuodelle 1907* (n.p., [1906]), pp. 46–47; J. K., "S. K.-R.-Weljeysseuran 21 yleinen edustajakokous ja wuosijuhla raittius-luentokursseinen Monessenissa, Pa., heinäk. 11–18 p:nä 1908," *Raittius-Kalenteri wuodelle 1909* (Hancock, 1908), pp. 116–18; *Sunday Mining Gazette* (Houghton, Michigan), July 28, 1907, p. 6; Minute Book of Iron Kauntin Raittius Liitto for 1907–17, minutes of February 6, 1910 (MS in possession of Finnish American Historical Library).

31 *Kolmannen Amerikan Suomalaisen Sosialistijärjestön edustajakokouksen pöytäkirja, Kokous pidetty Hancockissa, Mich., 23–30 p. elok., 1909* (Fitchburg, n.d.), pp. 76–81.

32 *Suomalaisten sosialistiosastojen ja työväenyhdistysten viidennen eli suomalaisen sosialistijärjestön kolmannen edustajakokouksen pöytäkirja 1–5, 7–10 p. kesäkuuta, 1912* (Fitchburg, n.d.), p. 310.

33 *Amerikan Uutiset* (Calumet), May 18, 1899, p. 7.

34 *New York Mills Journal,* August 10, 1904, p. 4.

35 Herman Montagu Donner, "The Crisis in Finland," *The Outlook,* LXXII (September 20, 1902), 157–63; Julius Moritzen, "The Plight of Finland," *Gunton's Magazine,* XVII (October, 1899), 266; John Jackol, "The Reign of Terror in Finland," *The Arena,* XXX (July, 1903), 37. See also petition quoted in John I. Kolehmainen and George W. Hill, *Haven in the Woods: The Story of the Finns in Wisconsin* (Madison, 1951), p. v.

36 Malbone W. Graham, *The Diplomatic Recognition of the Border*

*States,* Pt. I: *Finland,* Publications of the University of California at Los Angeles in Social Sciences, III, No. 2 (Berkeley, 1936).

37 *Työmies,* July 27, 1918, p. 5.

38 O. J. Larson, "What of Finland?" *Siirtokansan kalenteri, 1919* (Duluth, 1918), p. 150; *Työmies,* May 3, 1918, p. 3; *New Yorkin Uutiset,* June 27, 1918, p. 5; Torsten Hedengren, *Save Finland from Germany and Starvation* (New York, [1918?]), p. 2; Herman Montagu Donner, "The Tragedy of Finland," *The Outlook,* CXIX (May 15, 1918), 103–5; *New York Times,* June 4, 1918, p. 12; "The United States, Finland, and Russia: Suggestion for a New American Policy," *The Finland Sentinel,* I (July 4, 1918), 8; *Siirtolainen,* January 11, 1918, p. 2.

*Chapter VIII*

1 *Kalevala: The Land of the Heroes,* trans. by W. F. Kirby, I (London and New York, 1951), 1.

2 U.S. Dept. of Labor, Commissioner-General of Immigration, *Annual Report . . . ,* 1914–20 (Washington, 1915–20). See also Maurice R. Davie, *World Immigration with Special Reference to the United States* (New York, 1949), pp. 275, 376–78; Roy L. Garis, *Immigration Restriction: A Study of the Opposition to and Regulation of Immigration into the United States* (New York, 1927), p. 256.

3 Wilho Reima, "Suomalaiset maanviljelijöinä Minnesotan metsissä," *Kansanwalistusseuran Kalenteri, 1911* (Helsinki, 1910), pp. 211–19.

4 J. J. Hoikka, " 'Metsistö' suom. ew. lut. seurakunta," *Kirkollinen Kalenteri wuodelle 1907* (Hancock, Michigan, 1906), pp. 140–44; Alex Pantti, "Kansan Koti," *Raittius-kalenteri vuodelle 1899* (Brooklyn, New York, 1898), pp. 87–91; "Carneyvillen. Wyo., s. s. osaston toimintakertomus," *Toveri kymmenvuotias, 1907–1917: Muistojulkaisu* (Astoria, Oregon, 1917), p. 76.

5 *Siirtolainen* (Duluth), February 4, 1920, p. 4.

6 *New Yorkin Uutiset* (Brooklyn), March 9, 1920, p. 6.

7 M. I. Kuusi, "Vähän Lasten Ystäväin Liiton toiminnasta South-Rangen seurakuntapiirissä, Michiganin valtiossa Amerikassa," *Koti,* Nos. 11–12 (1913), 173; "Pääpiirteitä Amerikan suomalaisten raittiusliikkeestä," *Rauhankokous ja pääpiirteitä Amerikan suomalaisten raittiustyön historiasta* (Hancock, 1908), p. 46; P. Pennanen, "Hyvä Toivo ja Uusi Vartia raittiusseurojen Raittiuskoulu," *"Uusi Wartia" Juhla Julkaisu. S. K. R. W. seuran, 20teen, Wuosijuhlaan, 1907* (n.p., n.d.), p. 9; Wilho Reima, " 'Kellä on nuoriso, sillä on tulewaisuus,' " *Raittius-Kalenteri wuodelle 1907* (n.p., [1906]), pp. 123–25; Jukka Kotiranta, "Lasten valistustyöstä s. s. osastoissa,"

*Kalenteri Amerikan suomalaiselle työväelle, 1918* (Fitchburg, Massachusetts, n.d.), p. 135; S——a L——a, "Kesäkoulut," *Lasten Joulu, 1915* (Astoria, 1915), p. 12.

8 U.S. Dept. of Commerce, Bureau of the Census, *Religious Bodies: 1926*, II: *Separate Denominations, Statistics, History, Doctrine, Organization, and Work* (Washington, 1929), 803, 820, 825; "Co-operative Training School in the Finnish Language," *Co-operation*, IX (December, 1923), 210; M. A. [Matti Anttonen], "Seurakunnan koulut," *Fitchburgin, Mass. Suom. Ev. Luth. Seurakunnan 40-vuotisjuhlajulkaisu, 1886–1926*, ed. Matti Anttonen (Ironwood, Michigan, n.d.), p. 80, and "Valo- ja varjopuolia Fitchburgin seurakuntaelämässä," *ibid.*, p. 90.

9 A. H., "Kirkkokuntamme Suomi-Synodi," *Kirkollinen Kalenteri wuodelle 1920* (Hancock, 1919), pp. 126, 131.

10 Juuso Hirvonen, *Michiganin kuparialue ja suomalaiset siirtolaiset* (Duluth, 1920), pp. 68–73; *New Yorkin Uutiset*, March 29, 1921, p. 6; *Amerikan Suometar* (Hancock), 1927: February 5, p. 4; June 14, pp. 4–5; "Mikko Skytän ja Jaakko Kamisen hautapatsaiden paljastamistilaisuudessa," *Koitto*, II (October 15, 1919), 3; *Historiallisen seuran kaiku*, No. 1 (Detroit, 1926).

11 V. Rautanen, *Amerikan suomalainen kirkko* (Hancock, 1911); *Juhlajulkaisu suomalaisen kansallis-raittius-veljeysseuran 25-vuotisen toiminnan muistoksi* (Ishpeming, Michigan, 1912); *Juhla-albumi Suomi-synoodin 25-vuotisjuhlan muistoksi, 1890–1915* (Hancock, 1915); *Amerikan Suom. Ev. Luth. Kansalliskirkon 25-vuotisjulkaisu, 1898–1923* (Ironwood, 1923); F. J. Syrjälä, *Historia-aiheita Ameriikan Suomalaisesta Työväenliikkeestä* (Fitchburg, [1925]); *Suomi-opiston 25-vuotisjulkaisu, 1896–1921* (Hancock, 1921); *Uljas koitto raittiusseuran joulujulkaisu 25:n vuotisen toiminnan muistoksi, 1915* (Fitchburg, n.d.); *Ashtabula-Harborin bethania seurakunnan 25-vuotisjulkaisu; 1891–1916* (Hancock, n.d.); *Viisitoista vuotta New Yorkin suomalaisten sosialistien historiaa, 1903–1918* (Fitchburg, [1919]); *Raivaaja Kymmenen Vuotta* (Fitchburg, 1915); *Työmies kymmenvuotias, 1903–1913: Juhlajulkaisu* (Hancock, 1913); *Amerikan Suometar, 1899–1919: Muistojulkaisu* (Hancock, 1919); *S. s. o. saima 25 vuotias* (Fitchburg, 1919); *Waukegan'in s. s. o:n 10-vuotisjulkaisu, 1905–1915* (Superior, Wisconsin, n.d.); *Muistoja 30-wuotisesta Lähetystyöstä* (Fitchburg, 1920); *Juhlajulkaisu, 1888–1913: Vesi N:o 22* (Hancock, n.d.).

12 George Sjöblom, "Finnish-American Literature," *The History of the Scandinavian Literatures: A Survey of the Literatures of Norway, Sweden, Denmark, Iceland and Finland, from Their Origins to the Present Day, Including Scandinavian-American Authors, and*

*Selected Bibliographies*, ed. Frederika Blankner (New York, 1938), p. 313.

13 E. A. Hedman, *Amerikan Muistoja: Näkemiäni ja kokemiani neljänkymmenen vuoden täällä oloni ajalla* (Brooklyn, 1925); J. H. Jasberg, *Amerikoissa: Pakinoita ja puheita Amerikan suomalaisten siirtolaisoloista* (Hancock, 1923).

14 Martin Hendrickson, *Muistelmia Kymmenvuotisesta Raivaustyöstäni* (Fitchburg, 1909).

15 Kalle Potti, *Iloinen Harbori, I* (Duluth, 1924). This novel was first serialized in the *New Yorkin Uutiset* towards the end of World War I.

16 J. Lauttamus, *Amerikan tuulahduksia* (Porvoo, 1922); Kalle Rissanen, *Amerikan suomalaisia* (Superior, 1924); Hijoppi Rotilainen [*pseud.* of Moses Hahl], *Juttuja, I* (Port Arthur, Canada, 1913), and *Agitaattori Räyhäsuu: Juttuja 2* (Port Arthur, 1913); Koivun Visa [*pseud.* of Antti Lepistö], *Rauniola: Suomesta ja Amerikasta* (Hancock, 1915).

17 Hirvonen, *Michiganin kuparialue.*

18 His historical writings include "Amerikan suomalaisen raittiusliikkeen historia," *Juhlajulkaisu suomalaisen kansallis-raittiusveljeysseuran 25-vuotisen toiminnan muistoksi*, pp. 3–317; *Amerikan ensimäiset suomalaiset eli Delawaren siirtokunnan historia* (Hancock, 1916); *Amerikan suomalaisten historiaa, I* (Hancock, 1919); *Amerikan suomalaisten historia, II: Ja elämäkertoja* (Jyväskylä, 1923); *Amerikan suomalaisten historia, III. Yhdysvalloissa ja Canadassa olevat suomalaiset asutukset* (Hancock, 1926); *Amerikan suomalaisten sivistyshistoria: Johtavia aatteita, harrastuksia, yhteispyrintöjä ja tapahtumia siirtokansan keskuudessa*, 2 vols. (Hancock, 1930–31).

19 *Amerikan Sanomat* (Ashtabula, Ohio), February 22, 1905, p. 2; Ilmonen, *Amerikan ensimäiset suomalaiset*, pp. 102–13, 118; E. A. Louhi, *The Delaware Finns or the First Permanent Settlements in Pennsylvania, Delaware, West New Jersey and Eastern Part of Maryland* (New York, 1925), pp. 43–44, 327–28; Syrjälä, *Historia-aiheita*, p. 7; *Pohjan Tähti* (Fitchburg), January 18, 1906, p. 3.

20 J. H. J., "Suomalaisten kehitys Amerikassa," *Juhla-albumi Suomisynoodin 25-vuotisjuhlan muistoksi*, pp. 159–60; Ilmonen, "Amerikan suomalaisen raittiusliikkeen historia," pp. 5–6; F. J. S——ä [Syrjälä], "Pimeydestä suuria valoja kohden," *Kalenteri Amerikan suomalaiselle työväelle, 1918* (Fitchburg, n.d.), pp. 102–6.

21 *Ashtabula-Harborin bethania seurakunnan 25-vuotisjulkaisu*, p. 3; K. E. S. [Salonen], "Alkulause," *Amerikan Suom. Ev. Luth. Kansalliskirkon 25-vuotisjulkaisu*, pp. 5–6; F. V., "Lukijalle,"

*Waukegan'in s. s. o:n 10-vuotisjulkaisu,* p. 3; "Pääpiirteitä Amerikan suomalaisten raittiusliikkeestä," p. 64; Hirvonen, *Michiganin kuparialue,* p. 5; *Raivaaja* (Fitchburg), January 26, 1914, p. 6; Alvar Rautalahti, *Juho Kustaa Nikander* (Hancock, 1920), p. 6.

22 Hirvonen, *Michiganin kuparialue,* pp. 44–46; F. Tolonen, "Suomisynodin 'Kirkkohistoriallinen seura,'" *Kirkollinen Kalenteri wuodelle 1920,* pp. 154–57; *Raivaaja,* January 26, 1914, p. 6; "Mikko Skytän ja Jaakko Kamisen hautapatsaiden paljastamistilaisuudessa," pp. 3, 5.

23 Hirvonen, *Michiganin kuparialue,* pp. 34, 41, 109.

24 *Raivaaja,* February 16, 1920, p. 1.

# SOURCES

Besides using materials gathered for my personal collection, I have used the resources of various institutions. Most English-language items were used in the State Historical Society of Wisconsin, University of Wisconsin Library, Cornell University Library, and New York Public Library. Finnish-language items were used at the last three named institutions as well as in the Ashtabula (Ohio) Public Library, University of Minnesota Library, and Minnesota Historical Society. The Finnish Newspaper Company (Brooklyn, New York), American Finnish Publishers (Superior, Wisconsin), and National Publishing Company (Ironwood, Michigan) permitted me to use their newspaper files. In addition to its books and pamphlets, the Finnish American Historical Library in Hancock, Michigan, provided newspaper files. It also has manuscripts which I used originally in the archives of the Finnish Historical Society of Hiawatha Land in Crystal Falls, Michigan. Still certain other items were secured from various institutions or individuals on loan or through microfilming.

I used or checked many of the sources, especially those published before 1925, listed in John I. Kolehmainen's *The Finns in America: A Bibliographical Guide to Their History* (Hancock, 1947). Therefore, I am mentioning or listing only some of the sources used or cited in my footnotes, including some which do not appear in Kolehmainen's bibliography. I do not often mention items cited only once or twice in my footnotes. Frequently the same item serves both as a primary and secondary source. In both this bibliography and the footnotes the Finnish version is cited only in the case of bilingual titles and the reproduction of the original capitalization of all Finnish titles is attempted. Also in this bibliography there ordinarily is no indication of the variations occurring from year to year in the titles of serial publications and newspapers which, by the way, were not always found in complete runs.

## *Unpublished Sources*

The present writer has five "America letters" written by Wäinö J. Lehto and Antti Kangas (1882–1903) and two notebooks of Karl Siren (*ca.* 1913–20) and Oscar Keturi (*ca.* 1902). He also has the Nyrkkilehti of the Tyyni Raittius Seura, Erie, Pennsylvania (1911–19) as well as the minute book of the discussion meetings of the same society (1914–15). The National Archives in Washington has a bound volume of American Consular Correspondence and Reports from Helsinki (1851–1906). In the Minnesota Historical Society's manuscript division are several folders of notes and drafts for an incomplete study undertaken by the Works Projects Administration on the Minnesota Finns. Among the manuscripts in the Finnish American Historical Library is the minute book of the Antisosialistinen Liitto, Hancock (1914–15).

In the collection transferred to the Finnish American Historical Library from the Finnish Historical Society of Hiawatha Land are manuscripts dealing mainly with temperance activities. These papers include the minute books of the annual meetings and directors' meetings of the Suomalaisen Kansallis-Raittius-Weljeysseura (1888–1919) and the same organization's presidential reports (1907–34). Similar minute books are present for the Suomalaisen Raittius-Ystäwäin Yhdistys (1890–1902). Other minute books include those of the Iron Kauntin Raittius Liitto (1907–12), Marquetti Kauntin Raittius Liitto (1907–12), Onnen Alku Raittius Seura, Neihart, Montana (1899–1907), and the Discussion Club of Toivola Raittius Seura, Crystal Falls (1911–12). During the transfer of the collection some items were lost or misplaced, including the Nyrkkilehti "Oras" of Pohjan Tähti Raittius Seura, Hancock (1907–12).

Unpublished dissertations include Arne Halonen's study on Finnish Americans in the political labor movement (University of Minnesota, 1945) and Henry S. Heimonen's comparison of Finnish-American farming with agriculture in Finland (University of Wisconsin, 1941). Minnesota Finns are the subjects of Walfrid J. Jokinen's dissertation (Louisiana State University and Agricultural and Mechanical College, 1953) and Ralph H. Smith's study (University of Southern California, 1933). Some mention is made of them also in John Syrjamaki's dissertation on the Mesabi iron communities (Yale University, 1940). John I. Kolehmainen wrote his dissertation on the Ohio Finns (Western Reserve University, 1937).

### *Published Sources*

Official United States documents are largely useful for their statistics on Finnish immigrants. They include the annual reports of the United States Commissioner-General of Immigration (1896–1920) and the federal censuses (1900–20). Finns are also mentioned in official reports on mining industries, such as the studies of the United States Immigration Commission (1911) and in the congressional documents on the copper strike of 1913 and 1914.

The Finnish government also provides statistics in its official statistical yearbook (*Suomen Tilastollinen Vuosikirja*) and its annual report on emigration (*Suomen virallinen tilasto. XXVIII. Siirtolaisuustilasto*). Other pertinent official materials include the journals of the clerical and peasant estates (1882–1906) and of the Diet (1907–20) as well as the documents and appendices to the journals (1882–1920).

Immigrant newspapers include *Amerikan Kaiku* (Brooklyn, 1905–6), *Amerikan Sanomat* (Ashtabula, 1898–1913), *Amerikan Suomalainen Lehti* (Calumet, Michigan, and other places, 1886, 1888, 1894, 1897–99), *Amerikan Suometar* (Hancock, 1902–20), *Amerikan Uutiset* (Calumet, 1896, 1898–1906), *Auttaja* (Ironwood, 1909–20), *Industrialisti* (Duluth, 1917–20), *Kuparisaaren Sanomat* (Hancock, 1895–96), *Lännen Uutiset* (Rock Springs, Wyoming, 1896), *Lännetar* (Astoria, Oregon, 1897–1901), *New Yorkin Uutiset* (Brooklyn, 1912–21), *Päivälehti* (Calumet, 1902–4, 1913), *Pohjan Tähti* (Fitchburg, Massachusetts, 1902–6), *Raivaaja* (Fitchburg, 1909–20), *Sankarin maine* (Hancock, 1880–81), *Siirtolainen* (West Superior, Wisconsin, and other places, 1894–95, 1905–6, 1913, 1917–20), *Sosialisti* (Duluth, 1914–15), *Suomalainen* (Rockport, Massachusetts, 1896–97), *Työmies* (Worcester, Massachusetts, and other places, 1903–7, 1909–20), and *Uusi Kotimaa* (New York Mills, Minnesota, 1896, 1900–2, 1907, 1919–20).

Worthy of use are English-language newspapers published in communities with Finnish immigrants, like Conneaut and Ashtabula in Ohio; Hancock, Calumet, and Houghton in Michigan; and Hibbing, Eveleth, Duluth, Ely, and New York Mills in Minnesota.

Finnish periodicals include *Ahjo* (Duluth, 1916–20), *Aura* (Hancock, 1914–19), *Kalevainen* (Brooklyn and Duluth, 1916–20), *Kansan Henki* (Duluth, 1916–19), *Koitto* (Duluth, 1919), *Lapatossu* (Superior, 1916–20), *Opas* (Dassel, Minnesota, [1911?]), *Paimen-Sanomia* (Hancock, 1889–1920), *Pellervo* (Hancock, 1913), *Pelto ja koti* (Hancock and Superior, 1913–20), *Raittiuslehti* (Hancock and other places, 1896–1913), *Säkeniä* (Fitchburg, 1907–20), *Tähti* (New York Mills, 1907), *Teosofian valo* (Cleveland, 1913, 1915), *Tiedon henki* (Hancock, 1910–11), *Toveritar* (Astoria, 1916–20), *Työwäen Ystäwä* (Calumet, 1897); *Uusi aika* (Duluth, 1914), and *Viesti* (Brooklyn, 1915, 1917).

Among the more useful annuals and calendars are *Airut, I: Sibelius seuran julkaisu* (Duluth, 1917); *Amerikan Joulukaikuja 1904* (Brooklyn); *Kalenteri Amerikan suomalaiselle työväelle,* 1914–20 (Fitchburg); *Kalevainen,* 1913–15 (Hancock); *Kansan ääni* [*Kewät-Albumi*], 1899–1902 (Brooklyn and Hancock); *Kaukomieli jouluna 1913* (Hancock);

*Kesäjulkaisu* [*Juhlajulkaisu*], 1913–19, Ohion, Pennsylvanian ja West Virginian S. R. Liitto *et al.* (Hancock and other places); *Kirkollinen Kalenteri,* 1903–22, 1930 (Hancock); *Köyhälistön nuija,* 1907–12 (Hancock); *Nuori Suomi,* 1903–5, 1907 (Brooklyn and Duluth); *Raittiuden ystäväin kalenteri vuodelle 1900* (Brooklyn), *Raittius-Kalenteri* [*Raittiuskansan kalenteri*], 1897–1920 (Brooklyn and other places); *Raivaajan Työvainiolta,* 1905–11 (Fitchburg); *Rauhan Juhlalle, 1902* (Fitchburg); *Rauhan kilpi kalenteri* (Chisholm, [1910?]); *Siirtokansan kalenteri,* 1918–57 (Duluth); *Suomalainen Almanakka ja Kalenteri,* 1904–10, Nielsen & Lundbeck (New York); *Taisto: Ashtabulan Suom. Sosialisti Osaston Juhannusjulkaisu* (Fitchburg, [1908?]); *Tartu kiinni,* Suomi-Opiston Juhla-Julkaisu ([Hancock? 1911?]); *Työväen Kalenteri,* 1905–6 (Hancock); *Urheilu-viesti,* 1909–11 (Hancock); *Vallankumous,* 1908–10, 1912–15 (Hancock and other places); *Vuokkoja, I* (Hancock, 1903); and *Ylöspäin* [*Ev. Luth. Kansalliskirkkokunnan kalenteri*], 1904, 1908–11 (Ironwood and other places).

The following list includes some of the more useful articles, books, and pamphlets.

Alanen, Yrjö. *Siirtolaisemme ja kotimaa: Siirtolaisuuden vaikutuksesta kansamme oloihin ja luonteeseen.* Helsinki, 1910.

*Alexandra Gripenberg's A Half Year in the New World: Miscellaneous Sketches of Travel in the United States (1888).* Ed. and trans. by Ernest J. Moyne. Newark, 1954.

*Amerikan albumi: Kuvia Amerikan suomalaisten asuinpaikoilta.* Brooklyn, [1905?].

*Amerikan Suom. Ev. Luth. Kansalliskirkon 25-vuotisjulkaisu, 1898–1923.* Ironwood, 1923.

*Amerikan Suometar, 1899–1919: Muistojulkaisu.* Hancock, 1919.

*Ashtabula-Harborin bethania seurakunnan 25-vuotisjulkaisu, 1891–1916.* Hancock, n.d.

Dorson, Richard M. *Bloodstoppers & Bearwalkers: Folk Traditions of the Upper Peninsula.* Cambridge, 1952.

Edgar, Marjorie. "Finnish Proverbs in Minnesota," *Minnesota History,* XXIV (September, 1943), 226–28.

Engelberg, Rafael. *Suomi ja Amerikan suomalaiset: Keskinäinen yhteys ja sen rakentaminen.* Helsinki, 1944.

*Evankelis-Luterilainen kansalliskirkko: Ensimmäiset 50 vuotta.* Ironwood, [1949].

*Finland and Its Geography: An American Geographical Society Handbook.* Ed. Raye R. Platt. New York, 1955.

*Finland: The Country, Its People and Institutions.* Helsinki, 1926.

Frederiksen, N. C. *Finland: Its Public and Private Economy*. London, 1902.

Gates, William B. Jr. *Michigan Copper and Boston Dollars: An Economic History of the Michigan Copper Mining Industry*. Cambridge, 1951.

Graham, Malbone W. *The Diplomatic Recognition of the Border States*, Pt. I: *Finland*. Publications of the University of California at Los Angeles in Social Sciences, Vol. 3, No. 2. Berkeley, 1936.

Haavio, Martti. *Kansankirkkomme ja kansansivistystyö*. Helsinki, 1947.

Hendrickson, Martin. *Muistelmia Kymmenvuotisesta Raivaustyöstäni*. Fitchburg, 1909.

Hirvonen, Juuso. *Michiganin kuparialue ja suomalaiset siirtolaiset*. Duluth, 1920.

*History of the Finnish Settlement in Brown and Dickey Counties of South and North Dakota, 1881–1955*. New York Mills, 1956.

Hytönen, Viljo. *Yleinen Raittiusliikkeen Historia*. Helsinki, 1911.

Ilmonen, S. *Amerikan suomalaisten historiaa, I*. Hancock, 1919.

Ilmonen, S. *Amerikan suomalaisten historia, II: Ja elämäkertoja*. Jyväskylä, 1923.

Ilmonen, S. *Amerikan suomalaisten historia, III. Yhdysvalloissa ja Canadassa olevat suomalaiset asutukset*. Hancock, 1926.

Ilmonen, S. *Amerikan suomalaisten sivistyshistoria: Johtavia aatteita, harrastuksia, yhteispyrintöjä ja tapahtumia siirtokansan keskuudessa*. 2 Vols. Hancock, 1930–31.

*International Migrations*. Ed. Walter F. Willcox. 2 Vols. New York, 1929, 1931.

Järnefelt [-Rauanheimo], Akseli. *Suomalaiset Amerikassa*. Helsinki, 1899.

Jasberg, J. H. *Amerikoissa: Pakinoita ja puheita Amerikan suomalaisten siirtolaisoloista*. Hancock, 1923.

Johnson, Aili Kolehmainen. "Finnish Labor Songs from Northern Michigan," *Michigan History*, XXXI (September, 1947), 331–43.

*Juhla-albumi Suomi-synoodin 25-vuotisjuhlan muistoksi, 1890–1915*. Hancock, 1915.

*Juhlajulkaisu suomalaisen kansallis-raittius-veljeysseuran 25-vuotisen toiminnan muistoksi*. Ishpeming, 1912.

*Jumalan viljelysmaa: Suomen kirkko, 1155–1955*. Ed. Jaakko Haavio and Oskar Paarma. Pieksämäki, 1955.

Jutikkala, Eino. *Suomen talonpojan historia: Sekä katsaus talonpoikien asemaan Euroopan muissa maissa*. Porvoo and Helsinki, 1942.

*Kalevala: The Land of the Heroes*. Trans. by W. F. Kirby. Everyman's Library. 2 Vols. London and New York, 1951.

*Kansan laulukirja*. Comp. by Vilho Reima *et al.* Ishpeming, 1907.

Kilpi, O. K. *Suomen siirtolaisuus ja 19. vuosisadan kansantalous.* Taloustieteellisiä tutkimuksia, XXII. Helsinki, 1917.
[Kiwiranta, Eelu]. *Eelu Kiwirannan sepittämiä Kansan Runoja.* Nos. 3–4. N.p., n.d.
[Kiwiranta, Eelu]. *Eelu Kiwirannan sepittämiä Weitikkamaisia Runoja. Luikasta lukemista Hauskuutta haluawille.* Nos. 1, 5–6. N.p., n.d.
[Kiwiranta, Eelu]. *Eelu Kiwirannan tekemiä Kansan Runoja.* Nos. 1–5. N.p., n.d.
Kolehmainen, John I. "Finland's Agrarian Structure and Overseas Migration," *Agricultural History,* XV (January, 1941), 44–48.
Kolehmainen, John I. "The Finnish Immigrant *Nyrkkilehti,*" *Common Ground,* IV (Autumn, 1943), 105–6.
Kolehmainen, John I. "Finnish Immigrants and a 'Frii Kontri,' " *Social Science,* XXII (January, 1947), 15–18.
Kolehmainen, John I. "Finnish Temperance Societies in Minnesota," *Minnesota History,* XXII (December, 1941), 391–403.
Kolehmainen, John I. "Harmony Island: A Finnish Utopian Venture in British Columbia," *The British Columbia Historical Quarterly,* V (April, 1941), 111–23.
Kolehmainen, John I. "The Inimitable Marxists: The Finnish Immigrant Socialists," *Michigan History,* XXXVI (December, 1952), 395–405.
Kolehmainen, John I. *Sow the Golden Seed.* Fitchburg, 1955.
Kolehmainen, John I. *Suomalaisten siirtolaisuus Norjasta Amerikkaan.* Fitchburg, [1946].
Kolehmainen, John I. "Why We Came to America: The Finns," *Common Ground,* V (Autumn, 1944), 77–79.
Kolehmainen, John I. and Hill, George W. *Haven in the Woods: The Story of the Finns in Wisconsin.* Madison, 1951.
Laine Y. K. *Suomen poliittisen työväenliikkeen historia.* 3 Vols. Helsinki, 1946.
Landis, Paul H. *Three Iron Mining Towns: A Study in Cultural Change.* Ann Arbor, 1938.
Laurila, Jacob. *Massachusettsin suomalaisia liikemiehiä vuosina 1890–1945.* Fitchburg, [1946].
Lauttamus, J. *Amerikan tuulahduksia.* Porvoo, 1922.
Lento, Reino. *Maasamuuto ja siihen vaikuttaneet tekijät Suomessa vuosina 1878–1939.* Helsinki, 1951.
*Neljäkymmenta vuotta: Kuvauksia ja muistelmia Amerikan suomalaisen työväenliikkeen toimintataipaleelta, 1906–1946.* Ed. Leo Mattson. Superior, 1946.
Niemi, Clemens. *Americanization of the Finnish People in Houghton County, Michigan.* Duluth, 1921.
Nieminen, Armas. *Taistelu sukupuolimoraalista: Avioliitto- ja sek-*

*suaalikysymyksiä suomalaisen hengenelämän ja yhteiskunnan murroksessa sääty-yhteiskunnan ajoilta 1910-luvulle, I.* Helsinki, 1951.

*Oma maa: Tietokirja Suomen kodeille.* Ed. E. G. Palmén *et al.* 6 Vols. Porvoo, 1907–11.

Potti, Kalle. *Iloinen Harbori, I.* Duluth, 1924.

*Raivaaja Kymmenen Vuotta.* Fitchburg, 1915.

*Rauhankokous ja pääpiirteitä Amerikan suomalaisten raittiustyön historiasta.* Hancock, 1908.

Rautanen, V. *Amerikan suomalainen kirkko.* Hancock, 1911.

Riippa, Antero. "Books for the Finnish Immigrant," *The Interpreter,* II (February, 1923), 5–8.

Saarnivaara, Uuras. *Amerikan laestadiolaisuuden eli Apostolis-luterilaisuuden historia.* Ironwood, 1947.

Saarnivaara, Uuras. *The History of the Laestadian or Apostolic-Lutheran Movement in America.* Ironwood, 1947.

Sjöblom, George. "Finnish-American Literature," in *The History of the Scandinavian Literatures: A Survey of the Literatures of Norway, Sweden, Denmark, Iceland and Finland, from Their Origins to the Present Day, Including Scandinavian-American Authors, and Selected Bibliographies.* Ed. Frederika Blankner. New York, 1938. Pp. 311–18.

Sulkanen, Elis. *Amerikan Suomalaisen Työväenliikkeen Historia.* Fitchburg, 1951.

*Suomen maatalous.* Ed. J. E. Sunila *et al.* 2 Vols. Porvoo, 1922.

*Suomi-opiston 25-vuotisjulkaisu, 1896–1921.* Hancock, 1921.

Syrjälä, F. J. *Historia-aiheita Ameriikan Suomalaisesta Työväenliikkeestä.* Fitchburg, [1925].

Tarkkanen, Matti. *Siirtolaisuudesta, sen syistä ja seurauksista.* Kansantaloudellisen yhdistyksen esitelmiä, Sarja III, No. 16. Helsinki, 1903.

Tuomiokoski, Mrs. Aino. "Finnish [Proverbs]," in *Racial Proverbs: A Selection of the World's Proverbs Arranged Linguistically.* Ed. Selwyn Gurney Champion. New York, 1938. Pp. 134–40.

Turner, H. Haines. *Case Studies of Consumers' Cooperatives: Successful Cooperatives Started by Finnish Groups in the United States Studied in Relation to Their Social and Economic Environment.* New York, 1941.

*Työmies kymmenvuotias, 1903–1913: Juhlajulkaisu.* Hancock, 1913.

*Uljas koitto raittiusseuran joulujulkaisu 25:n vuotisen toiminnan muistoksi, 1915.* Fitchburg, n.d.

*Viisitoista vuotta New Yorkin suomalaisten sosialistien historiaa, 1903–1918.* Fitchburg, [1919].

*Voiton Kaiku: "Voiton Lippu" Raittiusseuran Juhlajulkaisu.* Fitchburg, 1908.

Wargelin, John. *The Americanization of the Finns.* Hancock, 1924.
Waris, Heikki. *Suomalaisen yhteiskunnan rakenne.* Helsinki, 1948.
Waris, Heikki. *Työläisyhteiskunnan syntyminen Helsingin pitkänsillan pohjoispuolelle, I.* Helsinki, 1932.
Wasastjerna, Hans R. *Minnesotan suomalaisten historia.* Duluth, 1957.
Wuorinen, John H. *Nationalism in Modern Finland.* New York, 1931.
Wuorinen, John H. *The Prohibition Experiment in Finland.* New York, 1931.
*Y. s. k. v. ja s.-liiton 50-vuotishistoria: Muistojulkaisu.* Duluth, 1937.

# INDEX

## SCANDINAVIANS IN AMERICA

***This is a volume in the Ayer Company collection***

Ander, O. Fritiof. **The Cultural Heritage of the Swedish Immigrant:** Selected References. [1956]

Ander, Oscar Fritiof. **T.N. Hasselquist:** The Career and Influence of a Swedish American Clergyman, Journalist and Editor. 1931

Barton, H. Arnold, editor. **Clipper Ship and Covered Wagon:** Essays From the *Swedish Pioneer Historical Quarterly*. 1979

Blegen, Theodore C. and Martin B. Ruud, editors and translators. **Norwegian Emigrant Songs and Ballads.** Songs harmonized by Gunnar J. Maimin. 1936

Christensen, Thomas Peter. **A History of the Danes in Iowa.** 1952

Duus, Olaus Fredrik. **Frontier Parsonage:** The Letters of Olaus Fredrik Duus, Norwegian Pastor in Wisconsin, 1855-1858. Translated by the Verdandi Study Club of Minneapolis. Edited by Theodore C. Blegen. 1947

Erickson, E. Walfred. **Swedish-American Periodicals:** A Selective Bibliography. 1979

Gjerset, Knut. **Norwegian Sailors in American Waters:** A Study in the History of Maritime Activity on the Eastern Seaboard. 1933

Gjerset, Knut. **Norwegian Sailors on the Great Lakes:** A Study in the History of American Inland Transportation. 1928

Hale, Frederick. **Trans-Atlantic Conservative Protestantism in the Evangelical Free and Mission Covenant Traditions** (Doctoral Thesis, The Johns Hopkins University, 1976, Revised Edition). 1979

Hogland, A. William. **Finnish Immigrants in America:** 1880-1920. 1960

Hokanson, Nels. **Swedish Immigrants in Lincoln's Time.** With a Foreword by Carl Sandberg. 1942

Hummasti, Paul George. **Finnish Radicals in Astoria, Oregon, 1904-1940:** A Study in Immigrant Socialism (Doctoral Dissertation, University of Oregon, 1975, Revised Edition). 1979

Hustvedt, Lloyd. **Rasmus Bjørn Anderson:** Pioneer Scholar. 1966

Jenson, Andrew. **History of the Scandinavian Mission.** 1927

Kolehmainen, John I. **Sow the Golden Seed:** A History of the Fitchburg (Massachusetts) Finnish American Newspaper, Raivaaja, (The Pioneer), 1905-1955. 1955

Kolehmainen, John I. and George W. Hill. **Haven in the Woods:** The Story of the Finns in Wisconsin. 1965

Koren, Elisabeth. **The Diary of Elisabeth Koren:** 1853-1855. Translated and Edited by David T. Nelson. 1955

Larson, Esther Elisabeth. **Swedish Commentators on America, 1638-1865:** An Annotated List of Selected Manuscript and Printed Materials. 1963

Lindeström, Peter. **Geographia Americae With An Account of the Delaware Indians.** 1925

Marzolf, Marion Tuttle. **The Danish Language Press in America** (Doctoral Dissertation, the University of Michigan, 1972). 1979

McKnight, Roger. **Moberg's Emigrant Novels and the *Journals* of Andrew Peterson:** A Study of Influences and Parallels (Doctoral Thesis, the University of Minnesota, 1974). 1979

Mattson, Hans. **Reminiscences:** The Story of an Immigrant. 1891

Mortenson, Enok. **Danish-American Life and Letters:** A Bibliography. 1945

Nelson, Helge. **The Swedes and the Swedish Settlements in North America.** 1943. 2 vols. in 1

Nielson, Alfred C. **Life in an American Denmark.** 1962

Olson, Ernst W., Anders Schon and Martin J. Engberg, editors. **History of the Swedes of Illinois.** 1908. 2 vols.

Puotinen, Arthur Edwin. **Finnish Radicals and Religion in Midwestern Mining Towns,** 1865-1914 (Doctoral Dissertation, the University of Chicago, 1973). 1979

Raaen, Aagot. **Grass of the Earth:** Immigrant Life in the Dakota Country. 1950

Scott, Franklin D. **Trans-Atlantica:** Essays on Scandinavian Migration and Culture. 1979

Strombeck, Rita. **Leonard Strömberg—A Swedish-American Writer** (Doctoral Thesis, the University of Chicago, 1975, Revised Edition). 1979

Svendsen, Gro. **Frontier Mother:** The Letters of Gro Svendsen. Translated and edited by Pauline Farseth and Theodore C. Blegen. 1950

Vogel-Jorgensen, T[homas]. **Peter Lassen Af California.** 1937

Waerenskjold, Elise. **The Lady with the Pen:** Elise Waerenskjold in Texas. Edited by C.A. Clausen with a foreword by Theodore C. Blegen. 1961

Weintraub, Hyman. **Andrew Furuseth:** Emancipator of the Seamen. 1959

Winther, Sophus Keith. **Mortgage Your Heart.** 1937